YORKSHIRE MONASTERIES

Exploring Historic Yorkshire

Yorkshire Monasteries
Cloister, Land and People

Bernard Jennings

Photography by Trevor Croucher

First published in 1999 by
Smith Settle Ltd
Ilkley Road
Otley
West Yorkshire
LS21 3JP

ISBN   Paperback   1 85825 105 2
       Hardback   1 85825 106 0

Set in Monotype Dante.

Designed, printed and bound by
SMITH SETTLE
Ilkley Road, Otley, West Yorkshire LS21 3JP

Contents

Preface & Acknowledgments

This is the first book in a new series with the general title *Exploring Historic Yorkshire*. The word 'Historic' has a double meaning, as the area covered is the historic county of Yorkshire, disregarding recent changes in local government boundaries. The books are aimed particularly at people who like to 'explore', ie to visit monasteries, castles, churches, historic houses, and generally to look for the history which is etched on the landscape.

The first part of this book is a broad-brush survey of the characteristics and development of the different orders of monks, nuns, canons and friars. The second. and most substantial, section consists of a detailed examination of the way of life, economic management and contribution to the life of the community of each of the orders or groups, concentrating in most cases on one or two examples, eg Selby Abbey and Whitby Abbey for the Benedictine monks, Bolton Priory and Bridlington Priory for the Augustinian canons, and Fountains Abbey and Rievaulx Abbey for the Cistercian monks. The third part is a gazetteer of about a hundred monastic sites in Yorkshire.

The preparation of this book would not have been possible without the generous help of English Heritage, other site owners, librarians and archaeologists. I would like to record my gratitude to the following:

The staff of English Heritage: Ms Hilary Lade, Mr Jeff West, Mrs Valerie Davies and the custodians of the Yorkshire monastic sites, Ms Lucy Bunning, Ms Celia Sterne, Ms Cathy Houghton. Ms Jane Whitehead of the National Trust at Fountains Abbey. Mr David R Wilson, curator, and Ms Francoise Hivernel, librarian, of the University of Cambridge Committee for Aerial Photography. Mr C R J Currie, general editor, Victoria County History.

The owners, administrators and neighbours of monastic buildings and sites: Bolton Priory, Mr J M Sheard of the Bolton Abbey estate; Coverham Abbey, Mr and Mrs Nigel Corner; Jervaulx Abbey, Mr and Mrs Ian Burdon; Malton Priory, Mr Dave Scott; Marrick Priory, Ms Cilla Withers; St Martin's Priory, Mr Robin Delf; Selby Abbey, Mr Brian Porter, Mr Wilfrid Staniforth and Mrs Peggy Morrill; Tickhill Friary, Mr and Mrs A de Mulder; Watton Priory, Mr and Mrs C R A Cherry; Wykeham Priory, Mr George Malcolm and Mrs Betty Early; Yedingham Priory, Mr James Lyall.

The staff of the libraries of the Universities of Hull and Leeds, and the cities of Hull and Leeds; Miss Pamela Martin, of the East Riding County Library; and Ms Susan Leadbeater, librarian of the Yorkshire Archaeological Society. Mr Peter Rowe of Tees

Archaeology, Mr Bob Yarwood of the West Yorkshire Archaeological Service, and the staff of the City of Leeds Museum at Kirkstall. My colleagues at the University of Hull: Professor V A McClelland, Mr Ian Marriott and Mr Jeff Lowsley. Mr John Earnshaw FSA, who has put his considerable knowledge of the history of the buildings of Bridlington Priory at my disposal.

Some of the research for this book was undertaken many years ago in partnership with WEA/university tutorial classes in Pateley Bridge and Harrogate, which wrote *A History of Nidderdale* and *A History of Harrogate and Knaresborough*. I would like to acknowledge with gratitude the contribution of the late Joanna Dawson, Stephen Good and Jack Hunter, and more recently of Muriel Swires. For practical help in a variety of ways I am grateful to Bert Hodge OBE and my wife Jean.

In this book, amounts of money are given in the original pre-decimal currency, twelve (old) pence (d) making one shilling (s), with twenty shillings to the pound. For the names of monasteries, most of which have had a variety of spellings down the centuries, the modern forms of the local place-name are used.

All of the photographs in this book, unless otherwise stated, have been taken by Trevor Croucher, who joins me in thanking the people included in the above lists, and in particular those who have given permission for the photography and been generous in their help:

English Heritage (Byland, Easby, Egglestone, Monk Bretton, Mount Grace, Rievaulx, Roche, Whitby); National Trust (Fountains); Wykeham Abbey Estate (Wykeham Priory); Mr Robin Delf (St Martin's Priory, Richmond); City of Leeds Museum Service (Kirkstall); Jervaulx Abbey Estate (Jervaulx); Mr & Mrs de Mulder (Tickhill); the owners (Sinningthwaite, Watton, Yedingham); and the administrator (Selby Abbey).

Bernard Jennings
Institute for Learning
Loten Building
University of Hull
October 1998

I

INTRODUCTION

In 1258 a group of Franciscan friars came to Richmond in North Yorkshire to begin building their friary on a site given to them just outside the town walls. Within two miles of the friary were two other religious houses, canons at Easby Abbey and monks at St Martin's Priory, a dependency of the great Benedictine abbey of St Mary in York. A short journey to the west along Swaledale brought the traveller to two nunneries, a Cistercian priory at Ellerton and a Benedictine priory at Marrick.[1]

Friars — canons — monks. These groups are sometimes lumped together as 'monks', but they were, in fact, quite different in organisation and function. The monk was committed to the internal spiritual life and working duties of the abbey or priory. Except in relation to the properties of the house, which could take up a lot of the time of the senior members, he had no responsibilities outside the walls. In the early days of Yorkshire Benedictine abbeys such as Selby, only a minority of monks became priests, but by the end of the twelfth century this practice had become general.[2]

Canons were priests living in communities under a rule — regula in Latin, and thereby known as 'regular canons' to distinguish them from the canons of minsters such as York and Beverley who were 'secular canons'. The regular canons carried out the normal priestly duties, sacramental and pastoral, at some of the parish churches they acquired.

The main function of the friars was preaching. Friars joined an order, not a house, and were expected to be much more mobile than the monks or canons. They lived mainly by begging. The Dominicans were a priestly order from the beginning. The friars of the other orders gradually adopted the same practice.

The main orders of monks, canons and friars were conveniently 'colour coded'. The Benedictine monks, the first order to appear in Yorkshire after the Norman Conquest, wore black. A major reform of their movement produced the Cistercians, the white monks. The original order of regular canons, the Augustinians, had a mainly black habit, and a reform of their calling was represented by the white canons, the Premonstratensians (from their mother house of Premontre in France). The Franciscan friars wore grey habits, the Carmelites white, and both the Dominican and Austin friars black. The street name Blackfriargate could therefore indicate the former presence of either of the latter orders. Nuns who called themselves Cistercians had white habits, the others probably wore black.

The independent Benedictine houses were called abbeys, and were headed by an abbot, with a prior as second-in-command. Dependent Benedictine houses were normally called priories, with a prior in charge. All of the houses of Augustinian (black) canons in Yorkshire were priories; all of the white canons' establishments in the county were abbeys. This difference simply reflects the customs of the two orders. Dominican and Trinitarian houses were often called priories, the houses of the other orders of friars normally friaries. 'Nunnery' is a general descriptive term, not a title. All of the Yorkshire nunneries were known as priories, and led by prioresses.

Villages, hamlets and country houses on the sites of medieval monasteries are often labelled 'abbey', irrespective of the correct medieval name. Examples include Bolton Abbey and Rosedale Abbey, both of which were medieval priories.

The Benedictine abbeys were normally located in towns, although at Selby the abbey was the main cause of the growth of the town. The Cistercian preference for remote rural locations is still evident, except in the case of Kirkstall, overrun by the expansion of Leeds. The friars went to the towns, where their buildings were so thoroughly quarried by the locals after the suppression of the monasteries that few traces remain. Eight monastic churches survived because they were used as parish churches — the whole of Selby and parts of the churches of Bolton, Malton, Bridlington, and four nunneries. Apart from the latter, only fragments remain of the twenty-four Yorkshire nunneries. The order with the most extensive remains is the Cistercian.

The history of monasticism in Yorkshire goes back six centuries before the arrival of the Franciscans in Richmond. In the middle of the seventh century, not long after the conversion to Christianity of the Anglo-Saxon rulers of Northumbria, monasteries were established, both to accommodate those drawn to the religious life and to provide a basis for evangelism. Bede, the monk-historian, mentions five monasteries on the eastern side of Yorkshire, at Whitby, Hackness, Lastingham, Watton and 'Inderawood' (probably Beverley, certainly in that neighbourhood); and three in the centre, at Ripon, 'Ingetlingum' (probably Collingham) and 'Calcacestir' (apparently Tadcaster, although the abbey itself may have been three miles away at Healaugh).[3]

The most important of these abbeys was Whitby, then known by its Anglo-Saxon name, Streonshalh. It was a double house of monks and nuns, each in their own enclosure, ruled by an abbess. The site was described in the eleventh century as consisting of 'nearly forty monasteries or oratories', roofless but with the walls still standing. It was therefore made up of a series of small cells, like an ancient Irish abbey. The first abbess, from the foundation in 657 to her death in 680, was Hilda, a relative of King Oswy of Northumbria. Before going to Whitby she had been abbess of Calcacestir, which was apparently another double house. Hilda was succeeded at Whitby by Oswy's daughter Elfleda, assisted by her mother Queen Eanfleda who had retired to the abbey after Oswy's death in 670. These royal ladies were formidable characters, influential in the affairs of the Church at large. Five men who had been monks at Whitby went on to become bishops.[4]

The monastery at Hackness was established by Hilda initially for nuns, although it may have become a double house later. Watton was a nunnery; Lastingham, 'Ingetlingum' and Ripon were apparently for

St Gregory's Church, Kirkdale. (Bernard Jennings)

monks only. There are contemporary references to other Anglo-Saxon monasteries, at Barwick-in-Elmet and Crayke near Easingwold. According to Bede, there were some pseudo-abbeys, households claiming to be monasteries to secure exemption from public service and taxation, but ruled by laymen and filled with renegade monks. Finding a true 'golden age' of religious observance is not easy.[5]

It has been suggested that Kirkdale, near Kirkby Moorside, was the site of another abbey, mainly on the strength of an inscription in Anglo-Saxon on a sundial, recording the rebuilding of 'St Gregory's Minster' in the period 1055-65. At that time, however,

the term 'minster' was used for any parish church. The Latin word for minster was *monasterium*. Translating that back into English as 'monastery' could create abbeys that never were.[6]

All of the Anglo-Saxon monasteries were either destroyed by the Danes, who conquered Yorkshire in 867-875, or abandoned as a result of the disturbed condition of the time. By the early tenth century the invaders had been converted to Christianity. Churches of secular canons were established during the same century at Ripon, York and Beverley, but there were still no monasteries in Yorkshire at the time of the Norman Conquest.

2
OUTLINE HISTORY I
Monks and Canons

In the South of England a monastic revival which began in the middle of the tenth century had created about thirty-five abbeys and nine large nunneries by 1066. It was only a matter of time before the North was re-colonised. However, the foundation of what became the three great independent Benedictine abbeys of Yorkshire — Selby, Whitby and York St Mary's — was far from being the orderly process whereby an existing monastery sent out a team of monks to establish a new house.[1]

The history of Selby Abbey, written there by a monk in 1174, tells the tale of Benedict, an Englishman who was a monk in the French abbey of Auxerre, serving as sub-sacrist in charge of the sacred relics. By far the most important of these was the body of St German, bishop of Auxerre in the fifth century, a finger of which had been severed. In nocturnal visions German ordered Benedict to leave the abbey, taking with him the finger, and go to 'a place in England called Selebia', where he was to establish a cell in honour of the saint. Benedict did so but, misunderstanding German's directions, he ended up in 'Salesbyria'. There he met Edward of Salisbury, a man of substance, who gave him a round, golden reliquary in which to keep the saint's finger. German had to appear in another vision, emphasising 'I did not say Salisbury', before his disciple

resumed the journey which brought him, by boat along the River Ouse, to Selby.

Benedict built a wooden shelter with a cross outside, which was noticed by the Norman sheriff of York, Hugh FitzBaldric. Hugh was impressed with the holy man and sent carpenters to build a small chapel. As Benedict had established himself on royal land without permission, the sheriff took him to meet King William, probably at York. The king decreed that a monastery should be founded, and gave for the purpose the site of the abbey, the village of Selby, the village of Rawcliffe and its lands, some land in Brayton on the south side of Selby, a fishery at Whitgift on the Ouse, and a wood called Flaxley. Benedict was consecrated as abbot by Thomas of Bayeux, appointed in 1070 as the first Norman archbishop of York, who gave to the fledgling abbey the territory of Selby Minor together with the townships of Monk Fryston and Ferry Fryston. Other Norman lords donated estates in Yorkshire and elsewhere, and Benedict travelled to London to secure a royal charter of confirmation for the foundation gifts.[2]

How much of this story should we believe? Selby Abbey was dedicated to St German, a popular saint in France but not so well known in England, which suggests that Benedict had been in Auxerre. It was an acceptable practice for monks to leave

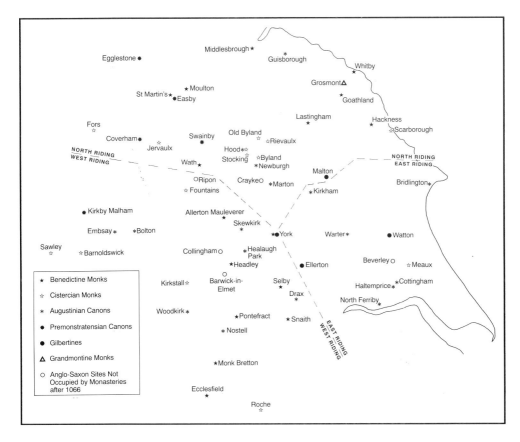

Houses of monks and canons in Yorkshire.

their abbeys to become hermits, and Benedict may have wandered about for some time before settling, perhaps fortuitously, in Selby. Edward of Salisbury was a real person, who witnessed the king's confirmation charter. Finally, we may be sure that in 1174 Selby Abbey had a golden reliquary containing a finger, which the monk-historian's account would serve to authenticate. Relics were valuable assets, attracting visits, and offerings, from pilgrims.[3]

Early medieval documents were not usually dated, and approximate dates have to be worked out from a study of the witnesses. There is good reason to believe, however, that Benedict had arrived in Selby by 1069, and that the king's decision to found an abbey, with the support of the archbishop, was made in the following year.[4]

Monastic life on the site of St Hilda's abbey at Whitby was re-established by Reinfrid, a Norman knight who had served in the army of the Conqueror during the latter's 'Harrying of the North' in the winter of 1069-70. After this 'scorched earth' campaign, designed to prevent any further rebellions in Yorkshire, Reinfrid became a monk at Evesham Abbey in Worcestershire where, as it happened, some Yorkshire refugees from William's onslaught had taken

Whitby Abbey, from the north-west. Some of the buildings of St Hilda's abbey were in the right foreground. (Cambridge University)

refuge. He and two companions went north about 1073-74, to set up a monastery on the site of the famous Anglo-Saxon abbey of Jarrow. In or shortly before 1078 Reinfrid went to Whitby. According to the foundation chronicle of Whitby Abbey, his decision was a consequence of having visited the ruins of Hilda's abbey in the winter of 1069-70. He may, however, have had a connection with the new Norman lord of Whitby, William de Percy. Reinfrid's son Fulk was a steward and tenant of William in 1086.[5]

Within a short time Reinfrid, given land in the vicinity of the old abbey by William de Percy, had been joined by a small band of followers over whom he ruled as prior. There are two conflicting accounts of subsequent developments, derived from the foundation chronicles of Whitby Abbey and St Mary's Abbey, York, respectively. If we

follow the Whitby account, when Reinfrid had been prior for several years, he was accidentally killed while helping to build a bridge over the River Derwent near Hackness. He was succeeded as prior by Serlo de Percy, brother of William, but some monks supported a man called Stephen as a rival candidate. Stephen secured from King William I a grant of the old monastic site at Lastingham, to which the dissidents moved, with Stephen as their abbot.[6]

The York version suggests, on the other hand, that Stephen took the monastic habit in 1078 under Reinfrid, a man of holy life but, by implication, with no great appetite for management. Reinfrid and the other monks persuaded Stephen, much against his will, to take command with the title of abbot. It was attacks by pirates and local robbers, and harassment from William de

Percy, that forced the monks to move to Lastingham.[7]

Stephen and his monks began building work at Lastingham, apparently concentrating on the church. It would have been normal practice for them to put up temporary wooden living quarters on the site. After a few years, however, they took advantage of the gift from Count Alan of Brittany, earl of Richmond, of the church of St Olave in Marygate, York, just outside the city walls. Their move to York upset Archbishop Thomas and the canons of York Minster, but a settlement was reached and in 1088 King William II gave Abbot Stephen the land on which St Mary's Abbey was built.[8]

There is one reason for believing that Stephen was at one time head of the Whitby community. In *Domesday Book* Stephen, described as abbot of York (ie St Olave's), held title to 'Prestebi' (the locality of Whitby Abbey) and 'Sourebi' (in the Ruswarp area). Some of the monks had clearly remained in the Whitby / Hackness area under Reinfrid and / or Serlo, and soon after *Domesday* William de Percy succeeded in transferring the title to Prestebi and Sourebi to his brother Prior Serlo. In the period 1091-96 William gave to his brother and 'the monks of Whitby' the townships of Whitby, Stainsacre, Newholm and Stakesby; the port of Whitby; Hackness with its two churches; five other places in the Hackness area; all the forests, pastures and other rights belonging to the parish church of Whitby; and the tithes of several other parish churches in Yorkshire and Lincolnshire. A township was a unit of manorial and civil administration, and at a later date of taxation. In lowland areas it normally consisted of a nucleated village and its lands, but upland townships frequently contained two or more hamlets or scattered settlements. The charter in favour of Serlo may be a repeat of the earlier grant to Reinfrid.[9]

St Mary's Abbey, York, from the south-east, c1880. St Olave's Church, Marygate, can be seen in the right background.
(Lefroy, *Ruined Abbeys*)

King William II (Rufus) gave to Whitby Priory the church of All Saints, near Fishergate Bar in York, on condition that it should be regularly occupied by a few monks as a 'cell'. Some years later Serlo retired to Fishergate with the title of prior of the cell, and was succeeded by his nephew William de Percy, son of the founder. At this point, not later than 1109, Whitby was re-named an abbey, the normal designation for a large Benedictine house.[10]

The hermit-turned-abbot of Selby had the same name as the hermit-turned-abbot who had devised the Benedictine Rule in the sixth century. Although some features of the rule might seem very onerous to us, St Benedict was aiming at a moderate and reasonable regime, in contrast to the extreme forms of self-denial and mortification practised by some groups. In the words of the American Cistercian Thomas Merton, 'St Benedict shifted the whole impact of asceticism to the interior — from the flesh to the will' . His monks did not have to survive without adequate food or sleep. The pursuit of holiness was largely a secret affair. The Benedictine Rule banned any private property within the monastery. No one was to claim anything as his own, 'whether book or tablets or pen or whatever it may be'. The monks were to sleep in dormitories, 'each one in a separate bed ... When they rise for the work of God, let them gently encourage one another, on account of the excuses to which the sleepy are addicted'.[11]

At every main meal there should be two cooked dishes, to give the monks some choice, plus a third dish 'if any fruit or young vegetables are available'. There was one main meal for part of the year, two for the remainder. Brethren doing heavy work could have increased rations, but all except the sick should 'abstain entirely from the flesh of fourfooted animals'. It would be better to abstain also from wine, 'but since nowadays monks cannot be persuaded of this, let us agree ... to drink temperately ... a hemina of wine a day is sufficient for each'. The size of a 'hemina' is uncertain. Estimates range from half a pint to a pint.[12]

The daily routine of the monk was divided between prayer services, sung in the choir of the church; spiritual reading; and manual work which could range from copying manuscripts to agricultural labour. The purpose of the work was not primarily economic. It provided a physical and mental balance to the monastic life. '*Otiositas inimica est animae*', wrote St Benedict. 'Idleness is the enemy of the soul. The brethren, therefore, must be occupied at stated hours in manual labour; and again at other hours in sacred reading.'[13]

The Benedictine Rule was adapted to meet English conditions, such as the longer summer day than in Italy. The mass was also given much greater prominence. In Benedict's scheme there was a single mass on Sundays and feast days. The *Regularis Concordia*, or monastic rule-book, devised in England about 970, provided for two daily masses. These and the eight sung services together took up over nine hours of the day. Work periods totalled about three to four hours, and spiritual reading one and a half to three hours, according to season. The monks had eight hours sleep in winter, just over five hours plus a siesta of one and a half hours in summer.

After the first of the two masses — in modern parlance a low mass; the second was a sung high mass — the monks assembled in the chapter house, to hear the reading of a chapter of the rule, to conduct the business of the monastery, and to have faults confessed and corrected. Two meals daily were provided in summer and one in winter, plus in each case a short break for a drink of ale. The meals were eaten in silence, apart from the voice of a lector reading from a spiritual work. This was part of a general feature, that only essential conversations were allowed. St Benedict had emphasised 'the great value of silence' in the pursuit of holiness.[14]

'A monk is a man who has given up everything in order to possess everything', writes Thomas Merton. His 'business is to empty himself of all that is selfish and turbulent and make way for the ... Spirit of God'. At first sight the monk had no social role. In the early Middle Ages, however, society was thought of as divided into three groups, according to function. The *oratores* prayed; the *bellatores* fought, and ruled; and the *laboratores* (craftsmen, merchants, but predominantly farmers) worked. The *bellatores* were too busy with their military and administrative tasks to have much time for prayer, even if they had the inclination. They could, however, divert some of the resources in land and rights which they held in return for service to the king or their superior lord, to support the *oratores*, the specialists in prayer, in the monasteries.[15]

The prayers and holy life of monks, nuns and other members of religious orders were therefore seen as earning divine favour and mercy, for society as a whole and particularly for the benefactors of the monasteries. This investment made good sense in the light of contemporary beliefs. Not only would souls face judgment after death, but the earth was subject to frequent interference from heaven. If there was too much rain or too little; if humans or animals were ravaged by disease; any blessings or misfortunes, collective or individual, could be seen as part of a system of divine rewards and punishments. In July 1348, a month or so after the bubonic plague known as the Black Death first broke out in the south of England, Archbishop Zouche of York wrote a pastoral letter to his flock, who were waiting with dread for the disease to spread to them. He did not explain — he did not know — that the plague bacillus was carried by fleas which lived on the black rat and suggest appropriate precautions. The epidemic was, he argued, 'surely ... the doing of the sins of men who, smiling amid prosperity, omit to remember the bounties of the most high giver'.[16]

The saints in heaven were not only valuable allies who could intercede for the faithful. They were seen as having a considerable measure of autonomy within the divine plan. St German's directions to Benedict of Selby have already been described. The anger of St Robert of Knaresborough at being treated with disrespect by the Trinitarian friars is mentioned on page 159. In the popular mind, the most effective way to make contact with a saint was at a shrine, such as that of St Hilda at Whitby Abbey.

The leading benefactors of the Benedictine abbeys in Yorkshire were nearly all French. As a result of the ruthlessness of the subjugation of the county by William I, all of the great barons who held land directly from the king were Normans, Bretons or Flemings, as were many of the landholders of the second rank. France had a much longer, and stronger, tradition of monasticism than northern England, and was seen as a source of both ideas and monastic personnel. In 1089 Ralph Paynel gave Holy Trinity Church in York, which before the conquest had housed a community of secular canons with substantial endowments, to one of the leading French abbeys, Marmoutier near Tours. Monks came from there to establish a dependent priory. In 1090 the lord of the Honour of Pontefract, Robert de Lacy, invited the Cluniac order, a branch of the Benedictines known for a great elaboration of the liturgy, to establish Pontefract Priory.[17]

The buildings of these Benedictine houses, powerfully supported by the new French masters of the county, came to dominate the local landscapes. Dr Janet Burton sees this as part of a deliberate strategy. 'Stone abbeys and cathedrals no less than stone castles were a symbol of conquest.'[18]

In the early twelfth century Whitby, Selby and St Mary's all acquired dependencies. Whitby, which already had All Saints, Fishergate, in York, was given the church of St Hilda in Middlesbrough by Robert de Brus,

on condition that some monks were stationed there. Hackness, where Whitby had two churches, was described as a cell in the middle of the twelfth century, but there is no evidence that a regular community was maintained there. Archbishop Gerard of York (1101-8) gave Snaith Church to Selby, on condition that at least two monks lived there. The operation of these small units, called cells or priory cells, was not conducive to the maintenance of monastic discipline, unless they were used for convalescent or semi-retired monks, and they were presumably accepted for financial reasons.[19]

A more substantial dependency was St Martin's Priory, on the south bank of the River Swale opposite Richmond. Its founder was Wymar, steward to the earl of Richmond, who gave the chapel of St Martin and

St Martin's Priory, Richmond.

other possessions to St Mary's Abbey. In the early years there seem to have been nine or ten monks at St Martin's, under a prior. Their responsibilities included a leper hospital.[20]

Several cells or priory cells belonged to French abbeys. Marmoutier owned Allerton Mauleverer directly, and Headley indirectly through Holy Trinity, York. St Wandrille acquired a cell at Ecclesfield, based upon the parish church there. Begar Abbey had a cell, apparently at Moulton, of which the only known asset consisted of the corn mills at Richmond. These small cells were staffed by French monks, singly or in small numbers. Some were little more than estate offices. A larger under-

Ecclesfield Priory: the east gable of the thirteenth century chapel.

taking was created in 1115 when Stephen earl of Albemarle (otherwise Aumale) gave fifteen churches and chapels in Holderness and other property to the abbey of St Martin at Aumale in the diocese of Rouen. To manage this estate a small priory was established at Burstall, the site of which has been washed away by the sea.[21]

A second Cluniac house was founded at Monk Bretton about 1155 by Adam Fitz-Swain. Pontefract Priory had an ill-defined supervisory role, and disputes about this led Monk Bretton to secede from the Cluniac order about 1279 and become an independent Benedictine priory.[22]

The Benedictine and Cluniac monasteries built up extensive estates, by a process which will be examined in more detail in chapter four. They acquired whole manors,

blocks of land large and small, corn mills, fisheries, churches and their tithes, tolls or exemption from tolls, and even a port and a ferry. Many of the tenants on the manors were bondmen, who were not allowed to leave their land without permission, and had no legal redress against their lords in matters of rents and services, although they might have some protection through the force of custom. They and some free tenants owed labour services, and both groups were required to have their corn ground at the manorial mill. In other words the monks had similar managerial responsibilities to those of the officers of large lay estates. The common practice with churches was to leave the rector in place, but to take an annual payment, known as a pension, out of the tithe — the delivery of one tenth of

Monk Bretton Priory: the gatehouse.

the produce of farming which had been compulsory since the tenth century — and other income of the church. St Mary's Abbey, which acquired forty churches in Yorkshire and several elsewhere, generally adopted this system.[23]

The second major monastic movement to affect Yorkshire began in 1113 or 1114 with the foundation of Bridlington Priory, a house of Augustinian canons. These men were priests who lived in communities, holding everything in common, according to the Rule of St Augustine. This was less comprehensive than its Benedictine counter-part, having been developed out of some advice, about the collective religious life,

given by Augustine (died 430) who was bishop of Hippo in North Africa.

The creation of Augustinian houses — in Yorkshire they were all known as priories — was encouraged by popes and reforming bishops, and in England by King Henry I (1100-35), as a means of dealing with some deep-rooted pastoral problems. The old-style minster churches, with a 'team ministry' serving a wide area, had gradually been replaced during the tenth and eleventh centuries by parish churches. The initiative was normally taken by the manorial lord, and for this reason parishes often coincided with lordships, even if the latter were large. The parish of Kirkby Malzeard originally coincided with the Honour of Kirkby Mal-zeard, which included nearly all of upper Nidderdale. The parish of Grinton in Swale-dale, stretching twenty-five miles to the head of the dale beyond Keld, was co-extensive with the manor of Healaugh.[24]

The establishment of a parish church could enhance the status of its founder. An Anglo-Saxon document dated between 1029 and 1060, called *On People's Ranks and Law*, declared that an upwardly mobile peasant who wanted to achieve the status of a thane, a minor lord, needed among other things to have a church on his estate. It was Orm, son of Gamel, who bought the ruined minster of St Gregory and had it rebuilt for the benefit of Brand, the parish priest. We know no more about the relationship be-tween Orm, a major landowner in Ryedale, and Brand, but many manorial lords regard-ed parish priests as their feudal retainers. The lords appointed the priests, and this right, known as the advowson, could be given away or sold. The lords could not legally lay their hands on the tithe, except indirectly by appointing a relative to the benefice, but they could charge a fee for the appointment and exact an annual rent. Successive popes and at least some of the bishops fought against this abuse.[25]

The other custom condemned by the Church was the marriage of priests. The sons of priests often went into holy orders themselves, providing an hereditary succes-sion in some parishes. This system had its advantages, as the only training which most of the rank and file clergy received was attachment to a serving priest. The Church authorities were, however, afraid of losing

control over the parochial clergy. Further clerical marriages were forbidden by the Council of Winchester in 1076, although parish clergy already married were allowed to continue in wedlock. The prohibition was difficult to enforce. One church in York, St Denis in Walmgate, remained an hereditary living until about 1170. Late in the twelfth century William the parson of Rudston, near Bridlington, was conveying land to his son John, who became a priest himself. In 1191 a married priest was ejected from Nidd Church, near Knaresborough.[26]

The gift of an advowson to a Benedictine abbey took care of the problem of lay con-trol, but a more radical approach was the transfer of both the assets and the responsib-ilities of a group of parish churches to the new-style team ministry, the house of Augustinian canons. The foundation charter of Guisborough Priory (c1119) declared that Robert de Brus, influenced by Pope Calixtus

Guisborough Priory: the outer face of the east end of the church, mid-nineteenth century.
(Grainge, *Castles and Abbeys*)

II and Archbishop Thurstan of York (1114-40), had endowed the priory with ten churches in addition to a substantial amount of land. Robert's second son, also called Robert, who was lord of Annandale (and ancestor of Robert Bruce, king of Scotland) gave six churches and their dependent chapels in southern Scotland. These were subsequently lost as a result of the Anglo-Scottish wars, but the number of churches acquired by the priory in Yorkshire (as far south as Hessle) and County Durham reached twenty-eight.[27]

Guisborough was the wealthiest Augustinian priory in Yorkshire, and the fourth richest monastery after St Mary's, Selby and Fountains. The second wealthiest house of the order was Bridlington, founded by Walter de Gant with the encouragement of Thurstan, with an initial endowment of five churches, rising eventually to eighteen. More representative, in terms of resources, was Bolton Priory, founded in 1120 at Embsay near Skipton by Cecily de Rumilly, lady of the Honour of Skipton, which had eight churches. The community moved to Bolton in Wharfedale in 1155. By that time seven more Augustinian priories had been founded, two in the North Riding: Marton (1135-54) and Newburgh (1142-43 at Hood near Thirsk, 1145 at Newburgh); two in the West Riding: Nostell (c1114, moving to a new site

The gatehouse at Kirkham Priory in the mid-nineteenth century.
(Grainge, *Castles and Abbeys*)

1120) and Drax (1130-39); and three in the East Riding: Kirkham (c1122), Warter (c1142) and North Ferriby (1140). Their endowments in churches and lands varied considerably. Nostell had twelve churches, North Ferriby only one.[28]

It can never have been envisaged that all of the churches acquired by the Augustinians would be served directly by the canons. The basic complement of a priory was a prior and twelve canons (modelled on Christ and the twelve apostles). The better-endowed houses often had larger numbers, twenty or more, but they also had more churches. The nearby churches could easily be served. At Bridlington and Bolton the priory church was also the parish church. At Guisborough they were separate but close. However, to station canons in ones and twos in the more distant churches would have destroyed the concept of the common life. It was not enough to send a canon riding ten miles or so to say mass on Sunday mornings. Parishioners, at least those who lived near to a parish church, expected to have a priest on hand for other purposes, not least to administer the last sacraments in case of sudden illness. For most of their churches, therefore, the Augustinians employed secular priests, paid either a fixed stipend or a share of the benefice income. At a later date the office of vicar — the word means deputy or substitute — was created in many of these churches. The vicar had a guaranteed source of income, and could be removed only by the bishop for good cause, unlike the stipendiary priests who held office at the pleasure of the priory.

Despite the unavoidable limitations on the pastoral role of the canons, their acquisition of about 110 churches in Yorkshire

and thirty or so elsewhere, achieved two objects of the reformers. First, clerical appointments and overall pastoral care were in these cases the responsibility of religious houses. Secondly, a message was delivered to the lords retaining advowsons that squeezing money out of churches in their patronage was no longer an acceptable practice.[29]

From the point of view of a lord wishing to found a monastery, it was much cheaper to establish an Augustinian priory than a Benedictine abbey of the same size. If, as was usually the case, a major part of the endowment was the income from parish churches, it cost the lord little to give much. During the twelfth and thirteenth centuries there was a considerable increase in the scale of farming in Yorkshire, with much new land cleared for cultivation. This boosted the tithe income, and together with the profits of the landed estates (the exploitation of which will be discussed in chapter six) gave the canons of the better-endowed houses a substantial surplus to spend on the priory buildings.

While the Yorkshire Benedictine abbeys were still in the pioneering stage, new movements were developing in France which were destined to have a profound effect upon monasticism across Europe. A common feature was a call to return to the literal observance of the Benedictine Rule, a threat to the easy-going lifestyle of some of the wealthier abbeys. Some reformers sought solitude, as a framework for a life of contemplation. This yearning led St Bruno and six followers, in 1084, to a lonely valley in the Alps, where the monastery of La Grande Chartreuse developed. The Carthusian monk spent most of his time in the isolation of his own cottage and garden. The order, by deliberate choice, spread slowly, and it was not until the late fourteenth century that its two Yorkshire houses, Hull and Mount Grace, were established. About 1100 St Stephen of Murat founded a similar contemplative order at Grandmont, near Limoges. The Grandmontines had three dependent priories in England, including one at Grosmont in the North York Moors set up about 1204.[30]

In 1098 a group of monks moved from the abbey of Molesmes in Burgundy, which in their view had become too busy and worldly, to seek a simpler life in the wilderness at Citeaux. They included an Englishman, Stephen Harding, who was abbot of Citeaux from 1109 to 1133, and was the principal architect of the Cistercian policy and system. In matters of diet this policy was stricter than the Benedictine Rule. Banning the flesh of four-footed animals allowed the easy-going abbeys to live well on poultry and game birds. The Cistercians prohibited all meat, except for the sick. The liturgy was stripped of elaboration, so that Cistercian monks spent much less time in church than did the Cluniacs. Church artifacts had to be simple — wooden crucifixes, not gold or silver; linen vestments, not silk.

The Benedictine practice of accepting boy recruits was rejected, on the grounds that poor vocations sometimes resulted and the presence of the boys disturbed the atmosphere of solitude. All recruits were to serve one year's novitiate. To prevent their abbeys becoming busy estate offices, the Cistercians renounced all feudal sources of income — labour services, corn mills, the profits of manor courts — and also refused to accept tithes. They sought for their abbeys sites which were remote from human habitation, and lands which could form part of a self-contained farming system. They recruited lay brothers, *conversi*, who combined a simple religious life with agricultural and other work. This vocation was intended to appeal to the unlettered peasant, but as the system developed, some of the *conversi* became managers of the granges, directing paid labourers. Perhaps as a result, some members of the knightly class in Yorkshire became lay brothers.

In the Cistercian system each abbey was inspected annually by the abbot of its mother house; Citeaux itself was visited by the abbots of its four oldest daughter houses; and all of the abbots were to meet each year at Citeaux for a General Chapter which regulated the affairs of the order. Some of the other orders emerging about 1100 adopted similar procedures, including the use of lay brothers. This was the case with the order of Savigny, an abbey founded in Normandy about 1112-13 by another hermit-turned-abbot, Vitalis.[31]

The first Cistercian house in England was established at Waverley in Surrey in 1128-29, but its impact was limited. The real Cistercian invasion was planned by St Bernard, appointed abbot of Clairvaux in 1114-15 at the age of twenty-five. He became the greatest propagandist for the Cistercian cause, as well as a man of great influence in Church affairs. As he had several Yorkshiremen amongst his colleagues at Clairvaux, Bernard would have known that Yorkshire was recovering from the Norman devastation, but was still underdeveloped, with extensive hunting forests and plenty of good Cistercian country. A site in the Rye Valley near Helmsley was given by Walter Espec, who had a castle at Helmsley and had founded the Augustinian priory of Kirkham. Sympathetic support came from Archbishop

Thurstan of York, a Frenchman who, Professor Knowles suggests, had gone native and shared an 'enthusiastic and ascetic temper' with some leading Yorkshire churchmen.[32]

In March 1132 a party of monks from Clairvaux arrived in the Rye Valley, to establish Rievaulx Abbey. Their first abbot was William, who had been St Bernard's secretary, and came apparently from the York area. They passed through York *en route*, no doubt calling on the archbishop. Their arrival had a profound effect upon St Mary's Abbey. It had been showered with gifts, and had become very wealthy in manors and other property. Some of the monks were stationed on the estates as local managers. Its situation made the abbey a busy place, with lay people coming and going on business or as pilgrims.[33]

As a result of discussion in the abbey about a return to the full observance of the Benedictine Rule, the leader of the reform group, Prior Richard (the second in command) approached the elderly Abbot Geoffrey, and by agreement a plan for reform was drafted. Food and drink were to be restricted to the allowance of the rule; silence was to be observed; and churches and tithes were to be handed over to the archbishop. These proposals outraged the majority of the monks, who included some who had retired to the abbey in middle life without a great appetite for sackcloth and ashes. Richard appealed to Archbishop Thurstan, who arranged with Geoffrey to visit the abbey in October 1132 for a conference. When he and his retinue arrived, feelings ran high and there was a disturbance. Thurstan withdrew, taking with him Prior Richard and twelve other reformers.[34]

The group stayed at the archbishop's house for the next three months, without any clear plan. They made no attempt to join the Rievaulx community, and may have hoped to go back to a reformed St Mary's. Two of them did return to the abbey, although one came back again, and two monks from Whitby joined them, one later canonised as St Robert of Newminster, the other Adam, the future founding abbot of Meaux. On the 27th December the archbishop settled the reformers on his land by the River Skell, to form the abbey which took the name Fountains from the local springs. Richard, the ex-prior, was elected abbot. The community had a hard time, trying to develop the land without the help, at first, of lay brothers, but it turned the corner with the recruitment of three rich clerics from York, who brought money, lands and the beginnings of a library. Abbot Richard had discussed with St Bernard the idea of moving the group to Clairvaux, but as the prospects improved it was agreed that Fountains Abbey would stay, and be formally admitted to the Cistercian order. This process was completed by 1135.[35]

The first community of Savigniac monks arrived in Yorkshire by a roundabout route. In 1135 the Savigniac abbey of Furness, in north Lancashire, established a daughter house at Calder in Cumberland, under Abbot Gerold. Raids by the Scots forced the monks, in 1137 or 1138, to return to Furness, which refused to take them back, either because it could not afford to feed them or because Gerold would not give up his rank. The Calder group therefore decided to go to York to seek the help of Archbishop Thurstan. On the way they met the steward of Gundreda, the widowed mother of Roger de Mowbray, who was under-age but about to inherit large estates, including the Honour of Kirkby Malzeard and the Barony of Thirsk. Gundreda, then living at Thirsk

Byland Abbey. In the foreground, the chapter house. In the background, from the left, the lay brothers' range, the west front of the church, and the nave.

Castle, and Roger settled Gerold and his monks on a hermitage at St William's Church, Hood, at the foot of Sutton Bank. The hermit was a relative of Gundreda, and had previously been master of St Michael's Hospital, Whitby, a creation of the abbey there. His consent and that of the abbot of Whitby were noted in the charter by which Roger conveyed the land to the Savigniacs,

and Roger and Gundreda bought out the interest of Whitby Abbey by giving to the latter a house in York.[36]

New recruits joined Gerold's community, including some veteran knights of the Mowbray entourage who brought material resources when they became lay brothers. The Hood site, however, proved to be too constricted for the necessary development.

After the death of Gerold in February 1142, his successor, Abbot Roger, secured from Roger de Mowbray the grant of the township and church of Byland on the Moor. The Savigniacs, unlike the Cistercians, had no objection to using parish churches as a source of income.

The community transferred to Byland on the Moor in September 1142, but moved on again after five years. The site was only a mile and a half from the Cistercian abbey of Rievaulx, and the story that each house was disturbed by hearing the bells of the other is well known. There were, however, other obstacles to a peaceful co-existence, including potential conflicts over the use of the River Rye for driving corn mills and other purposes, and the expansionist policy of Rievaulx. It should be remembered also that, in the early 1140s, Byland Abbey belonged to a rival order.

Roger de Mowbray gave to Abbot Roger and his brethren a better site at Stocking, near Kilburn, to which they moved in 1147, keeping the name Byland Abbey. In the same year the Savigniac order merged with the Cistercians. At Stocking 'a small stone church, a cloister and other houses and offices' were built, in the words of Philip, the third abbot. He wrote a history of the abbey in 1197, consisting mainly of the recollections of Abbot Roger, who had retired at an advanced age in the previous year. Philip's rather confused account is the source of the story of the bells.

At some stage, probably in the 1160s, the Byland community decided not to develop further at Stocking, but to build on a virgin site nearly three miles to the east. There the woods were cleared, and 'long and wide ditches' made to 'draw off the water from the marshes'. When the site was dry, 'they built from new their beautiful and great church as it now [1197] appears.' The long western range, accommodating the lay brothers, had been completed, and some progress made on the church and the eastern range (chapter house and monks' dormitory), when the formal move took place on the 31st October 1177. The abbey was still called Byland; in the course of time, Byland on the Moor became known as Old Byland.[37]

As the Byland story is complicated not only by the number of moves, but also by the change of affiliation in 1147, it may be useful to list its five locations:

Name and location	Date Order
Calder Abbey	1135-1137/8 Savigniac
Hood Abbey	1138-42 Savigniac
Byland (on the Moor) Abbey	1142-47 Savigniac
Byland (Stocking) Abbey	1147-77 Cistercian
Byland (New Byland) Abbey	1177- Cistercian

It was fortunate that the foundation of a Cistercian abbey, with its preference for undeveloped land, was not an expensive operation, as the order grew apace. The simplicity, enthusiasm and self-sacrificing spirit of the Cistercians — and probably, although the evidence is less certain, of the Savigniacs — attracted recruits in large numbers to both callings, as choir monks and as lay brothers. In one of his writings, St Ailred, abbot of Rievaulx from 1147 to 1167, put these words into the mouth of one of his novices: 'Our food is scanty, our garments rough; our drink is from the stream and our sleep is often upon our book ... everywhere serenity and a marvellous freedom from the tumult of the world.'[38]

By 1135 Rievaulx was able to send a party of monks to form Warden Abbey in Bedfordshire, also founded by Walter Espec. In the following year another group went to colonise Melrose Abbey, founded by King David I of Scotland, and in 1142 Revesby Abbey in Lincolnshire became another daughter house. Meanwhile Fountains had created new abbeys at Newminster in Northumberland (1138) and Kirkstead in Lincolnshire (1139).[39]

Ailred, the son of the hereditary priest of Hexham, was a steward to King David. On a mission for the king in 1134 he visited Rievaulx in the company of Walter Espec, and returned on the following day to offer himself as a novice. Waldef, the prior of the Augustinian house at Kirkham, who was a stepson of King David, was also attracted to the Cistercian cause. An agreement was drafted for the transfer of Kirkham Priory, and any canons who so wished, to the Cistercians, with Rievaulx building a new priory for the canons who preferred to remain Augustinian. However, the deal fell through, and only Waldef became a Cistercian, later serving as abbot of Melrose. Walter Espec, founder of both Kirkham and Rievaulx, became a monk in his last days at Rievaulx, and was buried there.[40]

The process of developing a second Savigniac house in Yorkshire began in or shortly before 1145, when several subordinates of Count Alan of Brittany, earl of Richmond, gave land in upper Wensleydale to recipients described in one charter as 'the monks of Savigny' and in another as 'the monks and brothers of Wensleydale'. Count Alan confirmed the gifts, and added the grant of pasture in his Forest of Wensleydale, otherwise known as the Forest of Bainbridge, with the right to take building materials, mine lead ore and iron, and take the flesh of deer killed by wolves. Peter de Quinciaco and two other Savigniac monks — what exactly they were doing in the area is unclear — set up house at Fors, between Askrigg and Bainbridge, but when Count Alan visited Savigny to report on the venture, he found Abbot Serlo reluctant to support it. In 1146 it was agreed that Byland would sponsor the new community.[41]

Serlo's attitude derived in part from the managerial problems in his organisation, which were resolved in 1147 when the Savigniac order was taken over by the Cistercians. It was not until 1150 that the three pioneers at Fors were joined by nine monks from Byland and the new abbot, John de Kinstan, a veteran of the Calder migration. The abbey at Fors was named 'Yore-valley', in French 'Jervaulx', after the old name for the River Ure, which flows down Wensleydale. Its members found the climate of upper Wensleydale too hostile, and in 1156 they migrated, keeping the same name, to a new site near East Witton, given by Conan, earl of Richmond.[42]

Between 1147 and 1151 four more Cistercian abbeys were established in Yorkshire. Henry de Lacy, lord of the Honours of Clitheroe (Lancashire) and Pontefract, gave the township and church of Barnoldswick to Fountains Abbey to form a new daughter house. The prior of Fountains, Alexander, went there with twelve monks and ten lay brothers. The occupiers of the intended site were evicted, and part of the parish church pulled down. The people of Barnoldswick protested, and appealed to the archbishop

Kirkstall Abbey from the south-west. Kirkstall has the most completely preserved original buildings of all the Cistercian abbeys in Yorkshire. (Cambridge University)

of York and the pope. The archbishop decreed that the chapels of Bracewell and Marton, hitherto dependencies of the parish of Barnoldswick, should become parish churches, and that the mother church of Barnoldswick should be appropriated to the use of the new abbey. The pope upheld the Cistercian claims. These decisions were not very surprising as Archbishop Henry Murdac and Pope Eugenius III were both Cistercians. It was equally unsurprising that the new abbey was unpopular locally, and matters were not helped by a spell of wet and cold weather. One of the monks, Serlo, who later wrote a history of the community, explained:

> We remained there for some years suffering many hardships through cold and hunger, both owing to the inclemency of the weather and the continued rain, and because of the disturbed state of the kingdom our goods were constantly carried off by prowlers.

Abbot Alexander found a better site at Kirkstall, near the River Aire, occupied by hermits and held under Henry de Lacy by William de Poitou. The hermits were either recruited to the Cistercians or bought out,

Kirkstall Abbey: the entrance to the twelfth century chapter house...

...and the interior of the chapter house.

William agreed to give the site, and Henry met most, if not all, of the cost of building the abbey church. The move took place in 1152.[43]

The next two foundations were staffed from the daughter house of Fountains at Newminster. In 1147 Richard de Buili of Tickhill and Richard FitzTurgis gave land near Maltby for the foundation of Roche Abbey. In the following January the usual

foundation party of abbot, twelve monks and ten lay brothers started Sawley Abbey, near Clitheroe. The founder-patron was William de Percy.[44]

The last abbey, at Meaux, might never have been founded if William, earl of Albemarle, had followed a Cistercian diet. William became known as Le Gros because of his weight, and by 1150 he could no longer ride a horse. He had a few years earlier made

The transepts of Roche Abbey from the south-west. The lay brothers' wing is in the foreground.

Adam and Eve, the serpent and the apple; a detail from the frescoes in Easby parish church.

a vow to go on pilgrimage to Jerusalem, but because of his age and girth he was persuaded to found a Cistercian abbey instead. According to the *Meaux Chronicle*, written in the fourteenth century, Adam, a senior monk of Fountains, chose a site at Meaux in Holderness which William had recently acquired for the purpose of making a park, and resisted the earl's suggestion that he might look elsewhere. This is just the kind of human interest tale beloved of the writers of monastic chronicles, whose motto seems to have been 'Never let the facts spoil a good moral story'. It was not necessarily true. The earliest relevant document is an agreement made in 1149-50, whereby William gave John de Meaux the land of Bewick in exchange for Meaux, 'for the making of a certain abbey'. Shortly afterwards he gave the Meaux site to the Cistercians 'for the souls of Ingram my brother, and of my mother and father and all my forebears', and added the wood of Routh and the marsh adjacent which he had obtained in another exchange. The earl had previously founded several religious houses in England and Normandy, and his devotion to monasticism is not in doubt. The population of the village of Meaux was moved elsewhere, and Abbot Adam with his twelve monks took possession on on the 1st January 1151.[45]

By 1152 there were over 300 Cistercian abbeys in Europe, and the General Chapter called a halt to new foundations. This order was sometimes disregarded, but no new abbeys were founded in Yorkshire. More than half of the thirty-six English abbeys existing in 1155, excluding the Savigniacs, had been colonised from Rievaulx, Fountains and their daughter houses.[46]

Ailred wrote that in 1143 the abbot of Rievaulx commanded about 300 men.

During his abbacy (1147-67), according to his biographer Walter Daniel, everything was doubled: monks, *conversi*, lay servants, lands and resources. By 1167 Rievaulx had 140 monks and 500 *conversi* and *mercenarii*, paid workers who, according to the Cistercian statutes, received spiritual benefits as well as wages. St Ailred, the St Bernard of Yorkshire, was a learned and holy man despite — or perhaps because of — a life of painful and disabling illness. He was also very tolerant. 'All, whether weak or strong, should find in Rievaulx a haunt of peace.' In Walter Daniel's words, '...those wanderers in the world to whom no house of religion gave entrance came to Rievaulx, the mother of mercy and found the gates open ... On feast days you might see the church crowded with the brethren like bees in a hive.' All the lay brothers (*conversi*) who could manage it would attend the abbey church for the major feasts.[47]

If other Yorkshire abbeys were following similar policies, it would help to explain the rapid expansion of the Cistercians, and their ability to colonise so much land. At the same time, potential trouble was being stored up. As the pioneering fervour cooled, the presence in an abbey of too many people with inadequately tested vocations could erode the Cistercian ideal. The very success of the *conversi* in making the wilderness blossom was itself a long-term threat to that ideal. As Thomas Merton says:

> ... the Cistercians became one of the most powerful economic forces in the Middle Ages
> ... the vast expansion and material power of the Cistercians could not help but corrupt the simplicity of their original spirit.[48]

Just as the Benedictine (black) monks were challenged by the Cistercian (white) monks, so a rival to the Augustinian (black) canons

*The south wall
of Egglestone
Abbey nave.*

arose out of the same ferment for reform which produced the Cistercians and Carthusians. St Norbert (c1080-1134), a German priest who gave his worldly goods to the poor and became a restless evangelist, was encouraged by the bishop of Laon, north-east of Paris, to establish a community at nearby Premontre in 1120. The order which emerged became known as the Premonstratensian or white canons. Like the Cistercians, they wore habits of undyed woollen cloth. Norbert chose the Rule of St Augustine as appropriate for canons, but his order adopted several Cistercian features: a stricter way of life; the use of lay brothers; and a federal system with Premontre as the mother house, and an annual General Chapter as the governing body.[49]

The order made a limited impact on Yorkshire. Its three houses were established in the north-west of the county, two of them in remote rural locations. (Beauchief Abbey, part of modern Sheffield, was just over the boundary in Derbyshire.) St Agatha's Abbey at Easby was founded by Roald, constable of the Honour of Richmond, in 1151, although it may have been the following year before the new abbot and twelve canons arrived from the first abbey of the order in England, Newhouse in Lincolnshire. The foundation charter explains that the *monasterium* of St Agatha was being given, along with other property, to build an *abbatia*. The existing *monasterium* was a minster, a team ministry, of secular priests, which can be traced back to 1135 and was probably much older. Fragments of an early Northumbrian cross found in the walls of the ancient parish church (which was not incorporated in the abbey buildings) indicate that the site had been used for worship as far back as the seventh or eighth centuries. The pattern of medieval parish boundaries suggests that when the town of Richmond was established, its parish was carved out of the territory of the minster at Easby.[50]

In the period 1184-87, Helewise, daughter and heiress of Ranulf de Glanville, the senior judge in England (whose relatives established several abbeys of white canons), and widow of Robert of Middleham, founded a Premonstratensian abbey at Swainby, in the parish of Pickhill. Here, too, there had been a minster of secular priests, but replaced before the foundation by a single rector. The original endowment consisted of the church of Coverham near Middleham; other land in Wensleydale; and land and pasture rights in Kettlewell, Wharfedale. Soon afterwards the canons were given Downholme Church. Between 1196 and 1202 the community moved fifteen miles west to Coverham, perhaps because it was a more convenient location for the management of its estates.[51]

Egglestone Abbey, on the River Tees, was founded in the 1190s, the only daughter house of Easby. At first the resources were adequate to support only three canons, but a few years later the gift by Gilbert de Laya of the manor of North Kilvington, near Thirsk, made it possible to increase the complement to the usual twelve canons. Egglestone remained, however, the poorest house of white canons in England.[52]

These three abbeys acquired a few churches, but nearly all were served by vicars or chaplains. The main sources of income were land and pasture rights. With their lay brothers, granges and flocks of sheep, they resembled small Cistercian abbeys.[53]

The only monastic order to originate in England was founded by St Gilbert of Sempringham in Lincolnshire. The son and heir of a Norman knight and his English wife, he was prevented by 'some repulsive physical deformity' from following a knightly career. His father gave him two churches, including St Andrew's at Sempringham, where he taught some local boys and girls. He eventually became a priest — his churches had been served by chaplains — and found himself responsible for 'certain maidens' who wanted to follow a religious life. About 1131 he erected a building for them alongside St Andrew's Church, and recruited some poor village girls to serve the seven apprentice nuns. On the advice of Abbot William of Rievaulx, he organised the girls into a lay sisterhood, with its own dress and rules, and copied the Cistercian idea of using lay brothers to do the manual work About 1139 Gilbert de Gant gave him a substantial area of land in Sempringham to endow a priory.

St Gilbert had no great appetite for management, and so in 1147 he asked the Cistercian abbots, meeting in General Chapter at Citeaux, to take over his infant movement. The Cistercians were reluctant to become involved with nuns, and in any case they had their hands full sorting out the merger with the Savigniacs. Pope Eugenius III, who was present at Citeaux, encouraged Gilbert to found his own order, and St Bernard helped him to draft its rules. When Gilbert returned to Sempringham a year later, he added a fourth element, regular canons, who would be chaplains to the nuns and manage external affairs. The canons followed the Augustinian Rule; the nuns, who were strictly enclosed, followed a basically Benedictine Rule; and Cistercian customs were adopted for the two lay sections. The canons wore white, the nuns a black habit with a white cowl.[54]

The first two Gilbertine houses in Yorkshire were both founded in 1150 by Eustace FitzJohn, a double house of nuns and canons at Watton, and a priory for canons only at Malton. It is said that Eustace was motivated by a guilty conscience. When Henry I died in 1135 he left no legitimate male heir. His daughter Matilda was opposed by his nephew Stephen, who secured enough support to be crowned king. A messy civil war followed, in which King David of Scotland intervened on the side of his niece Matilda. In 1138, with the support of a few barons, including Eustace FitzJohn, David invaded northern England. The atrocities committed by his forces were so appalling that Archbishop Thurstan raised an army to fight under the banners of popular saints. At what became known as the Battle of the Standard, on Cowton Moor north of Northallerton, the invaders were crushed. The estates of Eustace were confiscated, but later restored.[55]

It is worth noting that during the anarchy of Stephen's reign (1135-54), apart from the Gilbertine houses, ten abbeys and priories for men and about eight nunneries were established in Yorkshire. There was great scope for acts of repentance in the light of the considerable amount of sinning which was going on. If the story about Eustace's motives is true, however, his conscience moved at the speed of a tortoise rather than a hare.[56]

Eustace and his wife Agnes gave the substantial township of Watton, together with some land in North Ferriby, to 'the nuns of Watton'. The township of Watton had been held from Eustace's overlord, William Fossard, for the service of two armed knights, to be provided when required according to feudal rules. The obligation was cancelled by William, 'for the support of thirteen canons who will serve the nuns in divine and earthly matters'. The thirteen were the usual prior plus twelve. In the late fourteenth century there were sixty-one nuns, under three prioresses, who in turn were responsible to the prior.[57]

The initial endowment of Malton Priory consisted of the churches of Malton, Winteringham and Brompton, and the township of Linton near Sledmere. The priory was intended by St Gilbert to serve as a retreat house for his canons. Its responsibilities included three hospitals for the care of the poor — a Gilbertine speciality: one in Wheelgate in Malton; another in Broughton to the west; and a third on an island in the River Derwent facing Norton.[58]

Two small Gilbertine houses, both for canons only, which were founded at the beginning of the thirteenth century, were never of any importance. St Andrew's Priory in York, built next to Clementhorpe nunnery, was endowed with a church and some land in the city. It was intended for twelve canons, but there were only four in 1380-81. About 1208 William FitzPeter endowed a priory at Ellerton, on the east bank of the River Derwent south-east of York, to support a hospital for thirteen poor people. It had five canons in 1380-81. Nearly all of the eleven Gilbertine houses in Lincolnshire, the county of origin of the only English monastic order, were double houses of nuns and canons. In Yorkshire this distinctive feature was found only at Watton.[59]

OUTLINE HISTORY II
Nuns, Friars and Late Arrivals

Archbishop Thurstan, one of the keenest supporters of monasticism, founded the first post-Conquest nunnery in Yorkshire at Clementhorpe, just outside the walls of York, at some time between 1125 and 1133. As explained previously, most early medieval documents are undated, but can be given a range of dates from the circumstances of the witnesses. The archbishop gave the site, rents and tithes from his corn mills, and both land and rents in the city of York and in the widespread estates of the diocese. In 1133 William de Percy, grandson of the founder of Whitby Abbey, established a nunnery known at first as Grendale, but within a few years as Handale, about twelve miles west of Whitby. The endowment consisted of land in Dunsley and Staxton, and pasture for two hundred sheep in the fields of Grendale and Dunsley.[1]

If one doubtful case (Kirklees) is excluded, there were only two nunneries in Yorkshire before 1143, but eighteen houses for men, not counting small dependencies. Donors making a spiritual investment in monasticism expected a better return from monks or canons than from nuns. This was partly because only men could say mass, and great importance was attached to masses for the dead, but it also reflected the subordinate position of women in early medieval society. Some features of that position

helped to draw women of the knightly class towards the religious life as an alternative to marriage. It was the normal practice for marriages to be arranged for economic or other family reasons. If romance developed it was a bonus. Even if her husband was caring and considerate, a married woman faced the strain of frequent child-bearing and the dangers of childbirth itself. A girl whose father had died could find herself in a marriage arranged by the feudal overlord, sometimes, in effect, being sold to the highest bidder. Widows could face the same process, and sometimes paid the overlord for the right to remain unattached.

A nunnery could contain, therefore, not only women burning with zeal to serve God, but also some who had made a rational choice of a dignified lifestyle, and no doubt some responding to both motives. Landowners with too many daughters to provide each with an adequate dowry might guide one or more of them to a nunnery, accompanied by a modest gift, but those who made the much greater investment to found a nunnery, with the women of their family in mind, were clearly dealing with a stronger vocation, whether spiritual or social.[2]

With a few exceptions the founders of Yorkshire nunneries were one step down in the social scale from the great lords who had endowed the Cistercian abbeys. They were on the whole the wealthier tenants of the barons. For example Roger de Mowbray, founder of Newburgh Priory and Byland Abbey, had amongst his major tenants: Bertram Haget, founder of Sinningthwaite nunnery (at a date before 1155), Peter of Sand Hutton, founder of Arden Priory (1147-69), and William de Arches who with his wife Juetta established Nun Monkton (1147-53). Their daughter Matilda was the first prioress. The sister of William de Arches, Agnes, who married Herbert de St Quintin, founded Nunkeeling (1143-53), and their daughter Alice established Nun Appleton (1148-54), as well as giving land to Nunkeeling. These family networks played an important part in the promotion of monasticism.[3]

By about 1160 ten more nunneries had been established, six in the North Riding: Keldholme, Marrick, Moxby (initially at Marton), Rosedale, Wykeham and Yedingham (the village of Yedingham is in the East Riding but the priory is on the north side of the River Derwent, the Riding boundary); two in the West Riding: Arthington and Hampole; and two in the East Riding: Swine and Wilberfoss. Most of the twenty-four nunneries of Yorkshire were therefore founded between the early 1140s and 1160. Later in the century came five more:

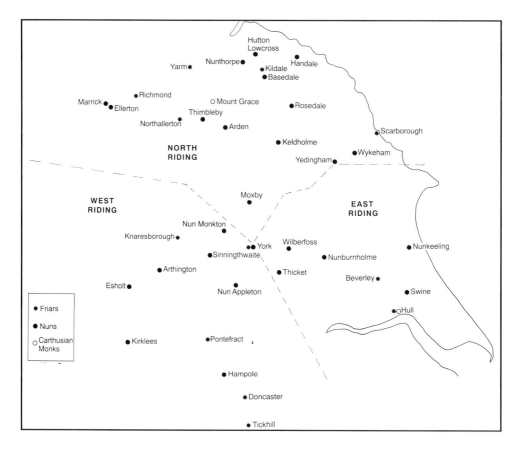

The distribution of nuns, friars and late arrivals in Yorkshire.

The nave of the nunnery church of Wilberfoss Priory survives as the parish church.
(Bernard Jennings)

Kirklees (taking the balance of evidence as to the date) and Esholt in the West Riding; Thicket and Nunburnholme in the East Riding; and a nunnery which began at Hutton Lowcross, migrated to Nunthorpe, and finally settled at Basedale in the North York Moors.[4]

The two remaining nunneries were Foukeholme, otherwise known as Thimbleby (the two places, near Osmotherley, are adjacent), which is first recorded in the reign of King John (1199-1216); and Ellerton-in-Swaledale *(see photograph on page 41)*. The latter has been confused with the Gilbertine priory of Ellerton near York and located even by modern scholars at Ellerton-on-Swale, south-east of Richmond. According to Dugdale, the priory was probably founded in the reign of Henry II (1154-89). Otherwise the earliest documented reference is dated 1227. However, between 1172 and 1183 Henry II made an annual grant of 4s to 'the nuns of Richmond'. There are three possibilities: there was a nunnery at Richmond which disbanded; the nuns lived near, not in, Richmond — Ellerton is six miles to the west; or the nuns moved from Richmond to Ellerton in or after 1183.[5]

Two of the nunneries were originally established as double houses of nuns and canons, Swine, which remained so until the late thirteenth century, and Marton. The nuns from the latter, founded about 1150, had moved to a separate convent at Moxby, a mile and a half to the south, by 1167. They continued to follow a version of the Augustinian Rule, but seem to have had little further connection with the canons at Marton. Some nunneries had a male head, called a prior or master, as well as a prioress. The foundation charter of Nun Appleton Priory was issued in favour of 'Brother Richard and the nuns of Appleton', and the next charter referred to 'the prior and nuns'. In such cases the prioress was responsible for the inner life of the nunnery, the master or prior dealing with business affairs.[6]

Apart from Moxby, and Arthington which followed a version of the Cluniac rule, the other nunneries were labelled as either Benedictine or Cistercian. Sometimes the evidence is no more than a single reference to the colour of the nuns' habit, eg Ellerton being described by John Leland as a 'priori of white clothid nunnes'. Cistercian abbeys were exempt from tithes on land which they farmed themselves (although they sometimes made compromise deals with the tithe owners) and some nunneries may have sought the Cistercian affiliation to secure the same privilege. It was granted by the pope to Sinningthwaite in 1172 and Swine in 1177. The Cistercian order showed no great interest in nuns. The first decree of the General Chapter providing for the affiliation of nunneries was not issued until 1213, and the policy of discouragement was resumed soon afterwards. The priests serving nunneries which called themselves Cistercian were always canons, secular clerks or friars, never priest-monks from a Cistercian abbey. Furthermore, the white monk abbeys were exempt from inspection by the archbishop. Cistercian nunneries were not.[7]

The differences in estate management between the Benedictine abbeys, with their manors, mills and churches, and the Cistercians, with their granges run by lay brothers, were not reproduced amongst the nunneries carrying the same labels. Both groups used lay brothers, especially if their endowment included undeveloped land or extensive sheep pastures. Most nunneries also had lay sisters at some stage.[8]

A hundred years after the foundation of St Mary's Abbey, York (1088), the county had fifty houses of monks, canons and nuns, not counting small dependencies. There were few additions during the next four decades: nunneries at Foukeholme and possibly Ellerton-in-Swaledale; two small Gilbertine houses, York St Andrew and Ellerton; and the white canons of Egglestone. These five houses had one thing in common: they were all poorly endowed.[9]

There is also the uncertain case of Healaugh Park Priory near Tadcaster. Bertram Haget endowed a hermitage there, with land and rights in the woodland, for the benefit of Gilbert, described as a monk of Marmoutier, and his successors. Gilbert may have come from one of the Yorkshire dependencies of the French abbey. Bertram's son Geoffrey confirmed his father's gift, together with the church of St John of the Park. The hermitage seems to have evolved into a small community of canons, but it was not until 1218 that, with the support of Bertram's granddaughter Alice, a fully-fledged Augustinian priory was in operation.[10]

The almost complete halt to new foundations after the end of the reign of Henry II (1154-89) need not be attributed to any fundamental change of attitude on the part of donors. In economic language, the market was fully supplied. Those families with the desire and the means to invest had already done so. The connections were maintained down the generations not only by tradition, and by contacts occurring naturally where a religious house was close to a family seat, but specifically by the fact that the office of 'founder' passed down by inheritance or by the sale of the lordship. We find, therefore, people in the sixteenth century describing themselves, quite accurately in terms of this convention, as the 'founders' of abbeys 400 years old. The founder was seen as having rights, eg hospitality, and sometimes consultation about the appointment of the head of the house; and also obligations, especially to defend the interests of the monastery.

Apart from the limited pastoral role of the canons, monasticism for men and women, until the early thirteenth century, meant withdrawal from the world into a regulated communal life. The new movements which then burst upon the Church and society had a very different character and purpose. The prime movers were St Francis of Assisi and St Dominic. Francis, described by David Knowles as 'one of the most familiar and admired figures in the history of mankind', was born in 1181 or 1182, the son of a prosperous merchant of Assisi. In 1205 he felt a call to abandon his comfortable life and spent three years in a prayerful search for his vocation, caring for lepers and rebuilding churches near his native city. When inspiration came, he conceived of a fellowship which would not withdraw into solitude, but would work amongst the people, persuading them as much by example as by preaching to repent and follow the teaching of the gospels. If not quite anti-intellectual, Francis had no sympathy with the niceties of academic theology.[11]

The rejection of material comforts had been a feature of earlier reform movements such as the Cistercians, but Francis recognised the limitations of personal vows of poverty taken in abbeys which had become wealthy. His followers therefore were to possess nothing, apart from the simple clothes they wore. For shelter and food they were to rely upon the people to whom they ministered. They therefore became known as the 'mendicant' (begging) friars. The humility of the Franciscans was expressed in their name, the 'lesser brothers' or Friars Minor. The Franciscan friar did not join a stable community, but was ready, in the words of the English Franciscan Thomas Docking, 'to travel about the whole world, preaching and hearing confessions, calming discords and bringing peace, spreading the faith and elevating the character of the people.'[12]

In 1209 Pope Innocent III (1198-1216) gave general approval to Francis's ideas for a new religious movement, but it was Pope Honorius III (1216-27) who worked out the rules, including a one-year novitiate and tight control by Ministers Provincial and a Minister General, which turned a brotherhood into an effective international order.[13]

St Dominic was born in 1171 or 1172 in Old Castile (north central Spain) into a landed family devoted to the Church. After about ten years of study he became a priest and an Augustinian canon. In 1206 he began preaching amongst the Cathars, an heretical sect also known as the Albigenses from the city of Albi, who were very strong in southern France. The Cathars, who held that the material world was evil, rejected the sacraments and marriage. They embarrassed the Church because the devotion and austerity of their preachers contrasted with the easygoing lifestyle of the rather ignorant parish clergy. A military campaign in 1209-14 forced Catharism underground.

In 1215 Dominic received papal approval for the creation of an international Order of Preachers. By 1220 they had followed the Franciscan example and become mendicant friars. There were, however, important initial differences between the two orders. The Friars Preachers were priests; few of the early Friars Minor were ordained. The Dominicans were essentially an intellectual order, with a doctor of theology in every friary. The Franciscans soon repaid the compliment of imitation and became, in John Moorman's words, 'one of the most learned institutions in the world'.[14]

The Dominicans arrived in England in 1221, the Franciscans three years later. By this time both orders had adopted the practice of acquiring or erecting simple buildings, including a church and living accommodation. In Yorkshire the first Dominican and Franciscan houses were established in the most populous town, York. The city, with the encouragement of King Henry III, gave to the Dominicans the chapel of St Mary Magdalen with some land adjacent, in Kingstoft inside the city ditch on the south bank of the River Ouse. They took possession of the property in 1227. The York house had an average of fifty friars in the late thirteenth and early fourteenth centuries, and was head of one of the four regions of the English province.[15]

The Franciscans came to York about 1230. In 1236-37 Henry III provided sixty oak trees for building, but the first site proved to be too constricted. In 1243 the friars were given another site, between the Ouse and the moat on the north-west side of York Castle, and the king paid £26 13s 4d towards the cost of the new building. In 1268 he gave some adjacent ground to make an elevated platform for open-air preaching. The number of friars in the period 1299-1337 ranged between thirty-six and fifty-two.[16]

The second Dominican house in the county was established in the second-largest town, Beverley. The exact date is unknown, but a Provincial Chapter was held there in August 1240, Henry III giving £6 13s 4d towards the cost. The founder was apparently a cleric called Master Stephen Goldsmith. Building work was still going on in 1263, when the king donated fifteen oak trees from the Forest of Galtres. There were about forty friars at the beginning of the fourteenth century.[17]

For their second house the Franciscans went to Scarborough, apparently by 1239, for on the 5th February 1240 the king ordered the sheriff of York to provide food on one day each week 'for the Friars Minor of Scarborough'. However, they soon encountered opposition from the Cistercians who, in common with the other orders of monks and canons, showed no great enthusiasm for the preaching friars. In 1189 King Richard I had given the parish church of Scarborough to Cîteaux Abbey, so that the revenues, less the cost of supporting a vicar, could be used to defray the expenses of the Cistercian General Chapter. Normally two or three Cistercian monks were stationed in the town to supervise the collection of the tithe and other parochial income. There was a potential for conflict between the friars and the parish clergy, not so much about preaching, in which many of the clergy in the early Middle Ages were neither competent nor interested, but in relation to other pastoral functions, especially hearing confessions and burying the dead. These activities could have resource implications, not only fees for interment in the priory church or cemetery, but also legacies and other gifts.[18]

The Cistercians made an almighty fuss about the Scarborough Franciscans, involving the pope and Bishop Grosseteste of Lincoln as well as their own General Chapter. To solve the problem Henry III, in 1245, gave the grey friars some land at Throxenby, two miles west of the town, to which they began to move in the same year. The new site was not very convenient for a preaching order. The friars could still walk into Scarborough to preach in the open air, but would not have so many hearers for sermons in the friary church. In or before 1252 the Dominicans settled in Scarborough, with the encouragement of the authorities of the borough. There is no record of any opposition to this move, and between 1267 and 1272 the Franciscans came back into the old town.[19]

Trouble with the Cistercians broke out again in the period 1281-83, when both friaries were planning extensions. Archbishop Peckham of Canterbury (a Franciscan) and Archbishop Wickwane of York intervened to protect the friars' right to celebrate divine service in their churches. In 1285 the Cistercian General Chapter complained that the activities of the friars had so reduced the revenues of Scarborough Church that instead of meeting their expenses for three days, they were sufficient only for one.[20]

Meanwhile two other orders of friars had established themselves in Yorkshire. The Carmelites, or white friars, originated in a group of hermits living on the slopes of Mount Carmel in Palestine in the middle of the twelfth century. Following the Saracen invasion, some Carmelites migrated, about 1238, to western Europe. The Friars Hermits of St Augustine emerged from a group of penitent communities in Italy, which became an order under papal guidance in 1243-44. Both orders became mendicants and preachers, and modelled their organisation on that of the Dominicans. (The name 'Augustinian' in relation to both canons and friars was often abbreviated to 'Austin'. For the sake of clarity, the canons are described in this book as Augustinian, and the friars as Austin.)[21]

The Carmelites were in York by 1253, at a site in Bootham, near the Horsefair. Henry III gave them eleven oak trees from Galtres Forest in 1253 and 1255. The Vescy family had been well disposed towards the Carmelites since meeting them as crusaders in Palestine, and in 1295 William de Vescy gave the York community a new site, bounded by Stonebow Lane, Mersk Lane, the River Foss and Fossgate, on which a church and friary buildings were erected. Edward I provided eight oaks in 1300, and the cemetery was consecrated in 1304. At that time there were about twenty-five friars.[22]

The first house of Austin friars in Yorkshire was probably that founded at Tickhill. The date is uncertain, but may have been as early as 1256. According to the traditions of the order, some friars from Tickhill established a friary in York near Lendal Bridge and the Guildhall. The earliest definite reference is in 1272. The house had thirty-five friars in 1300.[23]

By the end of the thirteenth century the Dominicans had friaries at Pontefract (1256) and Yarm (before 1266); and the Franciscans at Richmond (1258), Beverley (before 1267) and Doncaster (before 1284). Both orders now had five friaries, their maximum number. There was supposed to have been a short-lived Franciscan friary in Hull, but there is no real evidence for its existence.[24]

The first friary to be established in Hull was Carmelite. In 1289 the dean of York,

Master Robert of Scarborough, petitioned for licence to give a house in Wyke-upon-Hull to the white friars. A licence was required under the Statute of Mortmain, passed by Parliament in 1279 because Edward I was concerned at the amount of land which had been acquired by religious houses, thus denying the king the feudal profits which he enjoyed on the death of a tenant-in-chief.

Edward I was in fact a major supporter of the Hull Carmelites. In 1293 he bought the township of Wyke-upon-Hull and the grange of Myton from Meaux Abbey, and six years later created a free borough with a new name, Kingston-upon-Hull. The growth in the numbers of both friars and congregation prompted the king in 1304 to give the Carmelites a new site just outside the walls, in exchange for their property in the town. Building began near the Beverley Gate (at the city centre end of Whitefriargate) in 1307 and the church was consecrated in 1311. Other benefactors were Sir Richard de la Pole and his son William.[25]

A house of Austin friars was established in Hull about 1303, in Blackfriargate, south of the market place. The de la Poles are thought to have been the main founders. Excavations by the Humberside Archaeological Unit in 1994 showed that the friars began with a narrow timber church. The chancel was soon replaced by a larger building on stone footings, but probably built of

The Austin friary on Blackfriargate, Hull, in 1789.
(Tickell, *History of Hull*)

brick as the nearby Holy Trinity Church was. The timber nave continued in use for some time, and was then replaced by a larger nave with both north and south aisles, also on stone footings.[26]

Three more Carmelite friaries were established in the fourteenth century: at Scarborough in 1319, the Cistercian opposition having been bought off by Edward II; Doncaster in 1350, 'a right goodly house in the middle of the town' according to John Leland; and Northallerton in 1356. An Austin friary in Northallerton was licensed in 1340, but never built.[27]

The four main orders of friars therefore had eighteen houses in Yorkshire, with four in York, three in Scarborough, and two each in Beverley, Doncaster and Hull. They all depended mainly on begging, supplemented by garden produce. The Franciscans were the most devoted to the rule of poverty. Although they found the literal observance of the precepts of St Francis too difficult, they tried to avoid the taint of property by such devices as having the title to their buildings beld by trustees. The other orders had no objection to owning their own churches and domestic buildings, and all four accepted small gifts of houses or rents in their own towns. Because of mendicancy the founders of a friary had only to provide the site and give some help with the building programme. The fervour of the friars in their early days, and their obvious impact on the populations of the growing towns, made supporting them seem to be a good spiritual investment.[28]

The expression 'main orders' is used above because there were some lesser orders. The Brothers of Penance of Jesus Christ, usually known by the sackcloth which they wore over their habits as the Friars of the Sack, came to

York about 1260. A General Council of the Church, held at Lyons in 1274, forbade the order to recruit new members, and it gradually withered away. There were still two friars in York in 1300. They had died by 1312, when the property passed to King Edward II. The Friars of the Holy Cross, or Crutched Friars, were not suppressed by the Council of Lyons, but the English bishops thought that they should have been. Archbishop Greenfield discouraged a group of them from settling in York about 1307, and a few years later hounded them out of Kildale in the North York Moors where they had been given a base by a local landowner.[29]

The Order of the Holy Trinity and of the Redemption of Captives in the Holy Land had been founded in 1197 for the purpose expressed in their title. Although they were called friars and begged for alms, the Trinitarians had little in common with the preaching or mendicant orders. In both their rule and their economic organisation, particularly the acquisition of churches, they resembled the black canons. The Trinitarians came to Knaresborough in 1252, and built their church over the tomb of St Robert, a hermit who had died in 1218, and whose holy reputation attracted many pilgrims.[30]

Apart from the three Carmelite, and one Austin, friaries mentioned above, only three religious houses were founded in Yorkshire during the fourteenth century. In 1320 Thomas Wake began the process of establishing a priory of Augustinian canons in the manor of Cottingham. In 1326 the enterprise was moved to Newton, a short distance to the south, where Haltemprice Priory was built. It was endowed with the townships of Newton, Willerby and Wolfreton, and four churches: Cottingham, Kirk Ella, Wharram Percy and one in Lincolnshire.[31]

The slow spread of the Carthusians, resulting from their hermit-like way of life and their determination to maintain the highest standards, has already been mentioned. The order had only nine priories in England, all but two founded in the period 1343-1414. Sir William de la Pole, a member of a famous upwardly-mobile family already mentioned on page 36 in connection with friaries in Hull, made plans in the 1360s for a hospital in Hull serving poor people, to be managed, as was normal, by secular priests. He then decided to use Franciscan nuns instead. Whether any were actually recruited is uncertain, but work had started on the hospital buildings, known as the Maison Dieu, when Sir William died. His son Michael went ahead with the hospital scheme, for thirteen poor men and thirteen poor women, but now in association with a Carthusian priory, known as a charterhouse from the anglicisation of 'La Grande Chartreuse', the mother house of the order. In 1377 Michael de la Pole paid the king £5 for the licence.

The priory was built outside the north gate of the town, close to the Maison Dieu. The management of a hospital, particularly one for both sexes, did not fit in well with the Carthusian style of strict enclosure, and the priory seems to have had little to do with the Maison Dieu. John Leland, describing the Charterhouse shortly after its suppression in 1539, wrote: 'Most part of this monastery was builded with Brike, as the residew of the buidings of Hull for the most part be.' Demolition of the church and buildings had already started, but 'The hospital standith'. The building later known in Hull as 'the Charterhouse' was actually the Maison Dieu.[32]

The last religious house to be established in medieval Yorkshire was the Carthusian priory of Mount Grace, near Osmotherley. It could not have had more illustrious benefactors. The principal founder was Thomas Holland, duke of Surrey. His grandmother was Joan Wake, known in her younger days as the Fair Maid of Kent, who inherited the great estates of the Stuteville and Wake families. By her second husband, Edward the Black Prince, she was the mother of King Richard II (1377-99). In February 1398 the king granted a licence to his young relative to establish the priory, and in return for £1,000 paid by the duke, he gave the property of several alien priories, seized by the Crown because of the war with France. He also granted the new priory exemption from taxation.

By January 1400 both of the principal benefactors were dead: Richard II was deposed and murdered in 1399, and the duke of Surrey was killed in the course of a rebellion against the new king, Henry IV. Some of the endowment income was lost to Mount Grace Priory, and its financial position was not made secure until the reign of Henry V (1413-22).[33]

By this time all of the small priories in Yorkshire belonging to French abbeys had become independent or closed. Their situation had been precarious since King John lost Normandy in 1204. Their property was liable to be seized, and squeezed of resources, whenever the English and French kings were at war. Religious links with France were effectively broken in 1378, when an Italian pope, recognised in England, was elected in Rome, and a French pope appointed in Avignon. In the period 1386-95 Pontefract Priory paid the king a substantial sum to be declared independent of Cluny. Grosmont Priory repudiated its allegiance to Grandmont. Ecclesfield Priory was closed

Mount Grace Priory church. (Lefroy, *Ruined Abbeys*)

and its property given to the Carthusians in Coventry, and Burstall Priory was similarly treated to the benefit of Kirkstall Abbey.

In 1414 Parliament petitioned Henry V to expel all foreign monks. The lands of Allerton Mauleverer Priory were given to King's College, Cambridge. The property in Richmond, the only asset of the shadowy cell of Begar Abbey, went to Mount Grace. Holy

Trinity Priory, York, was made an independent Benedictine house in 1426, and kept its cell at Headley.[34]

Three forms of religious life and organisation which have some affinity with monasticism are not surveyed in this book, although a few references occur. They are hermits and anchorites; hospitals; and the military orders. The distinction between the first two was that an anchorite normally stayed in strict enclosure in a cell, whereas the hermit, although living in relative seclusion, was not withdrawn from the world. Most anchorites were women, often described as anchoresses. Hermits were men, living singly or in small groups. Some were seekers after a solitary, contemplative life, but others had a particular function, eg providing shelter for travellers, or maintaining roads or bridges. In the early fourteenth century the hermit of St Helen's Chapel at Shipton, north of York, was collecting money to repair a road through the Forest of Galtres 'where many accidents have occurred by reason of the depth of the ways'. Some hermitages evolved into, or attached themselves to, monasteries.[35]

There were basically three kinds of medieval hospital. Some cared for lepers. A few, such as the hospital at Spital, otherwise Rerecross, on Stainmoor (the responsibility of Marrick Priory), provided shelter for travellers. Most cared for 'the sick and the poor', providing spiritual solace as well as material help. Their function was care rather than cure, although the staff of some hospitals had skills in the use of traditional medicine and herbal remedies. A few hospitals were attached to monasteries. Most were freestanding, staffed by priests and sisters.[36]

There may have been as many as a hundred hospitals in medieval Yorkshire at one time or another. It is difficult to be more precise, as some were short-lived and others may have appeared under more than one name. By far the largest hospital in Yorkshire was St Leonard's, York (originally known as St Peter's), which was generously endowed. Its normal staffing was a master; thirteen priests following the Augustinian Rule; four secular chaplains;

The undercroft of St Leonard's Hospital in York.

*The church tower of
Marrick Priory rising out
of the farm buildings.*

*The fifteenth century tower of
Ellerton Priory stands alongside
fragments of the church*

Kirkham Priory: a lonely fragment of the east end of the church.

eight sisters; and an unknown number of lay brothers and female servants. There were usually about 200 inmates, often described as 'sick and poor', but including in the later Middle Ages some who had bought a place. The hospital also had an orphanage, and grammar and song schools.[37]

The military orders, which originated in Palestine after the First Crusade (1095-99), were the Knights of St John of Jerusalem, otherwise the Knights Hospitallers (c1113), and the Knights Templars (c1118). In Yorkshire their houses, known as preceptories (Templars) and preceptories or commanderies (Hospitallers), were essentially estate offices, administering property for the benefit of the international order. Following the military withdrawal from Palestine in 1291, the Templars no longer had a clear function. In 1308-12 the order, accused of heresy, idolatry and immorality, was suppressed. Some of their property was transferred to the Hospitallers. The Yorkshire houses of the two orders are listed at the end of the gazetteer.[38]

THE POST-CONQUEST PIONEERS
The Benedictines, especially Selby and Whitby

In the Benedictine system the abbot was in complete command. A great deal depended upon his qualities, as a spiritual leader, and as a manager of men and resources.

According to the monk-historian of Selby Abbey, writing in 1174, the first abbot, Benedict, was initially successful in both roles, but then things began to go wrong. King William II (1087-1100), known as Rufus, had no great affection for the abbey founded by his father at Selby, preferring to support his own foundation, St Mary's at York. In 1093 Rufus gave Selby Abbey to the archbishop of York, as part of a deal which prevented the archbishop exercising authority over the vast diocese of Lincoln. The archbishop therefore had a second lever of power, the first being his right to inspect and oversee a Benedictine abbey.

It is not clear whether these external factors contributed to the discord which developed within Selby Abbey, but matters came to a head when two monks absconded with 80 lbs of silver from the monastic treasury. After a successful pursuit, Benedict had the miscreants castrated. This did not improve morale in the abbey. Complaints were made to Rufus, who ordered Abbot Stephen of St Mary's to arrest Benedict. Stephen was dissuaded by Benedict from doing so, but the pioneer abbot of Selby realised that his position had become untenable. He resigned in 1096 or 1097 and left the area.[1]

His successor was Abbot Hugh, who had previously served as prior, the second-in-command in a Benedictine abbey. He has often been described as Hugh de Lacy, which would make him a member of the great baronial family which was one of the early benefactors of the abbey. There is, however, no medieval record of his surname. In charters he appears as 'Abbot Hugh' in the usual way. He was, in the words of the monastic historian, 'a simple man, God-fearing, rejecting evil, distinguished for his charity, remarkable for his humility, praiseworthy for his piety and glorious in his chastity'.

When Hugh took over, the monks were still living and worshipping in the temporary wooden buildings put up around Benedict's original hermitage on the banks of the River Ouse. The delay in starting on the permanent stone buildings may have been due to a shortage of resources, perhaps because for a time donors were favouring St Mary's. Hugh was able to attract new grants and new recruits, sometimes together, as when Nigel, the provost (administrator) of the archbishop of York, became a monk at Selby and gave half of the township of Hillam, near Monk Fryston, and other property. Archbishop Gerard of York gave the churches of the great parish of Snaith, which stretched seventeen miles from Hensall on the west to the River Trent beyond Adlingfleet.[2]

As more land was acquired, the possibility of moving to a more salubrious situation than the damp riverside in Selby was considered. King Henry I (1100-35) issued an order to Archbishop Gerard, the sheriff of York, and all his barons in Yorkshire, that the abbey of St German of Selby, founded by his father and mother, must not move to another place. This unusual instruction, and the reference in it to Henry's mother Queen Matilda, must be the source of the tradition that Henry, the youngest son of William the Conqueror, was born in Selby. This may be true, but one argument against is the absence of any reference in the 1174 history.[3]

Hugh and his monks were able to move a little, to a slightly higher site about 150 yards from the river, and there work began on a stone church. The stone used is magnesian limestone, which can be seen in many older buildings in York and Tadcaster. The initial supply may have come from quarries at Huddleston. Hugh acted as both *architectus* (perhaps best translated as 'master builder') and hod-carrier. Every day 'dressed in a workman's cowl he carried to the wall on his shoulders stones, lime and whatever was needed for the work'. On Saturdays he collected a labourer's wage, which he gave to the poor. The building operations included the chapter house, dormitory and frater (refectory).

In due course, 'with the greater part of the church completed with God's help, and the conventual buildings erected around according to the rule, the devout shepherd led his sheep into the fold on the vigil of the feast of the holy patron German', ie on the 30th July.[4]

Selby Abbey: the south side of the nave, with 'Abbot Hugh's Pillar' in the centre. (The Story of Selby Abbey)

Most of what Abbot Hugh built has disappeared, including the conventual buildings, all on the south side of the church, and the chancel, later replaced by a structure twice as long. Hugh built the wall of the south aisle of the nave for almost the whole of its present length, so that the cloister would be fully enclosed, but on the north side his work progressed just beyond the first two bays west of the transept. The original appearance of the church can be judged from these sections, and from the west wall of the north transept. (The south transept was destroyed by the collapse of

the central tower in 1690.) The similarities in detail between Hugh's work and Durham Cathedral led Charles C Hodges, an architect who made a thorough survey of Selby Abbey church in 1892, to conclude that the same architect had been involved in both.[5]

Hugh retired from the abbacy in 1122 or 1123. The next five abbots were outsiders, imposed on the abbey by the king and/or the archbishop of York. Herbert from St Alban's Abbey was a devoted contemplative but a hopeless manager. After his resignation Durand from St Mary's, York, was appointed. He was, according to the 1174 historian,

Selby Abbey's Norman west doorway.

The west front of Selby Abbey.

'a very prudent man in external matters ... erudite ... eloquent ... handsome in appearance', but on the debit side he was fond of the company of ladies of easy virtue. He was forced to resign in 1135 by Archbishop Thurstan. After a vacancy lasting for two years, the reason for which is not clear, the monks took Thurstan's advice and elected Walter, who had been head of Pontefract Priory. Abbot Walter, a good all-round performer according to the monastic historian, died in 1143. He was succeeded by Elias Paynel, a member of a leading Norman family, benefactors to Selby, who had been head of Holy Trinity Priory, York. He was 'almost completely a layman, except for his recollection of the psalms, having been converted from a soldier'.[6]

An ex-soldier was perhaps a good choice in the anarchy of Stephen's reign (1135-54), when in addition to what might be called the official civil war between the forces of Stephen and Matilda, there was much local disorder, and 'tyrants and robbers' roamed the land. Henry de Lacy, a relative of Elias, began to build a castle in Selby, which provoked an attack from William le Gros, earl of Albermarle. The earl was a consistent supporter of King Stephen, but may have been fighting a private war on this occasion. During the subsequent fighting, most of the town was burned down, but those who tried to violate the abbey or attack the townspeople who had taken refuge there received short shrift from St German. The monastic historian devotes several thousand words to describing the vigorous actions of the saint in rescuing the deserving and smiting the ungodly, and then apologises for the omission of many more miracles for considerations of brevity! In this context what people believed could be as important as what actually happened, and the saint intervening directly on behalf of those under his protection is a familiar figure in medieval chronicles.[7]

When the election of an archbishop of York was disputed in 1147, Abbot Elias opposed the candidate who was ultimately successful, the Cistercian Henry Murdac. The latter had his revenge in 1152 or thereabouts, when he forced Elias to resign and imposed German, prior of Tynemouth Abbey, as the replacement abbot. For over a year the Selby monks refused to recognise German, until Murdac compelled them, under threat of

The south side of the nave in Selby Abbey, looking east, showing pillars of different styles.

excommunication, to elect his appointee. Three months later Murdac died. In the vacancy Elias was restored by the archdeacon of York, only to be deposed six months later by the archbishop of Canterbury, acting as the papal legate in England. German returned, and gained a reputation for considerate and efficient management. He died in 1160, to be succeeded by Abbot Gilbert de Vere (1160-84), in whose time the monastic history was written.[8]

It is not surprising that between the retirement of Abbot Hugh and the election of Gilbert de Vere, work on the abbey church proceeded by fits and starts. Money for building may have been scarce, and problems were caused by the settlement of the foundations of the tower — the church is built on clay — which distorted the arches of the easternmost bay on either side of the nave. 'The gradual growth of the nave', writes Charles Hodges, 'has resulted in the multiplication of the different forms of columns to a remarkable degree, there being in the whole church no less than thirteen distinct varieties.' By about 1190 the work on the ground level of the nave, including the north porch and the lower part of the west front, had been completed. Soon afterwards the remaining section of the triforium (the arcade above the nave arches) was added in the Early English style, the pointed arch replacing the rounded arch characteristic of the Norman style.[9]

In 1213 King John gave the Selby monks the right to elect their own abbot. The archbishop could now interfere in the appointment only in the case of scandal. The abbey continued to receive grants of land, often from later generations of donor families. Some gifts were for a specific purpose, eg the purchase of communion wine or the provision of a light at night in the cloister. By the middle of the thirteenth century the estates had reached virtually their maximum extent. Most of them lay within the area of the map opposite. In addition the abbey owned property at six other locations in Yorkshire; in Lincolnshire, including Crowle Church and three other churches; Leicestershire; and Northamptonshire, with another church.[10]

The churches provided about forty per cent of the abbey's income, in the form of tithe, glebe (land belonging to the churches) and offerings, less the cost of serving the churches with chaplains or vicars. Snaith

Selby Abbey: the Lathom Chapel and window of the north transept, both c1470.
(The Story of Selby Abbey)

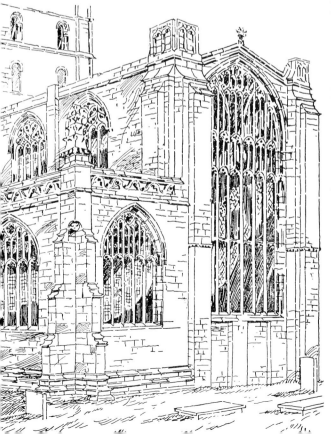

Church was constituted as a priory cell, staffed by two priest-monks, one of whom was called the prior. Chaplains were employed to say mass at the parish church in Selby, but the functions of the latter were gradually transferred to the abbey church. This is why the abbey church survived the suppression of the monasteries.[11]

The secular income came, in money and in kind, from a variety of sources: the produce of the demesne land (ie the land held by the lord of the manor, not his tenants), cultivated in part by the compulsory labour of bond tenants; rents and other dues from both free and bond tenants; the leasing of small manors; the profits of corn mills and manor courts; fisheries in the River Ouse and fish ponds; 1,100 acres of 'waste, moor and turbary' in the vast marsh of which Thorne Waste is the remnant — 600 acres at Inclesmoor within the manor of Rawcliffe and the rest at Eastoft on the eastern side; a ferry across the river at Selby — there was no bridge until 1792; and a small fleet of boats, used for carrying peat from Inclesmoor and Eastoft, tithe corn, fish and other goods. Because so many of the Selby estates were low-lying, most of the roads were impassable for wheeled vehicles in winter, and the rivers provided an essential lifeline.[12]

Medieval Selby never became a borough, and it remained under the control of the

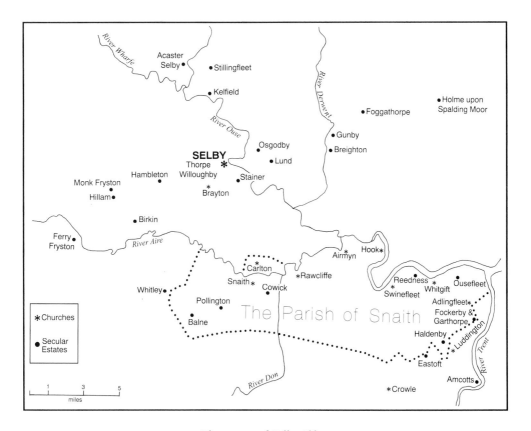

The estates of Selby Abbey.

abbey except for one aspect. It might have been expected that the abbey would have had the profits and the market and any fairs held in the town. In 1227, however, a charter for a two-day fair in July and a Wednesday market was granted to Brian de l'Isle, as a reward for his support of King John and the boy king Henry III in his role as constable of Knaresborough Castle.[13]

The twelfth century abbots of Whitby, after William de Percy, are less well known than their Selby counterparts. William's successor Nicholas died about 1139. The next abbot, Benedict, resigned in 1148 or 1149 after some trouble in the abbey, to become prior of the cell in Fishergate, York. Archbishop Henry Murdac then intervened to insist that the thirty-six monks should elect one of his

three nominees as abbot. They chose Richard, prior of Peterborough Abbey, who served as abbot until his death in 1175. During his time the abbey prospered in both spiritual and material affairs, save for the heavy damage inflicted in a raid by the king of Norway.[14]

There are no records of the abbey church in Abbot Richard's time. Excavations have shown that the nave of the first stone church was roughly the same in size and layout as its fourteenth-century successor, but the chancel was much smaller. Glyn Coppack has pointed out that the church at Lastingham, where Stephen and his followers built part of what was intended to be an abbey church between 1080 and 1086, gives a good idea of the style in which the first stone church at Whitby was begun a short time later.[15]

The twelfth century apsidal east end of Lastingham Church.

*The Norman crypt at Lastingham is the work
of Abbot Stephen and his colleagues.*

When a later abbot died in 1206, the abbey was taken over by King John. Normally he would have held the property for a few months until a new abbot was appointed, but John was beginning his quarrel with the papacy which led to England being placed under an interdict, banning all church services, from 1208 to 1213. John made allowances for the maintenance of the monks, and kept the rest of the revenues. In the two years to the 29th September 1212 the king took £231 out of a total income of £413. A new abbot was elected in 1213.[16]

About 1110, in the course of confirming previous grants, Henry I had made the abbey overlord of a large area, defined by boundaries 'from the port of Whitby all the coast to Blawic [Bleawyke] and so to Grendich [Greendyke] and along Grendich to Swinestischae [now known as the Druid's Circle] and to Thornelay [Thirley]' and so on. Lands within these bounds were designated later in the century as the Liberty of Whitby (see map overleaf), separate from the administrative sub-divisions of the county known as wapentakes. The king exacted a price for his charter by requiring

the abbey to surrender the right to hunt deer and wild boar. He was, in effect, extending his Forest of Pickering. A medieval forest was not a woodland, although it would contain some woodlands. It was a hunting ground, much of it consisting of open country, which was subject to special laws for the preservation of the beasts of the chase.[17]

It became the policy of the abbey to secure direct control, and not merely the overlordship, of as much as possible of the land within the Liberty. Between 1109 and 1114, Abbot William de Percy bought the townships of Hawsker, Normanby, Fylingthorpe and Fylingdales from Tancard the Fleming. About ten years later he made an agreement with Aschetin of Hawsker whereby the latter conveyed Newholm to the abbey, receiving in exchange Hawsker and Normanby to hold for 24s a year rent, plus labour services at ploughing and harvest times. Aschetin's relationship with the abbey was not purely economic. In the time of Abbot Benedict he built and endowed a chapel in Hawsker, where masses were said by priest-monks. Labour services from other rented lands were used to cultivate the abbey demesnes. The township of Broxa, for example, was let off for 10s a year and other dues plus the provision of all the ploughteams in the township 'once a year' (it is not clear whether this was for one day or several) and a reaper from each house in August.[18]

The abbey acquired land bordering the Liberty and just inside the Forest of Pickering through the accession of the hermitage of Goathland. When Henry I ordered his lordship of Pickering to be brought under forest law, the hermitage must have been either disturbed or threatened. The king issued a charter in the period 1109-14 to safeguard the hermitage, held by Osmund the priest and his brethren, and, probably by way of compensation, gave them some additional land and pasture rights. Soon afterwards Osmund and his colleagues surrendered themselves and the hermitage to Whitby Abbey, and took the Benedictine habit. The hermitage must still have been in operation later in the century, in effect as a monastic cell, because in the 1170s or 1180s a toft in Lockton, north-east of Pickering, was given to 'the brethren of St Mary of Goathland'. In 1205 the abbey gave King John

three horses in return for the confirmation of their title to Goathland.[19]

The most valuable resource outside the Liberty acquired by the abbey during the twelfth century consisted of eleven churches. About 1120 Robert de Brus, founder of Guisborough Priory, gave to Whitby Abbey the church of St Hilda the Abbess in Middlesbrough, together with some land in Newham, on condition that 'certain monks' should be in residence to provide services. Middlesbrough thus became the second priory cell of the abbey. The other churches are shown on the map on page 54. Sutton-on-Derwent and Seamer were given by members of the Percy family. Occasionally landowners managed to give the same property to different monasteries. Whitby paid 10s a year to Evesham Abbey to satisfy the latter's claim to the title of Huntington Church, near York.[20]

Whitby's principal holdings of land within Yorkshire but outside the Liberty are also shown on the map overleaf. The largest was at Cayton, near Scarborough, where the abbey held half of the township. Part of this land had been given, part bought. Gifts of land which were too small for direct exploitation were let off for money rents. Lands in Wold Newton and Hoveton, near Kirkby Moorside, were in the middle of estates being built up by Bridlington Priory and Rievaulx Abbey respectively, and were leased to those two houses.[21]

All of the donors of land expected prayers in return. Some

The Liberty of Whitby.

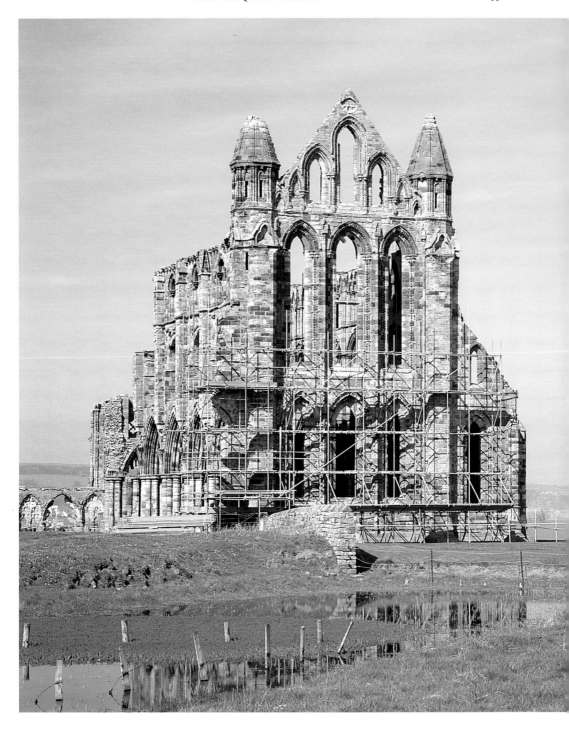

Whitby Abbey, the east end, which was built c1220 in Early English style (under repair during 1997).

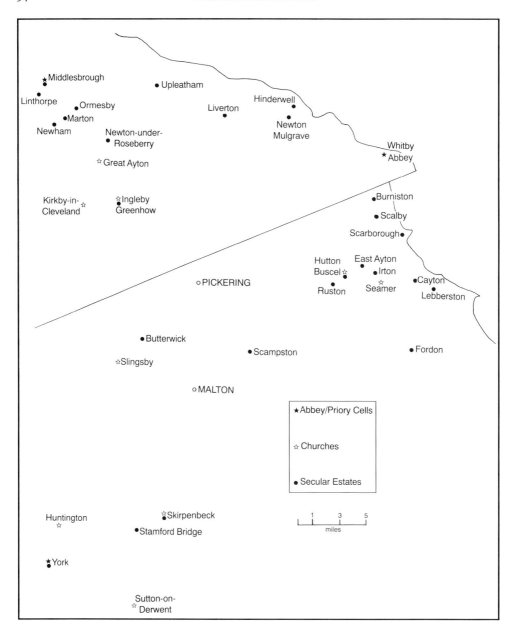

The Yorkshire estates of Whitby Abbey outside the Liberty of Whitby.

of them specified particular spiritual services. Amfrey de Chauncy, whose father had given Skirpenbeck Church and fifty acres of land in the township to the abbey, increased the grant of land to about 140 acres, on condition that each member of his household should have, on the anniversary of his or her death, the special services arranged on the anniversary of a monk's death. A lady named Pagana wanted material as well as spiritual comforts in return for the gift of land in Blake Street, York, including the subsistence allowance appropriate for one monk and one servant, and a clothing allowance. It was established practice for elderly people to take the habit of a monk or nun during their sunset days. Pagana's deal was a foretaste of the development of monasteries as retirement homes for older people remaining in the lay state. Some people became members of the monastic community posthumously. William son of Angot of Osgodby on his deathbed offered some meadow land in East Ayton to the abbey in return for burial there. His wife Beatrice laid the title deeds on the altar at his funeral.[22]

One of the less savoury features of monasticism was litigation between religious houses. In matters of finance, the eyes of the monks and canons were not always lifted up towards heaven. Whitby Abbey and Guisborough Priory fell out about tithes and the right to bury people — for a fee, of course — in the area served by St Hilda's, Middlesbrough, and the church of Stainton, which belonged to the priory. Robert de Brus called a meeting, and made a Solomon-like judgment by dividing the rights into two. There was a long-running dispute between the abbey and Bridlington Priory about the tithe of fish payable by the fisher-men of Whitby and Filey respectively. An agreement was made in the 1120s whereby Whitby fishermen 'plying to Filey' would pay tithe there to Bridlington, which owned Filey Church, and Filey fishermen 'plying to Whitby' would do the same to Whitby Abbey, which owned the parish church there. Unless it was intended that the tithe would be paid where the fish was landed, the agreement was unenforceable, and the matter rumbled on. In 1156 an adjudication was made by the heads of three monasteries to the effect that fishermen living in the parish of Filey 'plying to Whitby' would pay tithe to Bridlington. Whitby Abbey was fined £33 6s 8d for tithe unjustly taken.[23]

Abbot William de Percy provided a resource for the local community in the course of solving an internal problem. A monk called Geoffrey contracted leprosy. The abbot founded a leper hospital at Spital Bridge in Whitby in 1109, with the intention that after Geoffrey's death the institution should become a general hospital 'for healthy or infirm poor'. A medieval hospital was for care rather than cure. This became St Michael's Hospital, which was run by a group of secular priests.[24]

Abbot Richard de Waterville (1176-90) did a good turn to the townspeople of Whitby which his successor regretted. The town was a proprietorial borough, ie it contained burgages (borough-houses), the owners of which were free men and had certain privileges, but control rested with the abbot. Within a few years of his appointment Abbot Richard issued a charter which made the burgage-owners virtually self-governing. He retained control, however, of fairs and markets. The charter was confirmed by King John at the beginning of his reign in 1199, but immediately Abbot Peter, Richard's

Whitby Abbey: the north wall of the nave (fourteenth century), and part of the north transept and east end (both thirteenth century). The original Norman east end was only about half as long, and narrower, ending in an apse.

successor, tried to have it cancelled. He gave the king 100 marks for a hearing into the validity of the charter, and the townspeople paid 80 marks, seeking a confirmation of their liberties. (A mark, worth 13s 4d, was frequently used as a monetary unit in the early Middle Ages.) Peter raised his stake to £100, and in 1201 King John cancelled the charter as contrary to the dignity of the abbey.

In 1204 the king restored to the abbey the hunting rights which had been taken away by Henry I. The abbot was now lord of the Forest of Whitby, which meant in practice all the common and waste land within the Liberty.[25]

About 1220 work began on the replacement of the chancel of the, abbey church with a much larger structure in Early English style. The massive Norman-style buildings, such as can be seen, for example, at Kirkstall Abbey, could, with proper maintenance, have stood for a thousand years. The newer styles of architecture let in more light. If more space was needed, eg for chapels in which monks could say their private masses, it made sense to take advantage of this. As time progressed, and the builders learned how to throw more of the weight of the church roof on to buttresses, so the windows grew in size, and where they had stained glass, in splendour.

The rebuilding of the north transept began towards the end of the abbacy of Roger of Scarborough (1223-44), and the new work was carried on down the first three bays of the nave. There it stopped, probably for financial reasons. The reconstruction of the nave was resumed in the early four-teenth century, but the work received a violent setback at the end of November 1334. A canon of Bridlington who wrote a chronicle of the period described how 'a great tempest with snow everywhere and a westerly gale', worse than anyone could remember, blew down 'the columns within the exterior walls and all the work placed above them'. These were the columns between the centre of the Whitby nave and the aisles.[26]

The nave and west end of Whitby Abbey, with two fourteenth century Decorated-style windows.

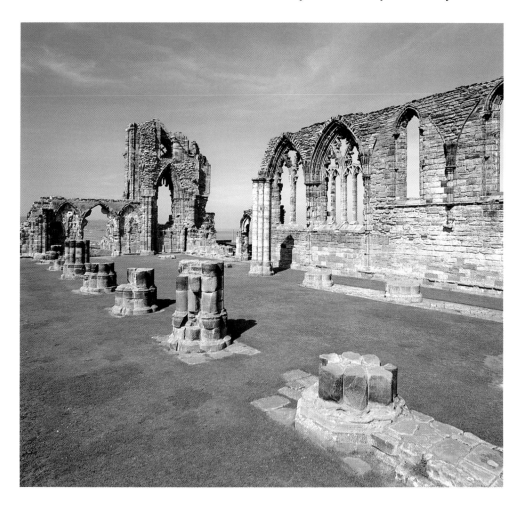

Whitby Abbey from the west, showing the outline of the large Perpendicular window inserted in the west front in the fifteenth century. A late eighteenth century drawing. (Atkinson, *Old Whitby*)

As explained below, Whitby Abbey was heavily in debt in 1320, and in 1328 the new king Edward III ordered the archbishop of York to arrange a survey of those churches belonging to the abbey the income of which had suffered from raids by the Scots in the previous reign, as neither the churches nor the abbey could afford to pay taxes on the old valuation. It is quite possible that the structure flattened by the gale had been standing incomplete for some time, which would, of course, have made it more vulnerable. Abbot Thomas of Haukesgarth (Hawsker) and his monks would not have found it easy to raise the funds to clear the damage and resume work on the nave. The west front, judging from the style of the windows, was not completed until the beginning of the fifteenth century.[27]

The importance in a Benedictine abbey of the spiritual qualities and managerial ability of the abbot has already been noted. As each house was independent, there was no external control except from the bishop when cases of scandal or serious incompetence came to his attention. In 1215 the Fourth Lateran Council of the Church ordered the black monk abbots of each province to meet every three years, and to make provision for the proper observation of the Benedictine Rule. The archdiocese of York formed one province until 1336, when England became a single province.[28]

One feature of the system which developed after 1215 was the inspection of Benedictine abbeys by visitors appointed by the Provincial Chapter. The archbishops of York also visited, but at irregular intervals. The reports of these inspections provide the main source of information about the internal condition of the abbeys. The surviving reports are few, and they are usually snapshots of the situation at the time of the visit. The other limitation is that they were concerned with faults, not achievements. If there were no faults to record, the visitors normally made no distinction between shining zeal and what David Knowles calls 'a decent mediocrity'.[29]

In 1233 Archbishop Gray visited Selby Abbey and laid down detailed rules for the proper conduct of its affairs. In 1256 the abbot, Thomas of Whalley, and his successors were granted by the pope the right to wear, or carry, the mitre, ring and pastoral staff, in other words to enjoy the dignity, but not the power, of a bishop. At about the same time the rights of the abbey over the churches and parishes of Selby and Snaith were confirmed, and the abbey was allowed to appropriate one of its Lincolnshire churches at the next vacancy. These grants were not secured by a polite written request to the pope. They were negotiated by two representatives sent to Rome by the abbot, who incurred considerable costs, probably including 'fees' to Vatican officials. In June 1256 the pope authorised them to take out a loan of £200 'in consideration of their expenses at Rome', binding the abbey to repay the money, within a specified time, with costs and interest — so much for the prohibition of usury. The abbots of Whitby enjoyed the same mitred status at the end of the fourteenth century, although the date of the award is unknown. The abbots of Selby, Whitby and St Mary's were amongst the spiritual peers regularly summoned to Parliament.[30]

Abbot Thomas of Whalley had a chequered career. He was forced to resign in 1263, for unspecified faults. After the death of the next abbot in 1269 he was elected again, although there was a dispute about procedure. Archbishop Giffard sent his officials in 1275 to inspect Selby Abbey and the priory cell at Snaith. They found both places in a sorry state. At Selby the abbot and four monks were accused of affairs with local women, some of them married. The abbot and another monk had fathered children. Two of the four priests at Snaith were married. Abbot Thomas must have promised to mend his ways, for he was left in place.[31]

Archbishop William Wickwane, who succeeded Walter Giffard in 1279, took his duties seriously. In the early months of 1280 he inspected, in person or by deputy, seventeen religious houses in Yorkshire and six elsewhere. At Whitby and St Mary's the report was 'omnia bene', 'all is well'. The archbishop visited Selby himself in January 1280. He made no reference to the conduct of the monks, which may have improved since 1275, but concentrated on the misdeeds of Abbot Thomas. He did not sing the mass, neither preached nor instructed, rarely attended chapter and corrected no faults there, rarely ate in the refectory, and never slept in the dormitory. It would have been difficult at this time to find abbots who did not commit the last two faults by living in their own quarters, but Wickwane was strong on discipline. The abbot of Selby rarely joined the monks in choir, or heard matins out of bed, ignored the rules about eating flesh meat, and treated his colleagues with contempt. He had appointed unsuitable *obedientaries* — departmental officials — and had diverted the income of the abbey to his relatives. He was guilty of immorality with two women and had fathered a child.

He had paid a large sum of money to a sorcerer to locate the body of his brother who had been drowned in the Ouse. The archbishop deposed him on the spot, and sent him to the Benedictine abbey at Durham to undergo penance.[32]

The new abbot was William of Aslakeby, who had been prior. He set about building a new chancel, constructed around the old one which continued in use until the operation was completed. In 1291 the abbey paid £12 to work three acres of quarry of magnesian limestone at Thevesdale near Tadcaster, which was used also by several other monasteries and York Minster. William died in 1293, and the work was continued intermittently by his successors, to be completed by Abbot Geoffrey of Gaddesby (1342-68).[33]

Two interesting points to emerge from the 1275 visitation were that the baptismal font had been removed from the parish chapel to the abbey church, and that there was no graveyard at the chapel. All the deceased of Selby were buried in the abbey precincts, where there was a 'town cemetery' in addition to the 'monks' cemetery'. As a result, the fees for baptisms and burials accrued to the abbey.[34]

One method used at this time to raise money for building work or other purposes was the sale of corrodies, annuities in kind. Corrodians paid a capital sum, or occasionally gave land, to secure accommodation, food and clothing for themselves, and sometimes for their families and servants. When Abbot Simon of Scarborough died in 1320, Selby Abbey had fifteen corrodians, eight receiving food and drink for themselves and their servants, and seven for themselves only. Eleven of them received an annual issue of clothes. The abbey was heavily in debt. When Archbishop Melton

paid a visit in 1335, he found six monks guilty of immorality, drunkenness, malicious talk or a combination of these. He imposed severe penalties. On the material side, the roof of the abbey church was in a poor condition, and the latrines of the infirmary smelt badly. This was the last episcopal visitation of Selby to be recorded, but the inspection carried out by a Benedictine team in 1423 reported that 'the highest peace is found, charity is nourished and the other virtues belonging to men of religion are daily augmented'.[35]

Archbishop Wickwane found no fault on a visit to Whitby Abbey in 1280. When Archbishop le Romeyn sent an erring monk from Monk Bretton Priory to Whitby in 1293 to undergo his penance (Monk Bretton paying 50s a year for his keep) he noted that the Rule at the abbey was well observed. Archbishop Melton found some faults in 1320, although not on the Selby scale. He decreed that monks should draw their clothing from the monastic store, and not be given a clothing allowance. Monastic alms were to be given to the poor and not used to pay abbey servants. Hunting dogs were not to be kept in the precinct, and the monks were forbidden to go out with bows and arrows. It is clear that the community had not been content to be merely the overlords of the Forest of Whitby. Melton noted also that the abbey was heavily in debt.[36]

The abbot, Thomas of Malton, resigned two years later after eighteen years in office. In retirement he was to have comfortable quarters at the abbey, decent clothing and an allowance of £8 a year, the provision of a monk-companion, valet, cook and servant, the profits of the manor of Eskdale, with horses to travel between there and the abbey, and wood and peat to keep him warm in both places. This kind of provision, which was not unusual, could be a considerable burden on an abbey, particularly as the next abbot would still expect what had become the traditional lifestyle of the office. An inspecting bishop, seeing an abbot who was inadequate but not so delinquent that he could be deprived, might be reluctant to persuade him to resign because of the cost of the retirement package.[37]

The replacement of abbots at Selby was an expensive business even without provision for retirement. In 1340 Edward III gave up his right to take over the revenues of the abbey during a vacancy in return for a payment of £80 on each change of abbot. In addition the king could by custom demand a corrody for one of his servants, and a benefice or pension for a priest in royal service. The archbishop of York could claim a similar pension for one of his priests. The total cost was about £100, one eighth of the gross annual income of the abbey. Whitby does not seem to have been so heavily burdened, but when Peter of Hartlepool was elected abbot in 1393, the abbey had to pay annual pensions of 5 marks (£3 6s 8d) each to clerics nominated by Richard II and the archbishop respectively. The monks would have felt more than filial regret when Abbot Peter died a year later.[38]

Thomas of Hawkesgarth, abbot of Whitby from 1322 to 1355, was involved in a dispute about hunting rights with the officers of the neighbouring Forest of Pickering. He was accused in 1335 of directing his men to trap the deer which strayed from Pickering Forest into the Forest of Whitby. He produced charters to show his title to the hunting rights, and secured a writ of confirmation from the king. He enquired acidly of the court of the Honour of Pickering

whether he ought to be required to answer an accusation that he had poached in his own Forest. The case dragged on for two years, at which point the Pickering jury decided that, as the wild beasts of the forest were no respecters of boundaries — it would have been quite impracticable to fence a boundary so many miles in length — the deer belonged to the forest in which they were found.[39]

In the 1360s a feud developed at Whitby between Abbot William of Burton and Prior Matthew Dawnay and their respective supporters. The abbot was accused of selling wool and corrodies without consulting the community. The prior's party included monks accused of immorality and/or assaulting the abbot. Visits by Archbishop Thoresby and officials from the Provincial Chapter failed to restore order, but the abbot of St Mary's and the warden of the Benedictine college at Oxford made more progess. Penances were ordered, and promises of good behaviour made, but when, as part of the deal, Abbot William produced a detailed analysis of the finances of the abbey, the monks refused to endorse it.[40]

The financial statement showed that 54% of the gross income came from churches. Most of the land was let off for money rents, but four manors, three granges — Stakesby, Lathgarth and Whitby Laithes — and the vaccary (dairy farm) of Goathland were still farmed directly. Accounts for the period 1394-96 show that the abbey then had 3,229 sheep and 394 cattle. There were corn mills at Ruswarp and Hackness, and a fulling mill at Ruswarp. The value of the fish tithe is shown by the 1394-95 accounts. The abbey's fish house contained 93,000 herrings on the day the accounts were made up, 53,000 described as good fish and the rest as offal.

Selby Abbey from the south-west, looking across the site of the cloister.

During the year 52,000 herrings had been sold for £17, and total fish sales came to over £42. Cod, codlings and coley are also mentioned, and stake-nets were hung in the River Esk to catch salmon and salmon-trout. In addition to the sales, a good deal of fish would have been consumed within the abbey, by the monks and servants.[41]

By the 1340s Selby Abbey had let off a substantial part of its estates, but was still farming some manors directly, especially near Selby. Abbot Geoffrey of Gaddesby (1342-68) was keen on draining the marsh-land in the Rawcliffe and Crowle areas, especially by means of the 'Mardik', which discharged into the Trent near Amcotts. The abbey lost over £200 when incomplete drainage works were swept away by floods, and

in recompense it was allowed to appropriate the church of Brayton. Geoffrey's successor, John of Sherburn (1369-1408), improved the Mardik, but there was a long-running dispute about the effect of the drainage works with the men of Thorne and Hatfield, who responded with both lawsuits and direct action, wrecking the sluices.

The Black Death of 1349 led to an acute shortage of labour. Increasingly Selby Abbey resorted to letting off its demesnes, and also its tithe collection, for money rents. Labour services were commuted to money payments. By 1460 only land in Selby, Thorp and Wistow was still farmed directly.[42]

In 1398-99 the Selby cloister was pulled down and rebuilt with stone from a quarry at Monk Fryston. It was roofed, as before, with sheets of lead. At the same time the refectory was re-roofed, using 'slate-stone', thin sandstone slabs, brought from Pudsey. The last major additions to the structure were the Lathom Chantry Chapel, built about 1470 under the will of John Lathom, a wealthy canon of Beverley, and the Perpendicular-style window in the adjacent north transept, of about the same date. Charles Hodges has pointed out that this window resembles the east window at Beverley Minster and the west window of Bridlington Priory.[43]

The accounts of Selby Abbey for the fourteenth and fifteenth centuries show that its administration was carried on through over twenty offices held by about sixteen monks. In addition to the abbot and prior, there were sub-prior, third prior and prior of Snaith. The two bursars handled about two-thirds of the total income, but several 'obedientaries' had their own earmarked revenues. The kitchener was in charge of the kitchen and food stores, and was also responsible for a fishery in the Ouse, which caught some of the salmon used in the abbey. He was helped by the granger, who supplied grain for bread and ale, and the extern cellarer who bought the livestock used for meat. The keeper of the refectory, keeper of the guest house and infirmarer were obedientaries whose role is described

A reconstruction drawing of the Selby Abbey buildings in the late fifteenth century, seen from the south-east. (The Story of Selby Abbey)

in their title. The sacrist and keeper of the fabric looked after church fittings, vestments, bread and wine for communion, organs and minor repairs. The precentor was responsible for the choir and choir books.

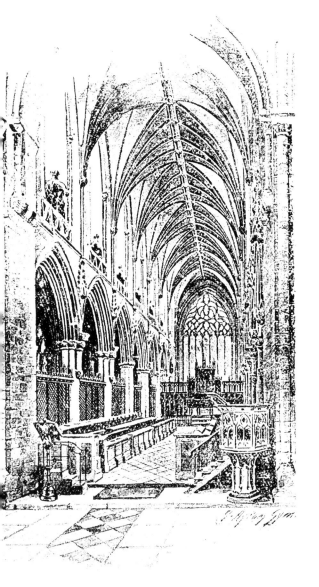

The choir at Selby Abbey in the late nineteenth century. (Tweedie, *Selby Abbey*)

The almoner gave alms to the poor, mainly in the form of a general distribution at certain times. One account shows meat, rye and 1,000 red herrings given out on one feast of St German (31st July), with a similar provision made on the other feast (1st October). The kitchener provided 1,200 red herrings for the poor on Maundy Thursday, a time of greater need as food was scarcer than in the summer or autumn. The almoner was also, in the early fifteenth century, in charge of the chantry founded at an altar in the church by Bishop Walter Skirlaw of Durham in 1398. Another duty of his office was the management of a school, in which boys were educated in return for acting as altar servers for the numerous masses said daily in the abbey church. There was a similar school at Whitby Abbey.[44]

The functions of two officers, the pittancer and the chamberlain, demonstrate how different was the lifestyle of the Benedictine monks at the end of the fourteenth century from that of the simple, heroic pioneering days. Pittances were originally small tasty dishes, added to the normal monastic meals. In the course of time the name was transferred to an allowance made for personal expenses. The chamberlain had once issued clothing, but now paid money allowances instead. By 1431 the two issues had been merged into payments of £3 6s 8d a year to the abbot, £2 13s 4d to 'the lord prior', £2 to each priest-monk and £1 to each novice. The latter became a full member of the community only when ordained priest. In addition some office-holders drew salaries. In 1398-99 the two bursars received 20s each and the prior 10s.

The abbot and prior of Selby each had their own buildings, and several obedientaries had their own, more modest, quarters.

The abbot lived in splendour, after the style of a manorial lord, and the monks lived in relative comfort. The accounts for 1398-99 show an average of thirty gallons of wine per week drunk in the abbot's hall, mainly, no doubt, by his guests, both monks and lay visitors, and the provision of a wide range of foodstuffs, including sturgeon and 'green ginger and other things bought at Hull', where this trade is commemorated in the street name Land of Green Ginger. Several payments were made to minstrels and other entertainers, including one 'lowest grade fiddler'. The abbot's hunting dogs, used no doubt when he went for a change of scene to his manor at Rawcliffe, and fur bought to line his clothing, figure in the same accounts.[45]

Also in 1388-89 Brother William Pygot graduated at Oxford as a bachelor of common law, having been supported by the abbey through an annual allowance of £10. Each Benedictine abbey had been required since 1336 to maintain one monk at university for every twenty members of the community. Pygot became abbot in 1408, and a later abbot, John Ousthorp (1436-66) had also studied at Oxford.[46]

The struggle to maintain the dietary rules of St Benedict had long been recognised as lost, although in 1421 Henry V made an unsuccessful attempt to put the clock back. Lip service was paid to the banning of red meat by eating it in places other than the refectory. If the monks had sought some justification for wanting more or better food, they could perhaps have found it in the climate. To stand in winter on the cliff top at Whitby, amongst the ruins of the abbey, and to think of spending several hours a day in an unheated church, eating in an unheated refectory, reading or working

The north transept and east end of Whitby Abbey in the early nineteenth century. (Grainge, *Castles and Abbeys*)

in an open cloister and sleeping in an unheated dormitory, is a good way of working up an appetite for a joint of beef or lamb.[47]

Selby had twenty-seven monks and novices in 1362, and the numbers remained at roughly the same level in the fifteenth century, ranging between twenty-three and thirty-six. There was never any problem with recruitment. As vacancies occurred through death, novices were admitted in groups of five or six, for the convenience of organising the training programme. In 1362, when most novices were still identified by a

Whitby Abbey from the south-east, in a late eighteenth century drawing. The tower finally collapsed in 1830. (Atkinson, *Old Whitby*)

topographical name, eg John of Rawcliffe, more than two-thirds bore the name of places within thirty miles of the abbey, and nearly half within fifteen miles. The 1381 clerical subsidy returns give a similar picture. Not much is known about their social origins, but Professor Dobson considers that in the later Middle Ages most of them came from the middling ranks of urban and village society, eg farmers and skilled craftsmen. It was possible for someone of relatively humble origin to progress from the almoner's school to a place in the abbey.[48]

Because of the number of obedientary posts, a monk with administative ability could count on having some specific responsibility while still relatively young.

Some monks progressed through several positions, of increasing importance. Those of a scholarly bent could be catered for, with the prospect for a few of a university place. Neither Selby nor Whitby, however, was renowned for its scholarship. In other words, what a black monk abbey offered to its recruits in the later Middle Ages was as much a career as a vocation. The monk carried out priestly duties, and was required to be celibate and obedient to his superiors. He was expected to be conscientious, competent and reasonably devout. He was not expected to achieve the standards of the distant, almost legendary past. The fifteenth-century monk was not seriously challenged to tread the hard, self-sacrificing road to sanctity.

A note on the measurement
of land and stock

Carucates Grants of land to monasteries were often expressed in carucates, each normally consisting of eight bovates. In Latin *caruca* is a plough, and *bos*, genitive *bovis*, an ox. As a farming term a carucate was roughly the amount of land which could be cultivated with one eight-ox plough team. In the early Middle Ages, however, carucates were used as units for the assessment of taxation (the geld) and feudal obligations. *Domesday Book* distinguishes between carucates used in this sense and the number of plough teams required for the land. In some parts of Yorkshire, eg south Holderness, the figures are often the same, but in others they differ. In the Bridlington area, for example, entries such as 'six carucates for geld and land for three ploughs' are common. Where carucates are mentioned in grants of land to monasteries, they are nearly always fiscal/feudal carucates. It is useful to know what fraction of a township, of what size in terms of its geld assessment, is being conveyed, but in the absence of other evidence the carucates cannot be translated into acres.

Bovates In grants to monasteries, a bovate could be either one eighth of a fiscal/feudal carucate, or a farming unit. In the latter sense bovates varied in size, commonly falling in the range 12 to 15 acres, but with plenty of examples greater and smaller. The size of a bovate is rarely specified in monastic charters, but may be known from other sources.

Acres The standard, or statute, acre was based upon a perch of five and a half yards.

Forty perches equal one furlong — 'a furrow long' — and four make a chain of twenty-two yards. A furlong multiplied by a chain gives an acre. In Yorkshire the local perch was frequently more than the statute measure, hence the label 'the county of broad acres'. Perches of 18, 20, 22 and 24 feet are recorded, and it was not unknown for different measures to be used in the same area. In North Cowton, for example, some land was measured by the perch of 20 feet (giving an area nearly 50% larger than the standard), and some by the perch of 22 feet (78% larger). Some transactions include the words 'according to the size of the local perch', but in relatively few cases is the actual size given.

It follows from the above survey of carucates, bovates and acres that statistics of the area of land acquired by monasteries should be used with caution. There is no problem when a whole township was given or bought, and smaller units can sometimes be identified on a modern map and measured from that. Otherwise the data are useful to give a quantitative dimension to a broad-brush treatment, but to feed figures of carucates, bovates and acres, of uncertain and undoubtedly variable size, into one calculation of area, is of no value.

Livestock Livestock, especially sheep, were frequently counted by the 'long hundred' of six score, ie 120 by our measurement. In this book, where the long hundred was probably used in the grant of rights of pasture, the numbers are given in words, eg 'two hundred', not 200. At Bolton Priory, and probably elsewhere, long hundreds were used for grain stocks.

5

'FAR FROM THE HAUNTS OF MEN'

The Cistercians, especially Fountains and Rievaulx

The initial and early endowments of a Benedictine abbey such as Selby or Whitby included manors which were going concerns, other land which could be let off, and churches which yielded tithes and other profits or at least a pension in money. There was therefore some income, in cash and in kind, from the earliest days. The experience of Cistercian abbeys was normally quite different. The favoured location was 'far from the haunts of men' — Barnoldswick, the first site of Kirkstall Abbey, was an exception — with undeveloped land which could be brought into cultivation by the lay brothers and servants, or used as pasture for cattle and sheep. The Cistercians refused to accept churches (although the Savigniacs, from whom Byland and Jervaulx were derived, sometimes did so), therefore denying themselves one regular source of income.

It was as well that the austerities prescribed by the Cistercian order were accepted cheerfully by the pioneering monks and lay brothers in Yorkshire, as their economic circumstances left them with no alternative. The initial needs for livestock, seedcorn and equipment must have been met either by the gifts of the lay founders or through the money which some recruits brought with them.

When Ailred went to Rievaulx Abbey a little over two years after its foundation

(1132), it had a guest house. We may be sure that a wooden church, dormitories and refectories for monks and lay brothers, and some kind of chapter house, had already been built. An excavation of the south transept at Fountains Abbey in 1980 found the post-pits of a timber church. Running south from it was a row of post-pits, the depth of which suggested the existence of a two-storey building, probably with the monks' dormitory on the upper floor. The early timber buildings of a Cistercian abbey, although not intended to have a long life, should not therefore be thought of as a collection of flimsy huts.[1]

The long process of constructing the church and monastic buildings in stone began at Fountains in the period 1135-38. Suitable stone was available locally. Eustace FitzJohn, constable of Knaresborough Castle, who had helped to feed the monks in their first year, and Adam FitzSwain, who later founded Monk Bretton Priory, provided some of the necessary funds. The work began, as normal, with the transepts and east end of the church, which accommodated the monks' choir stalls and the high altar. The structure was seriously damaged by fire in 1146.

William Fitzherbert, who had been treasurer of York Minster, became archbishop of York after the death of Thurstan in 1140. His appointment was opposed by the Cistercians and Augustinians on the grounds that it had been secured by royal favour and bribery. The conflict went on for several years, with the Cistercians using their considerable influence at Rome against the new archbishop. Henry Murdac, elected abbot of Fountains in 1144, was particularly aggressive in this campaign, and in 1146 the supporters of William attacked Fountains Abbey and set it on fire. According to the foundation chronicle, it was completely destroyed 'except for the oratory with some adjacent buildings'. The 'oratory' may have been the choir / presbytery or a chapel. The 1980 excavations found burnt material, including melted glass.[2]

After repair work, construction was resumed. Within a few years the transepts and a short presbytery — the eastern arm — had been built, and the south wall of the nave carried down the whole length of the cloister. This strategy, already described at Selby Abbey on page 45, allowed the buildings round the cloister to be developed without waiting for the completion of the nave. On either side of the cloister were dormitories at first floor level, for the monks in the eastern range and the lay brothers in the western range. By about 1150 the latter was about half of its ultimate length of 300 feet. The nave was completed about ten years later.[3]

Building in stone at Rievaulx began about 1140. The church consisted of an aisled nave of nine bays, north and south transepts, and a presbytery of two bays, a typical early Cistercian church constructed in the massive Norman style. As the abbey was built on a terrace in a narrow valley, it was not possible to keep to the conventional east-west axis for the church. The alignment is nearer

The north aisle of Fountains Abbey's nave, looking west. (St John Hope, YAJ, vol 15)

north-south. However, the usual descriptions were used, so that the nave occupies the 'west' end and the presbytery with the high altar is at the 'east' end. The stone used came from a quarry half a mile further up the valley, transported by a specially-cut canal. This particular coarse sandstone was suitable for plain styles, but difficult to use if elaborate carving was required. By the

The north transept of Rievaulx Abbey, showing the junction between the original coarse sandstone and the finer-grained stone used in rebuilding the east end c1220.

death of Abbot Ailred in 1167 the church had been completed, together with the chapter house and the monks' refectory, which at this time, as at Fountains, had its long axis parallel to the church.[4]

It is necessary only to look around at the ruins of great abbeys such as Rievaulx and Fountains to realise that the initial construction of church, cloister and outbuildings must have taken a considerable time. Although the monks and lay brothers helped in the early days, they were needed for other duties, and so specialist masons and other craftsmen were increasingly used. The main determinant of progress was the availability of spare money, over and above the needs of the monastic community, coming from the estates.

It is possible to identify, tentatively, three phases in the development of the Cistercian estates during the twelfth century. The caution is necessary because of uncertainties about the dating of documents. Two transactions dated to 1160-75 could have been made in the same month, or be fifteen years apart. The first phase was the intensive cultivation of the land close to the abbey, which became the home farms. The second involved the acquisition and development of two kinds of property which came to characterise Cistercian land management: granges and extensive upland pastures. In the third phase the abbeys engaged in two operations. They had to fight off by legal means, or buy off, attempts by lords to recover land or rights given by their predecessors. Secondly, they no longer relied on spontaneous gifts, or the quiet persuasion of charismatic abbots. A systematic policy of estate development in target areas was pursued through the purchase of land and rights, either directly or through the Jews. The latter were not allowed to farm land, or to rent it out as landlords. If they foreclosed on a mortgage, sometimes because the king demanded special taxes or forced loans, they had to sell the land. Some of their keenest customers were Cistercian abbeys.

If the monks had been pedantic, they would have used the term grange (which has the same root as grain) for a farm that was

Looking across the ruins of Rievaulx Abbey's nave, with its massive Norman pillars, to the north end of the frater.

mainly arable; vaccary (from the Latin *vacca*, a cow) for cattle, especially dairy, farms; and bercary (*berca*, a sheepfold) for sheep stations. In fact, although the terms vaccary and bercary were sometimes used, it became the practice to describe all three types as granges. They had one feature in common: they were self-contained units, designed to be worked by the lay brothers and servants of the abbey.

Walter Espec's foundation grant to Rievaulx included the two adjoining townships of Griff and Thillestone, now represented on the map by Griff Farm and Stiltons Farm respectively, and an extensive tract of Bilsdale, which he confirmed by another charter in 1145. A valuable gift made in the period 1154-60 was the meadow of Oswaldeng to the south of the abbey site, which gave the monks control of the adjacent stretch of the River Rye, allowing them to divert the river and make a second canal. This provided water power to drive a mill, as well as transport for stone.[5]

In the period 1145-52, Rievaulx acquired land to the north-west on which the granges of Morton and Hesketh were developed, the latter being augmented by grants of pasture along the western edge of the Hambleton Hills, north of Sutton Bank. An agreement made in 1178 fixed the stock numbers of Hesketh Grange as eight oxen (the standard plough team), thirty-two cows with their issue, two bulls, six horses, six sows and four hundred sheep — the latter probably reckoned by the 'long hundred' of six score, and therefore equivalent to 480.

Before 1154 Roger de Mowbray gave pasture rights in Farndale, 'saving [reserving] the wild game', plus woodlands at Douthwaite, north of Kirkby Moorside, and Middle Head. Substantial grants of land at

East Cowton and Crosby, near Northallerton, were secured from the Bishop of Durham, who was lord of Allertonshire. On land in the East Harlsey/Ingleby Arncliffe area, Morton Grange and two sheep stations were established.[6]

The abbey began to build up a valuable estate, used mainly for arable cultivation, at the western end of the Vale of Pickering, with the gift by Gundreda, mother of Roger de Mowbray, of land in Welburn in the period 1138-43. She had previously given two bovates in Hoveton, just across Hodge Beck from Welburn, to St Michael's Hospital, Whitby. Abbot Ailred leased this land from the hospital, promising to help with supplies for the poor there. By grants and purchase (eg five acres bought for £4 and a cow) Rievaulx gained Hoveton, nearly all of Welburn, land for a grange at Wombleton, meadow at Rook Barugh, and pasture rights on a great sweep of moorland from Welburn, through Gillamoor, Fadmoor and Bransdale, to join up with Farndale Moor at Middle Head.

The question may be asked: 'What happened to the peasants of Hoveton and Welburn?' Hoveton is a 'lost village' and counts as a presumed Cistercian depopulation. The bondmen of Welburn were given permission by Roger de Mowbray c1155 to leave and settle elsewhere. Unless suitable land was on offer, this was not an attractive proposition. A bondman could not leave his land without permission, but would not normally wish to do so. The burdens of bondage in Yorkshire were generally light. The fate of the Welburn peasants is unknown.[7]

Rievaulx could not push its colonising effort beyond the River Dove, which flows down Farndale. St Mary's Abbey owned the lordship of the area between the Rivers

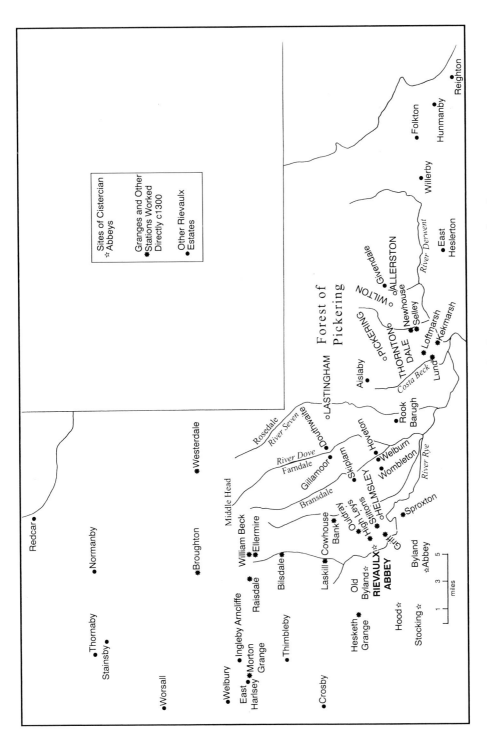

The estates of Rievaulx Abbey. (See also the maps on pages 85 and 132.)

The east end and south transept of Rievaulx Abbey, one of the finest examples of the Early English style. The buildings in the foreground were part of the abbot's lodgings in the later Middle Ages.

Dove and Seven, which includes Hutton-le-Hole, Spaunton and Lastingham. The interest of St Mary's in this area went back to the period c1080-86, when the community was located at Lastingham. East of the River Seven was the Forest of Pickering, which was used for large-scale pastoral farming as well as hunting. Its royal lords showed no disposition to allow Cistercian flocks and herds into this Forest. King Henry II was willing, however, to part with 'the king's waste below Pickering'. This was a flat, badly-drained area, much of which was waterlogged in winter. The drier spots could bear spring-sown crops, but the main use of the land was as rich summer pasture. In 1157 the king gave Rievaulx this 'Marishes' area, stretching from Costa Beck on the west side of Pickering to Allerston Beck which flows down Givendale. A few years later Torphin of Allerston gave some land in his township, including a site for a sheepfold and pasture for five hundred sheep in Givendale Dyke. Other holders of land within the Marishes surrendered their interest to the abbey for a mixture of money, livestock and spiritual services.[8]

The lay brothers and servants of the abbey undertook a major programme of drainage works in the Marishes, which has left traces on the modern map as several 'Friars Dykes'. As the land was drained, the question of boundaries in areas which had previously been shared as common pasture between several townships became important. Agreements were made in 1180 to define the boundaries between the monastic land and the territories of Wilton and Thornton Dale respectively, in both cases mentioning the ditches which had been made by Rievaulx.[9]

The land so far described, with the exception of East Cowton, lay within a radius of twenty miles from the abbey, convenient for maintaining contact with the lay brothers. Offers of property further afield were not refused, however. Grants of land and rights along the northern edge of the Wolds at Reighton, Hunmanby, Folkton, Willerby and East Heslerton were valuable for their access to large sheep runs, but there was good arable land as well. In the 1160s Rievaulx bought sixteen extra acres in the field of Folkton. In Willerby the abbey found itself in competition with Bridlington Priory, which was building up a large estate there, and sold out to the priory in 1175.[10]

There was a very different motive for acquiring land in the Wakefield/Barnsley area. The abbey was given the right to mine iron ore and use dead wood for making charcoal in Shitlington and Flockton, together with land and pasture in both townships and the site of a grange at Shitlington. Rievaulx also had iron-smelting forges by the River Dove in Stainborough (at the bottom of the hill below Wentworth Castle), and at Blacker in Upper Hoyland 'in which they may make iron and utensils needed for their house at Rievaulx'. Most, if not all, of these grants were made in the time of Abbot Ailred.[11]

The Tankersley ironstone, averaging one foot in thickness, outcrops on a line running through Flockton and Stainborough. It was worked along the outcrop and by shallow pits, the traces of which still pock-mark the landscape. Three other Cistercian abbeys became involved in the exploitation of the Tankersley ore, Kirkstall at Ardsley, Byland at Emley and Bentley, and Kirkstead (Lincolnshire) at Kimberworth. Fountains Abbey worked the Black Bed and Clay Wood ironstones at Bradley Grange and Kirkheaton. Rievaulx had another ironworks at

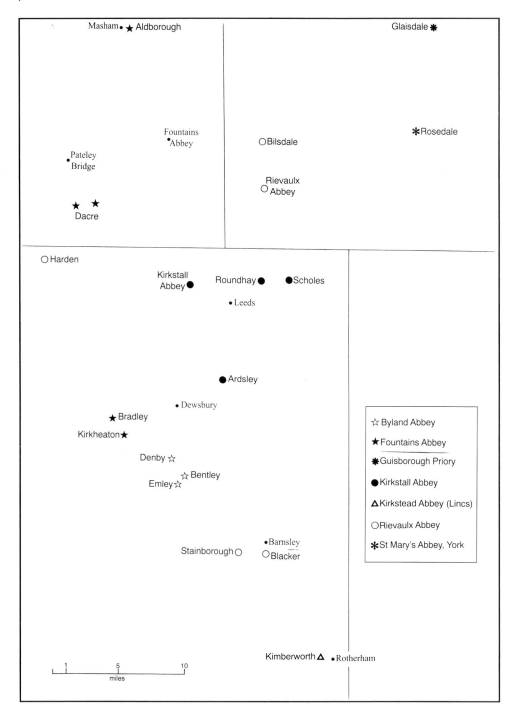

Monastic iron-smelting forges.

Harden, near Bingley, and Kirkstall built its famous forge near the abbey shortly after 1200, to exploit ironstone deposits in the Leeds area. In the early fourteenth century Kirkstall opened another forge in Scholes Park.[12]

In the last years of Ailred's abbacy, Bernard de Balliol gave to the abbey extensive pasture rights in his Forests of Westerdale and Teesdale, including the right to keep sixty brood mares in the latter, and to make lodges and folds in both places. The estates continued to expand after the death of Ailred in 1167. For example, about sixty acres of arable land, some meadow, the site of a sheepfold and pasture for four hundred ewes and twenty-four rams, in East Bolton (now Castle Bolton) in Wensleydale, were given in the 1170s. At about the same time two families holding land in Normanby in Cleveland gave land in Saltcote Flatts and Saltcote Hills, sheep pasture and fisheries in the River Tees. From other sources Rievaulx acquired fisheries at several places further up the Tees. It seems that Ailred's saintly reputation (he was canonised in 1191) made Rievaulx an attractive prospect for landowners wanting to make a spiritual investment.[13]

Although the Cistercian abbeys were quite happy to accept, and sometimes to depopulate, established farming villages, their main source of wealth was the improvement of 'waste' lands. In economic terms, 'waste' was a misnomer. Moorland, 'carrs' (seasonally-flooded land) and marshlands all had some value, as common pasture, for digging stone or peat, or for fishing and fowling. In the hands of the Cistercian lay brothers, however, their value could increase greatly. The economic balance of a Cistercian abbey — this could apply to other orders as well — depended in part on the nature of its 'waste' hinterland. In the case

of Rievaulx this was the North York Moors and the wetlands of the Vale of Pickering. Meaux Abbey was surrounded by the carrs and marshes of Holderness, and in its economic records drainage and the making of canals loom large.[14]

Fountains Abbey had the advantage of a position almost on the line dividing the main upland zone of Yorkshire from the Vale of York. The 'foothill' lands immediately north and south of Fountains had themselves considerable potential, and several granges were established there in the early years of the abbey. They included Sutton and Morker Granges, the land for which was given by Archbishop Thurstan and Robert de Sarz, one of his tenants, respectively. By about 1150 William de Percy, the founder of Sawley Abbey, had added some land in the adjacent township of Markingfield. Between 1154 and 1172 Fountains increased its holding there by a typical Cistercian deal. Roger le Bret of Markingfield was in financial difficulties. He gave to the abbey thirty-six acres of land adjoining a stretch cleared by the lay brothers, receiving in return £14 13s 4d, an eight-ox plough team and a horse 'so that he could retain the rest of his inheritance'. A few miles to the south, the land for Cayton Grange was given by Eustace FitzJohn.[15]

The township of Aldfield, immediately to the west of the abbey, did not pass to Fountains until 1356, but during the second half of the twelfth century, part of Sawley, to the south, was acquired for five oxen, five cows with their calves, 120 sheep with sixty lambs, and 20s. The lay brothers dammed the valley of Dene to create a fish farm. The townships of Galphay and Winksley passed to the abbey by a roundabout route. Part of Winksley was initially rented from Geoffrey de Bellun. The Fountains records contain

twenty charters from Geoffrey's son Nicholas, each conveying a portion of the townships or some associated rights to the abbey.
It might be thought that Nicholas was generous only in fits and starts, but the true
explanation is provided by an accompanying
disclaimer from Henna, widow of Aaron,
Jew of York, and Isaac, her son-in-law and
attorney. Nicholas had progressively mortgaged his land to the Jews, and when Fountains bought the debt each transaction was
re-written as a charter in favour of the abbey.
When Nicholas died, to be buried as a brother at Fountains, the abbot agreed to pay his
widow an annual pension of £5 in respect
of her right of dower, ie one third of the
income from her late husband's lands.[16]

Between 1136 and 1145 Count Alan, earl
of Richmond, gave a substantial estate in the
Masham area for the establishment of a new
abbey. It included Roomer and Bramley on
the west side of the Ure, and on the other
side a woodland 'where Burton stood'. The
new abbey was never created, and the land
was developed by Fountains as the granges
of Aldborough, Nutwith and Bramley. Iron-
smelting forges were at work at Aldborough
in 1181.[17]

It is possible that the build-up of the
Fountains estates slowed in the late 1140s and
early 1150s because of the Murdac affair. The
role of Abbot Henry Murdac in the dispute
with William Fitzherbert over the arch-
bishopric, and the burning of the abbey,
have been mentioned on page 69. In 1147
Murdac himself was appointed archbishop
of York, but there was so much opposition
that he was not formally enthroned until
1151. A new abbot of Fountains was elected,
but Murdac treated him as a deputy and
continued to oversee the affairs of the abbey
until his death in 1153.[18]

In 1154-56 William de Percy confirmed the
gift of Gikel de Baldersby of six acres in the
field of Baldersby, between Ripon and
Thirsk. This was the nucleus of what became one of the richest arable granges of
the abbey. Over the next 100 years sixty
charters from about twenty families conveyed over 800 acres in Baldersby and the
adjacent townships of Easby and Birkhow
to the abbey, which made modest payments
for a few of the grants. Other lowland arable
granges were established in the twelfth
century at Marton-le-Moor, North Cowton,
Middleton Tyas and nearby Moulton, where
a carucate was bought for fifty marks (a
mark was 13s 4d), Thorpe Underwood, and
Green Hammerton, the latter augmented
in 1238 by the purchase from a Jew of two
bovates for ten marks.[19]

A walk of about four miles west from
Fountains Abbey brought the brethren to
the edge of Nidderdale. After a further trek
of about nine miles, down and up steep hills,
they could look down into Wharfedale.
Upper Nidderdale, carved out of the rocks
of the millstone grit series, was excellent
cattle country. On the west side of Wharfedale and extending across the top of Airedale was nutritious and healthy grazing for
sheep on the springy turf of the high limestone pastures. All this dales area was thinly
populated, much of it being included in
hunting forests. It should be remembered
that at this period 'forest' meant 'hunting
ground' and not 'woodland', although
forests contained varying amounts of woodland. Whatever forests may have existed in
the high Pennines before the Norman Conquest had been greatly expanded by the new
French lords.

Most of the area was described in *Domesday* as 'waste'. In the Vale of York, 'waste'

was mainly the result of William the Conqueror's devastation in the winter of 1069-70. As the small French army could not, in addition to carrying fire and sword through the central plain, have destroyed every settlement in every corner of the Yorkshire Pennines and North York Moors in a midwinter campaign, some at least of the waste in the Dales must have another cause. There has been much speculation about possible organised or spontaneous movements of people from the uplands to redevelop the fertile lowlands. In parts of the Dales, eg Nidderdale, there is clear evidence that depopulation and the creation of forests went together, although it is difficult to say which was the cause and which the consequence.[20]

What is not in doubt is the value to the Cistercians of thinly-populated forests which were valued by the lords primarily for sport. Fountains secured a foothold in Nidderdale before 1140, with the gift from Robert de Sarz of what became the grange of Warsill. In 1145 Bertram Haget, who ended his life as a monk at Fountains and whose son Ralph was successively abbot of Kirkstall and Fountains, gave the township of Dacre to the abbey, subject to an annual payment of two marks. This was later surrendered by another son, William, in return for twenty-five marks and a horse. Dacre was part of Roger de Mowbray's Chase of Nidderdale and Roger confirmed the grant. 'Chase' was the correct name for a baronial hunting ground, as distinct from a royal forest, but the term 'forest' was commonly used for both.[21]

About 1150 the lady of the Honour of Skipton, Alice de Rumilly, and her husband gave Fountains nearly half of the township of Kilnsey in Wharfedale. The lands of the grange there were augmented by smaller grants, eg from Edulf de Kilnsey in 1174, who stipulated that he should join Fountains as a lay brother and his son as a monk, with his wife being found a place in a nunnery. Between 1164 and 1175, William de Percy granted land in Malham, the tarn and its fish, and pasture rights over a great expanse of moor bounded by Darnbrook Beck, Cowside Beck and Arncliffe. The western half of this became known as Fountains Fell. When William's daughter Maud and her husband the earl of Warwick confirmed these grants in 1175, Fountains paid sixteen marks and agreed that the earl and countess could fish in the tarn whenever they visited the area. This was a bargain, especially as Maud added half a carucate of land in Malham soon afterwards.[22]

Fountains built up large flocks of sheep, which were managed from Kilnsey and Malham. It would have suited the abbey to absorb the rest of the Chase of Nidderdale, but there was an obstacle. By two charters dated 1143-66 Roger de Mowbray gave to his foundation Byland Abbey extensive rights throughout his Chase of Nidderdale, including pasture, building timber, a salt spring and 'iron ore and a tenth of my lead house'. The local leadmines were clearly being worked, with the lord taking his share.

Byland Abbey greatly increased its control of the area known as Stonebeck Up and Stonebeck Down, principally by buying from Roger in 1172, for £200, all of the rights except hunting in Stonebeck Down. The financial pressures which led Roger de Mowbray to sell to Byland also gave Fountains its opportunity. In 1175 the abbey bought Fountains Earth and Dallowgill for 120 marks paid to Roger to help finance a journey to Palestine, and eleven marks to

Byland Abbey from the south. A good example of a Cistercian plan. To the left of the cloister, the long lay brothers' range. To the south, the kitchens, refectory (at right angles to the cloister) and warming house. On the east side, the chapter house, with the monks' dormitory above. The small rooms at the bottom right of the eastern range may have accommodated corrodians.
(Cambridge University)

his two sons. Soon afterwards, in return for eighty-three marks and in compensation for some corn belonging to Fountains taken by Mowbray's men, the abbey was granted 'all copper, iron, lead and every kind of metal and stone' in the Chase of Nidderdale, presumably meaning in the parts of it occupied by Fountains. At about the same time the abbey bought the township of Bewerley for £100, plus ten marks to Roger's wife Alice de Gant. In the grants of Dacre, Bewerley and Fountains Earth, Roger's hunting rights were reserved, but he promised to give the carcasses of six stags yearly to the Fountains infirmary.

Between 1175 and 1181 Fountains secured the complete title, including hunting rights,

to 'the land of Brimham', later known as the township of Hartwith-cum-Winsley, for the payment of 355 marks to Roger de Mowbray, and five marks to the Knights Templars to secure a perpetual lease, at 10s a year, of half a carucate which had been given to them by a tenant of Roger. In six years the abbey had spent nearly £600 in the systematic acquisition of a large tract of land, of great potential value for farming, and containing the rich leadmines of Bewerley and the iron ore deposits of Dacre. The reference to copper seems to have been purely speculative.[23]

Considering the sweeping nature of the early grants to Byland, and the loose wording of the conveyances of mineral rights, it is not surprising that disputes arose between the two abbeys. The most serious of these, about five leadmines in the 1220s, was said to be a disgrace to the Cistercian order. It was settled in 1226 by arbitration, the terms of which provide the first detailed evidence of medieval leadmining in Nidderdale. Lead ore was found normally in veins, narrow, near-vertical fissures in the rock. Five 'grooves', or stretches of vein, were in dispute, two of them on the north (Byland) side, and three on the south (Fountains) side, of Ashfold Gill Beck, which separated the territorial interests of the two abbeys. The first two, apparently in the Merryfield area, where the main vein runs north of the beck, were to belong to Byland. Two grooves in Coldstones, on the south side of the boundary, were to be worked jointly by the two abbeys, dividing all the expenses and the lead ore 'except the king's share', for a period of seven years from the 2nd February 1226, after which Byland was to withdraw. A third groove at Coldstones, previously worked in common, was to be exploited in the same way until exhausted.

Roche Abbey from the west. The overall plan is similar to Byland Abbey, opposite. The transepts (c1170) are the most prominent surviving feature. As the short eastern arm was never extended, the monks' choir occupied the eastern part of the nave. The division between it and the lay brothers' choir can clearly be seen. The stream on the right ran under the lavatories of the monks and lay brothers. (Cambridge University)

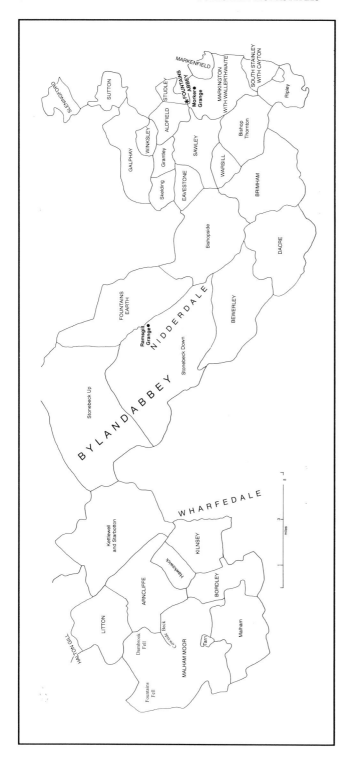

The Fountains empire in the Yorkshire Dales. Townships in which the abbey was the sole, or a major, landowner are shown in capital letters.

Looking across a corner of the cloister at Byland Abbey, to the lay brothers' choir and west end.

Any monk or lay brother who violated the agreement was to be sent on foot to the other abbey to apologise, and then to be put on bread and water every Friday for a year. The monks and lay brothers would probably be involved in a managerial role, as leadmining was a specialist craft.

It is clear that Byland, taking advantage of the broad wording of its grants of mineral rights from Roger de Mowbray, had for some time been mining lead ore within the township of Bewerley, in which Fountains had, subsequently to the Byland grants, bought both the mining and mineral rights, from Roger. The joint working of one of the grooves at Coldstones represented an earlier attempt at a compromise. The reference to exhaustion should be understood in terms of contemporary mining technology, which used trenching, 'hushing' (releasing a flood of water to gouge out the upper horizons of the vein) and a succession of shallow shafts sunk along the vein. It was not normally possible to penetrate to any considerable depth because of the problems of drainage and ventilation. The mention of 'the king's share' is evidence of an attempt by the monarch, not generally successful, to claim an interest in all leadmines on the grounds that gold and silver mines belonged to the Crown, and most lead contained at least a trace of silver.

The two abbeys were also in competition in Sleningford, where land acquired by Byland would have made a convenient way-station between the abbey and its granges in upper Nidderdale. However, Fountains put on the pressure and bought out its rival for 140 marks. Agreements made in the late twelfth century allowed Byland to have several rights of way across the land of Fountains in upper Nidderdale, and to build

a bridge over the Nidd near its principal grange of Ramsgill. Byland's animals were not to eat the grass belonging to Fountains, except when they were held up by flood water at the fords. The two Cistercian communities might have regarded each other as brothers in Christ, but such ideas do not seem to have influenced their economic relationships.[24]

Roger de Mowbray died in 1188. His heir Nigel lived for only three more years, to be succeeded by his son William (c1171-1223). The latter did not share his grandfather's affection for Byland Abbey, and in 1204 he tried to evict the brethren from all or part of their Nidderdale lands. To secure confirmation of its title, and the full use of Stonebeck Up apart from hunting rights, Byland had to pay £266 13s 4d, and hand over some land elsewhere in Yorkshire. Fountains encountered fewer difficulties, but clashed with William de Mowbray about the methods used to defend the granges against wolves. It was eventually agreed that the lay brothers and monastic servants might use bows and arrows within the enclosed ground of the granges, and keep two mastiffs at each, tied up by day but let loose at night.[25]

Some lords followed the Cistercian example and established their own cattle farms, usually known as vaccaries, in their forests. During the thirteenth century the population of the country increased, towns were growing, and the rising demand for food and raw materials made large-scale farming profitable. In 1218 a complex agreement was made between Jervaulx Abbey and Ranulph FitzRobert, who held the Forest of Bainbridge under the earls of Richmond. Both parties could establish vaccaries anywhere, although the abbey kept mainly to the area which became known as Abbotside. The pasture rights for Ranulph and his men of the village of Bainbridge were defined in detail. The abbey was to have the fishing in the River Ure, except that otter-hunting was reserved to Ranulph. At the end of the century Jervaulx and the earl of Richmond each had ten vaccaries or granges in the Forest of Bainbridge. The lords of the Forest of Swaledale had twelve vaccaries in the late thirteenth century, despite having given, in 1241, an extensive tract at the head

of the dale to Rievaulx Abbey, which established five granges there.[26]

Fountains Abbey extended its holdings in Wharfedale and upper Airedale by means of a mixture of gifts, exchange and purchase. About 1170 eighteen bovates in Arncliffe were bought for £18, plus a yearly charge of 24s of which the first six payments were made in advance. Before 1175 William de Rilston gave half a carucate in Bordley in return for being received as a monk or lay brother, with his son Alan taken on as a

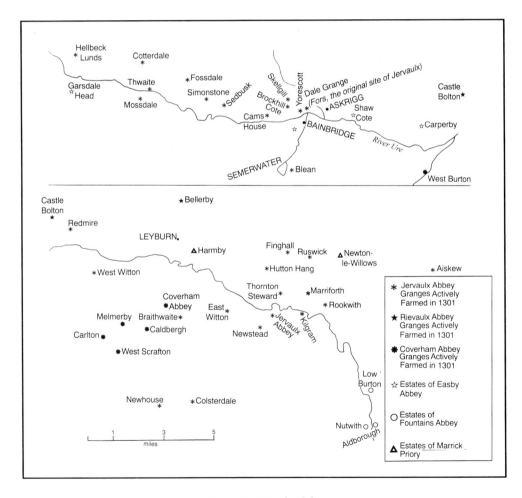

Monastic Wensleydale.

The largest surviving fragment of Jervaulx Abbey, the southern part of the eastern range, with the twelfth century lancet windows of the monks' dorter on the upper floor, and day stairs to the left.

lay servant for a year or two to see whether he wanted to become a lay brother. Examples like this, which show that the *conversi* were not recruited only from the lower ranks of society, are far from rare. In the years 1175-95 six bovates of land in Kettlewell (annual charges 5s 4d) cost eighteen marks, forty sheep, two cows, an ox and a horse. An exchange of arable lands in the same township cost the abbey ten marks.[27]

It is clear that Cistercian abbeys such as Fountains were ploughing back the profits

Jervaulx Abbey: the chapter house.

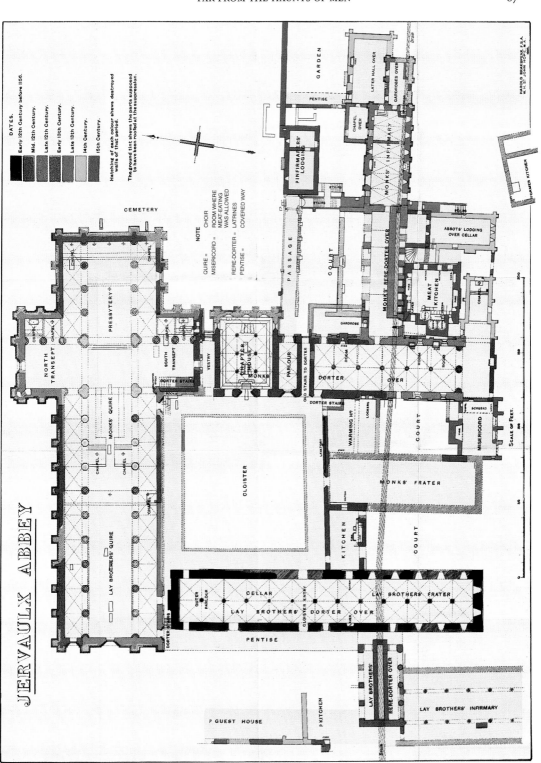

JERVAULX ABBEY

DATES.

Early 12th Century before 1156.
Mid. 12th Century.
Late 12th Century.
Early 13th Century.
Late 13th Century.
14th Century.
15th Century.

Hatching of each colour shews the parts destroyed walls of that period.

The ground tint shews the parts supposed to have been roofed at the suppression.

NOTE

QUIRE = CHOIR
MISERICORD = ROOM WHERE MEAT-EATING WAS ALLOWED
RERE-DORTER = LATRINES
PENTISE = COVERED WAY

CEMETERY

HAROLD BRAKSPEAR, F.S.A.
W. H. ST. JOHN HOPE, M.A.

Brakspear and St John Hope, YAJ vol 21.

The sub-vault under the lay brothers' dormitory at Fountains Abbey, looking south.
(St John Hope, *YAJ*, vol 15)

of their earlier economic efforts into the acquisition of new land, particularly to consolidate their hold on target areas. Clearing land for cultivation, building granges and making enclosures also involved material costs, as well as an immense amount of labour. Although the granges in the Pennines were mainly pastoral, small-scale arable cultivation was practised to feed the men and animals of the granges. A taxation return of 1297 shows that nearly all of the corn grown in the dales was oats, which survived damp conditions better than other grains, and as a bonus provided a straw which was a nutritious feed for stock.[28]

By about 1200 the basic building scheme at Fountains Abbey had been completed. It included a monks' refectory built at right angles to the cloister, which had become a characteristic Cistercian feature, made

necessary because a long western range was required for the *conversi*. This range at Fountains was widened, from 25 feet to 42 feet, and its length doubled to 300 feet. The upper floor was used as the lay brothers' dormitory, the lower floor housing their refectory as well as large stores. The final stages of this work were completed by Abbot Ralph Haget (1190-1203).[29]

Haget is praised for his sanctity and wisdom in the chronicle of Fountains. This is not a wholly unbiased source, but he is known for one great act of charity. In 1194 famine led to the outbreak of an infectious disease — called plague, but this term was used for any major epidemic — and 'a great concourse' of poor people came to the gate of the abbey. It had no building capable of holding them, and so temporary shelters were erected. The poor were fed and nursed, and priests went amongst them daily, hearing confessions, administering the last rites and conducting burial services.[30]

This work was put on a permanent basis. In the early thirteenth century Simon de Mohaut made a donation, together with his body for burial, of a bovate of land, and the bondman who occupied it, in West Morton, near Keighley, together with pasture for two hundred sheep and land for a sheepfold, all 'for the use of the secular poor lying in the infirmary'. The latter was situated by the west gate of the abbey, one of a group of buildings, which included 'the Chapel of St Mary at the Gates', designed to meet the needs of lay people and especially women, who were allowed into the main precinct only for special reasons. Further gifts for 'the poor at the gate of the abbey' increased the endowment of the lay infirmary. Other Cistercian abbeys, including Meaux, had similar infirmaries.[31]

The reign of King John was a difficult time for the Cistercians. His exactions cost Meaux Abbey 1,000 marks and Fountains 1,200 (£800). The Fountains chronicle records, however, a marked increase in the number of monks in the early thirteenth century. As a result the choir stalls were overcrowded and there was a shortage of altars for private masses. It had gradually become the custom for the monks to be

Fountains Abbey, the south-east corner of the cloister, showing, from the left: the chapter house, parlour, door to the monks' dorter, warming house, lavatorium for washing, and door to the frater (refectory) above. (St John Hope, YAJ, vol 15)

The presbytery and Chapel of the Nine Altars, Fountains Abbey.

ordained as priests. The response at Fountains was the replacement of the short, aisleless eastern arm with one twice as long, flanked by aisles and therefore with about four times the area of the original, ending in the spectacular Chapel of the Nine Altars. At the same period the infirmary block was rebuilt on a much larger scale, with a great hall measuring 180 feet by 78 feet, one of the largest halls in medieval England. According to the chronicle, this major building programme was begun by Abbot John of York (1203-11), continued by Abbot John of Hessle (1211-20), and brought to a glorious conclusion by Abbot John of Kent (1220-47). In the plan drawn by St John Hope (on page 98), all of this work is for convenience attributed to the last-named.[32]

Alan Sorrell's impression of the Chapel of the Nine Altars at Fountains c149
after the rebuilding work of Abbot John Darnton. (English Heritag

The north side of the choir and presbytery at Rievaulx Abbey, showing the flying buttresses which made larger window-openings possible. The last bay on the left accommodated five chapels.

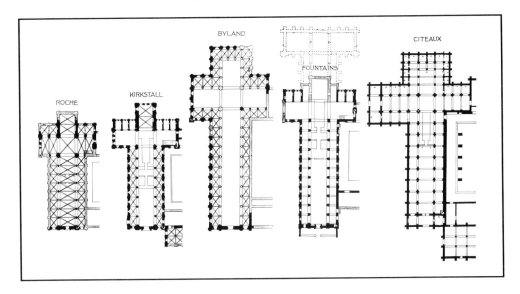

Comparative plans of Cistercian churches. The thirteenth century extension at Fountains which created the Chapel of the Nine Altars is shown in outline. (Bilson, Arch J, vol 66)

There were major building developments at Rievaulx Abbey, roughly in parallel with those at Fountains. At about the end of the twelfth century the south side of the cloister was remodelled, with a new frater (refectory) measuring 124 feet by 38 feet placed at right angles to the cloister, and flanked by a new kitchen and warming house, where the brethren were allowed to thaw out from time to time. The basement of the refectory building may have been used as a dining room for the *conversi*. One of the mysteries of the Rievaulx site, with its short western range, is where its lay brothers slept.

In the second quarter of the thirteenth century, according to St John Hope, the short eastern arm of the abbey church was replaced by a new seven-bay aisled structure in Early English style. The floor was paved with yellow and green tiles in a geometric pattern. The more elaborate buildings at Rievaulx and Fountains have been regarded as an abandonment of the Cistercian ideal of simplicity. Perhaps; but we need not rush to judgment. Assuming that more space was needed for priestly functions — and the remodelled transepts and east end at Rievaulx accommodated nine additional chapels — to erect the new building in the original Norman style would have been reactionary and inefficient. The new style let in much more light.[33]

An important influence on the planning of extensions to the abbey churches at Fountains and Rievaulx was probably the church at Byland, built about three decades later than the first stone structures at the other two abbeys. It was much bigger, had large transepts with space for four chapels, and an extra bay at the eastern end, behind the high altar, which accommodated five more. The extended Rievaulx church was only fractionally longer than the Byland church. The Chapel of the Nine Altars at Fountains

Coloured tiles in the south transept of Byland Abbey.

Rievaulx Abbey: the south side of the choir and presbytery.

was a more elaborate version of the east end of Byland.

Whether a Cistercian abbey went for such extensions would depend upon two factors, the number of monks and the financial position. Kirkstall managed with its original structure, built in the period 1152-c1170, but the design allowed for six chapels in the transepts. Fountains and Rievaulx were comparatively wealthy, and when expenditure on the acquisition and development of their estates had eased, more money was available for work on monastic buildings.[34]

The secret weapon of the Cistercian economy was the *conversus*, the lay brother. As already explained, not all of the lay brothers came from the lowest ranks of society. It is wrong to see them, after the first hectic days when monks and *conversi* alike worked

Kirkstall Abbey church from the east.

The west front of Kirkstall Abbey church. (Lefroy, *Ruined Abbeys*)

until they dropped, essentially as muscle-men. A survey of the number and size of the granges shows that they could not possibly have been staffed wholly, or even mainly, by the lay brothers. The main labour force consisted of hired servants, supplem-ented at busy times by the compulsory labour of the bondmen, who had been acquired in violation of Cistercian rules. In 1289, for example, the abbot of Kirkstall sued three men for forcibly rescuing one of his bondmen in Bardsey, whom the abbot 'for a certain act of rebellion had put in the stocks in order to whip him'.[35]

Apart from the problem of recruiting enough of them, there were two other reasons for not staffing the granges wholly

with *conversi*. As Colin Platt points out, they were full members of the monastic comm-unity. 'In youth and in age, in sickness and in health, the community was bound to support them.' Secondly, they were needed for managerial and specialist tasks. They developed collectively a wide range of expertise, in every kind of farming including sheep rearing and horse breeding; land drainage; fisheries, in both rivers and fish farms; salt making; quarrying; the mining and smelting of iron and lead; and not least the management of granges, and groups of granges with dependent lodges.[36]

Illustrations of the skills required are given by the records of iron and lead smelt-ing on the Fountains estates in Nidderdale.

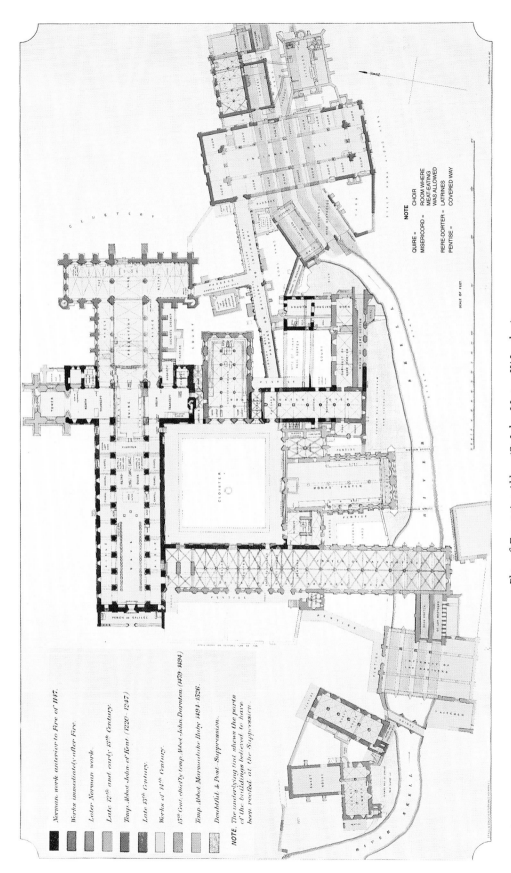

Plan of Fountains Abbey. (St John Hope, *YAJ* vol 15)

In 1309 the abbey made an agreement about iron smelting with John de Mowbray, lord of the Chase (hunting ground) of Nidderdale, who was concerned mainly with the preservation of the woodlands which sheltered the wild game. Fountains had an iron-smelting works at its grange of Dacre, and was allowed to have 'one other forge with two furnaces, which may be moved from place to place for making iron where convenient'. The fuel used was charcoal, and the abbey was allowed to make as much as it wished between 29th September and Easter, in the woodlands on its Nidderdale estates. The 'two furnaces' would have been a bloom-hearth and a string-hearth respectively. In the former the iron ore was alternately heated until it was white hot (about 1,400° C) and hammered to remove impurities. It was then re-smelted at a higher temperature in the string-hearth. Both hearths were blown by bellows. A static forge could use a water wheel, but a moveable one would obviously rely on a foot-blast.

Lead ore was smelted, using 'white coal' (kiln-dried wood) as a fuel, in furnaces known as 'boles' or 'bales'. These were built, in the form of a low circular wall of stones with openings at the base, on exposed hillsides, and originally relied upon the wind for the draught. In the early fourteenth century it became the practice to fit bellows to provide a better blast and allow more regular working. The next step was to remove the operation to the side of a stream so that a water wheel could drive the bellows. In the fifteenth century Fountains was using both boles and a stream-side smelting mill, which has given its name to the hamlet of Smelthouses, near Pateley Bridge. The accounts for the mill include payment for the making of a *sufflatorium*, a bellows pipe.[37]

A substantial proportion of the output of the Cistercian economy was consumed by the great human machine of the abbey — the monks, lay brothers, servants, guests, the lay infirmaries where they existed, and other charitable provisions. Surpluses for sale might have been produced from time to time in almost any area but the main sources of cash were rents from lands which did not fit into the grange economy, minerals and, especially, wool. Although one of the grants of iron ore made to Rievaulx mentioned the needs of the abbey for ironware, it is probable that lead and iron workings were carried on primarily to make money. Lead ore was mined when no building work was in progress at the abbey concerned. This was inevitable, as production depended so much on the fortunes of discovery. In the 1360s lead from the Fountains mines at Coldstones in Nidderdale was bought for use in roofing Windsor Castle.[38]

The principal 'cash crop' of the Cistercians was wool. In the early Middle Ages most English wool was exported, mainly to the textile industries of the Low Countries. The trade was in the hands of Flemish and Italian merchants, who offered to the monasteries long-term contracts sweetened by large cash sums in advance, which carried hidden interest charges. A regulation made in 1181 by the Cistercian General Chapter forbidding abbeys to contract for more than one year at a time was ignored. A ban on buying wool from small producers, known as *collecta*, to increase the scale of the contract was no more effective. The Cistercians and Gilbertines graded their wool into three qualities. An Italian account of c1300 shows that, amongst the Cistercians, Fountains received the highest prices, £14 for the

Rievaulx Abbey from the notional south-east. (Because of the lie of the land, the church was aligned nearly north-south instead of west-east.) The chapter house, ending in an apse, can be seen to the left of the south transept. The frater (refectory) is the most prominent building on the south (left) side of the cloister. (Cambridge University)

best quality, and Meaux the lowest, £10 for the same, in each case for a sack of 364 lbs.

The same Italian account listed the number of sacks each monastery could be expected to supply annually. This could be less than the actual production, because wool was sold or used elsewhere (cloth was woven at Meaux to meet the needs of the abbey) or more because of *collecta*. Houses other than the Cistercians also had tithe wool to sell. It is, in any case, imprudent to place too much reliance on a single source of this kind. All this is to suggest that the much-quoted Italian list should be used with caution, mainly to indicate the relative scale of operations of different abbeys. Fountains headed the list with seventy-six sacks, Rievaulx and Jervaulx coming next with sixty and fifty respectively. These three abbeys had sixty per cent of the Yorkshire Cistercian total. If seventy-six sacks had been produced wholly from the sheep of Fountains, that would indicate a flock, excluding lambs, of over 18,000.[39]

The availability of cash in advance from wool merchants was one temptation too many for some abbeys. At an earlier stage the main cause of indebtedness was building operations. Kirkstall, for example, despite substantial help from Henry de Lacy, had borrowed money from Aaron of Lincoln to complete the monastic buildings. Richard I took over this debt, and allowed the abbey to settle it for 1,000 marks (£666 13s 4d). The indebtedness which became widespread in the third quarter of the thirteenth century seems to have been due more to extravagance and mismanagement than to building work. It is noteworthy how quickly debts were reduced when an austerity programme was instituted.[40]

In 1274 King Edward I appointed Philip de Willerby custodian of Fountains Abbey because it had debts of about £6,000, including £900 owed to Jews in York The latter had been paid off, and the debt reduced to under £1,300, by 1290. A new custodian was appointed in the following year, and at the same time the king told his officers to stop sponging off the abbey by staying at Fountains or the granges.[41]

The problems faced by the Cistercians and other monasteries specialising in wool production, notably Bridlington, Watton and Malton, were increased from about 1276 by outbreaks of sheep scab, thought to be the result of a run of cold and wet seasons. In that year Henry de Lacy, earl of Lincoln, the 'founder' of Kirkstall Abbey, agreed to take over the management of its finances because it was so heavily in debt. Eventually he made what would be called today a re-financing arrangement. In 1287 he took over land and rents yielding £41 a year in return for an annual payment to the abbey of £53, and advanced money to pay off the most pressing debts.[42]

Bad weather, animal diseases and raids by the Scots combined to make the lives of the Yorkshire Cistercians, in common with many other monastic communities, miserable in the period 1314-22. Exceptional rains in 1314-16 ruined crops and caused heavy losses of sheep. According to the *Lanercost Chronicle* (which was mainly the work of Franciscans in Yorkshire, but ended up at Lanercost Priory in Cumberland) 'there was such a mortality of men in England and Scotland through famine and pestilence as had not been heard of in our time'.

The Scots were able to replenish their stores by raiding into Yorkshire, left defenceless after the victory of Robert Bruce at Bannockburn in 1314. They attacked the Richmond area in 1314 and 1316, and, emboldened by their success, swept down the Vale of York in 1318. Towns, including Northallerton and Knaresborough, were burned down. The raiders returned, with much livestock and other booty, via Bolton Priory and the Pennine valleys. In 1319 they came again, crushing a makeshift English force at Myton, near Boroughbridge, and reaching as far south as Castleford. Once more they returned via Airedale and Wharfedale. The lowland granges of Fountains were pillaged, and the Jervaulx estates suffered badly. In a revaluation of tax assessments in 1318 — which did not, of course, take account of the 1319 raid — the figure for Fountains was reduced from £343 to £100, and that for Jervaulx from £200 to £100. The valuation of the poorest Cistercian abbey, Sawley, was cut from £54 10s to £4.[43]

As if this were not enough, an outbreak of cattle plague in 1319-22 killed large numbers of oxen and cows. The Scots invaded twice in 1322, on the second occasion coming close to capturing Edward II in the neighbourhood of Rievaulx and Byland abbeys.

They went as far as Beverley, causing great damage on the eastern side of Yorkshire, and returned home 'laden with spoil and with many prisoners and much booty'.[44]

The next catastrophe was, in human terms, the worst of all. The Black Death — bubonic plague carried by fleas which lived on the black rat — swept across Europe and reached Yorkshire in May 1349. Three-quarters of the monks and lay brothers at Meaux Abbey died. A heavy mortality in an enclosed community was to be expected, but where the records are sufficient to calculate the proportion of peasant land vacated by death in the plague year, figures of 40% and more are found. The death rates of rectors and vicars in three archdeaconries were: East Riding 48%, York 45%, Cleveland 35%. Five of the eight Cistercian houses in Yorkshire appointed new abbots in 1349: Byland, Kirkstall, Meaux, Rievaulx and Roche.[45]

One effect of the Black Death, and the resultant shortage of labour, was to hasten the decline in the numbers of lay brothers. Their role was also changing. In 1310 Fountains made an agreement with Brother Robert of Morton, keeper of Cowton Grange in the North Riding, one of the most distant from the abbey, whereby he managed the grange for a fixed annual payment, taking his profit out of the remainder. In a Fountains rental of 1361, and another undated rental of about the same time, we find Brother Roger paying 40s a year for the grange of Coldstonefold, on Greenhow Hill, and 26s 8d for the leadmines there. These are round figures — 26s 8d is two marks — and it is clear that Brother Roger was not simply returning the net annual income, but was holding some kind of lease. In the same rental five granges in the Nidderdale area, some at least holding abbey livestock, were

leased to laymen. Why bother to become a lay brother if you could negotiate the same arrangement as a layman? By the late fourteenth century, no Cistercian abbey in Yorkshire had as many as ten lay brothers.[46]

An alternative to letting granges as going concerns with monastic stock was to split them into peasant holdings. In 1336 Clairvaux Abbey, as mother house to Fountains, allowed the latter to let the granges of Kilnsey, Marton and Baldersby in this way, thus reversing the piecemeal depopulation of Baldersby. In 1363 a similar licence was issued for Kilnsey and eight other granges, including Sleningford, another suspected depopulation, and Sutton. The application declared that since the Anglo-Scottish wars the nine granges had been 'lost, burned and reduced as if to nothing'. Fountains may simply have repeated the wording of 1336. The decay of granges four decades after the last Scottish attack in the areas concerned may have been caused by the shortage of both lay brothers and lay servants after the Black Death and the second, less severe, attack of plague in the winter of 1361-62. Not all of the granges were permanently split up. Sutton was still being farmed directly by the abbey in its last years.[47]

One device used by the Cistercians when in financial difficulties was the appropriation of churches, whereby the abbey took part of the benefice income (tithe, glebe and offerings), leaving a portion for a vicar. This practice had been rejected by the Cistercians in their pioneering days, but in 1239 the poorest Yorkshire house, Sawley, had appropriated Tadcaster Church. Because of the damage caused by the Scots, the same abbey was allowed to appropriate the church of Gargrave in 1320. Byland was given leave to do the same with Rillington in 1344, the

er Dunn's impression of the appearance of the east end of the abbey church at Rievaulx in the thirteenth century: monks' choir stalls in the foreground, with the presbytery and high altar beyond. (English Heritage)

Scots' damage being cited as the reason. Profits from churches accounted for one-sixth of the cash income of Meaux Abbey in 1393-94. Kirkstall acquired seven churches in Holderness when it was given the property of the suppressed alien priory of Burstall in 1395.[48]

The Cistercians followed the Benedictine example in the later Middle Ages by selling corrodies (annuities in kind). In 1526 Rievaulx sold one to a married couple for the term of their lives. They were living at the grange of Skiplam, but had leave to move into the abbey precinct if they wished. Their allowances included, weekly, six gallons of convent ale, two gallons of abbot's ale, four gallons of 'greenhorn' (apparently the weakest brew), ten wheaten loaves and six rye loaves.[49]

Much less is known about the internal affairs of the Cistercian abbeys than of the Benedictines, because they were exempt from visitation by the archbishop. The murder of Abbot Philip of Jervaulx by one of his monks in 1279 was happily untypical. In 1306, for an unstated reason, Archbishop Greenfield excommunicated the abbot of Sawley, together with the prior, sub-prior, cellarer, sub-cellarer, sacrist, sub-sacrist, bursar and others. The Cistercian obedientaries (departmental officers) did not, like some of their Benedictine counterparts, hold separate funds. There was a common treasury.[50]

The archbishops of York had an excuse to meddle in the affairs of Fountains Abbey because they were 'founders', as successors in title to Archbishop Thurstan. In 1290 Archbishop John le Romeyn wrote to the abbot of Clairvaux, the mother house of Fountains, and to the Visitors, the senior officers of the order in England, alleging

that Fountains was in a bad spiritual and material condition. The reduction of its debts, and the appointment by the king of a new custodian in 1291, are mentioned above. In March 1294 the archbishop informed the abbot that he intended to spend a night at the abbey on his way to his manor house at Otley, to be entertained at the expense of the community as it was his first visit as founder. The news would not have been received with pleasure. Apart from the threat of interference, archbishops usually travelled with a substantial retinue. John le Romeyn seems to have carried out an unauthorised inspection, as he wrote again to the Cistercian Visitors with a catalogue of criticisms. The monks had wasted their resources, showed contempt for charity, neglected the rule and their devotions, formed conspiracies, and expelled any sincere and zealous brethren.[51]

There were several disputes at Meaux Abbey about the appointment of abbots in the second half of the fourteenth century. The most serious trouble occurred in 1396 when some monks objected to the election of Thomas Burton, who had been bursar. When two abbots were sent by the General Chapter to investigate, they found the abbey defended by armed men under the orders of Robert Burley, abbot of Fountains (the mother house of Meaux) and Burton. The appointment of the latter was confirmed, but because of continued unrest he decided to resign in 1399, and devoted himself to compiling the *Meaux Chronicle*. As the record of events comes from his pen, he had the last word.[52]

Burley died in 1410. When the monks of Fountains met to elect his successor, they had seven nominations, including John Ripon, abbot of Meaux and a former cellarer of Fountains. Roger Frank, a Fountains monk, secured the highest number of votes, thirteen, and Ripon only four. Frank did not have the necessary two-thirds majority, but the abbots supervising the election exercised their discretion and declared Frank elected. Ripon refused to yield, and pursued his case in the king's court and at Rome. Frank and thirteen supporters were turned out of the abbey, the supporters of the rivals came to blows, but by 1416 Ripon had gained control. He remained abbot until his death in 1434.[53]

After these unedifying events, Fountains achieved greater stability under a succession of able administrators, Abbots John Greenwell (1442-71), Thomas Swynton (1471-78) and John Darnton (1478-90). Greenwell's era is well recorded through the survival of the memoranda book of Thomas Swynton for the years 1446-58, and the bursar's books for 1456-59. The abbots lived like lords, with comfortable quarters in the abbey, country houses on the former granges at Baldersby and Thorpe Underwood, and a hunting lodge at Brimham Park. Abbot Greenwell may have been in delicate health. He was supplied with a variety of ointments and

medicines, as well as a diet including oysters, partridges, quails, venison, raisins, figs, nuts, apples, pears, plums and a range of wines.

The abbots were men of power and influence, not only with their own communities and extensive estates, but also in regional and national affairs. Since the fourteenth century they had worn the mitre and ring, the insignia of a bishop, and had served as spiritual peers in Parliament.[54]

When John Darnton became abbot, parts of the abbey church, especially the tower over the crossing, the presbytery and the Chapel of Nine Altars, were in a poor, indeed a dangerous, condition. He carried out extensive repair work and remodelling, and installed great new windows, in Perpendicular style, in the west wall of the nave and the east end, ie in the centre of the Nine Altars Chapel. To support the east wall of the latter, large external buttresses were constructed.[55]

Sir John Pilkington, the lessee of Bradley Grange, left £10 towards Darnton's building work in 1479. He also bequeathed 'To every monke in Fontaunce Abbey 6s 8d, so that ilkone of thame severally say messe of Req-

The frater, Fountains Abbey. (Walbran, *Guide to Ripon*)

*Fountains Abbey: an elevation of the east side
of the south transept, showing the effects of
settlement and the alterations of the fifteenth
century.* (St John Hope, *YAJ*, vol 15)

uiem for my saule within five days they have
knaulege of my deth ...' It is not surprising
to find Fountains monks with private funds
at this time. The obedientaries and senior
monks had their own rooms. The aisles of
the infirmary hall had been made into separate rooms, possibly for the benefit of elderly
monks. The restrictions on meat eating,
gradually eased from the middle of the fourteenth century, had become a dead letter,
except for the formality that meat was
normally eaten not in the refectory, but in a
separate room, the misericord.[56]

Darnton's successor, Marmaduke Huby
(1494-1526), inherited the problems of the
crossing tower. He reinforced the pillars and
arches, but decided to build a new tower in
an unusual position, at the end of the north
transept. It was constructed in magnesian

limestone, 170 feet high, and survives, apart
from its floors and roof and the tracery of
some windows, as a paradox. Huby's motto
'*Soli Deo Honor et Gloria*', 'Honour and glory
to God alone', appears on the tower, as well
as on other buildings, eg the chapel of
Bewerley Grange. The lord abbot of Fountains could not, however, avoid sharing in
the honour and glory. The great windows
of late medieval monastic churches may
have represented in part a response to grandiose urges, but at least some justification
could be offered, in terms of the better light,
and the pious stories told in the stained glass.
Huby's tower held the bells of the abbey,
but they could have been hung in a much
simpler belfry. It is difficult to see his magnificent structure as other than a declaration
of power.[57]

Although most of the Fountains granges
were let for money rents by the late fifteenth
century, some still carried monastic stock.
The records of the granges in Nidderdale
and Wharfedale for the period 1454-1537
show two systems of management at work.
At two granges within a few miles of the
abbey, Warsill and Haddockstones, the keepers were essentially foremen, being paid
partly in kind, partly in money and partly
by being allowed to use some of the land
for themselves. These granges were probably regarded as part of the 'home farm'. The
other Nidderdale granges were let by an
arrangement first recorded in 1454, when
two men leased Lofthouse Grange for a five-
year term, holding forty cows and eighteen
young cattle of three different ages — all
abbey stock — and delivering stirks, cheese
and butter to the abbey 'according to the
customary usage of old time'. More details
are given in later agreements, for example,
the lease of Bouthwaite Grange granted in

Fountains Abbey from the west, showing, from the left: Abbot Huby's tower at the end of the north transept, the west front of the nave, and the lay brothers' wing.

1512 to a widow and her son for the term of fifty years. They were to keep the following abbey stock: two bulls, sixty cows and twenty-seven young cattle of three different ages, and to deliver to the abbey annually eighty stones of cheese and forty of butter, and thirty stirks, or pay in default 1s a stone for butter, 8d for cheese and 4s for a stirk. At Whitsuntide the stirks were to be driven to the abbey (to be allocated to their summer pastures), together with nine of the oldest and most 'crochy' cows, which were to be fattened on pastures near the abbey for killing in the autumn. At Michaelmas the old cows were replaced by nine heifers. In Nidderdale 'stirk' meant cattle one to two years old. As the cows presumably calved in the spring, the stirks would be just over a year old when taken to Fountains. They would, of course, be of both sexes. The Bouthwaite agreement was more complicated than most, because two mares and their foals were wintered there, and the keepers had to pay £3 6s 8d extra per year for the pasturing of their own cattle. They were to have all the arable land, and any profit from the abbey herd beyond the quota.

The other dairying granges were let at different times in the period 1454-1537 on a similar basis, with stocks of 60, 40 or 20 cows and the other figures in proportion. The basic principle was that the keepers made their living out of the use of some of the grange land, and any extra yield of milk or stirks beyond the quota — that for milk products was quite modest. The reference in 1454 to 'the customary usage of old time' suggests a long-established custom, which may have originated when the lay brothers managed the granges. It was an established practice on large estates in the thirteenth and fourteenth centuries to have standardised herds and production targets, for the convenience of managerial control.

In addition to the dairy herds, Fountains used its Nidderdale lands to winter both sheep and steers and bullocks pastured in the summer on the Craven uplands. In 1496 about 1,700 sheep, and 380 steers and bullocks, were kept in Nidderdale from Michaelmas (29th September) until the feast of the Finding of the Holy Cross, or St Helenmas (3rd May). The flocks always kept to the same two seasonal locations. For example, one which spent the summer above North Cote, Kilnsey, was wintered on Bewerley Rigg in Nidderdale. Another moved from Darnbrook Fell to spend the winter at Bollershaw. The management of sheep on unenclosed ground was based upon 'hoofing', that is herding the sheep with dogs on to a stretch of ground which became so familiar that the flock would not easily stray.

For the keepers of the Fountains granges there were three key dates in the year. On 3rd May the sheep and store cattle were driven to their summer pastures. At Whitsuntide the oldest and youngest cattle went to the abbey. At Michaelmas the keepers and their families gathered at Toft Gate, on the boundary between Bewerley Rigg and Greenhow Moor and by the side of the road from Pateley Bridge to Grassington, to see the sheep come over the hill from Craven

and collect a new bunch of heifers. Whatever entertainment was arranged on these occasions would be covered by 'the customary usage of old time' and is not recorded.[58]

The chapel of Bewerley Grange, mentioned above, was one of several built by Fountains Abbey at its principal granges. There were others at Bouthwaite and Brimham in Nidderdale, and Kilnsey in Wharfedale. Byland Abbey had a chapel at Ramsgill, its main Nidderdale grange. None of these chapels is recorded before the fifteenth century, and it is not clear whether they were built for the benefit of the lay brothers and other staff, or whether they served the convenience of visiting monastic officials in the later Middle Ages.[59]

For the lands stretching from the Ripon area to Fountains Fell, which had been dominated by the abbey since the twelfth century, the abbot of Fountains was, right up to the eve of the dissolution, a man of great power and influence. When a boundary dispute about leadmining rights on Greenhow Hill was investigated by commissioners appointed by the Crown in 1530, one of the parties complained that they had no chance against the influence of the prior of Bolton and the abbot of Fountains, William Thirsk. 'The prior appeared there with Sir Thomas Clifford, with many other gentlemen and men to the number of 300 persons or above ...and the said abbot appeared ... with many gentlemen ... to the number of 500 or above.' Even allowing for the considerable exaggeration usual on such occasions, there is no doubt that when required the abbot could call out many tenants and other supporters as the army of the Fountains empire.[60]

SAINTS, SCHOLARS AND SCOTS
The Black Canons, especially Bolton and Bridlington

The first house of Augustinian canons to be established in Yorkshire, Bridlington Priory (1113-14), made a flying start in the build-up of resources, in both parish churches and lands. When its founder, Walter de Gant, confirmed his own grants and those of his men in the 1120s, the list of Yorkshire churches included Bridlington with chapels at Bessingby and Grindale, Filey, Willerby (west of Filey), Ganton and Grinton in Swaledale. There were also three churches in Lincolnshire and Derbyshire plus a half interest in South Ferriby. Walter's principal grants of land were thirteen carucates in Bridlington, nearly eight around Muston, five and a half and a mill in Filey, five in Fordon and three in Reighton. His men had given amounts of land ranging from two to ten bovates in Hilderthorpe, Bessingby and Easton to the south of the priory, and Grindale, Buckton and Reighton. 'Grinton and all lying adjacent to it' went with the grant of the church there. Upper Swaledale was part of the marriage portion of Matilda, daughter of Count Stephen, earl of Richmond, when she became the wife of Walter de Gant.[1]

It is clear from the local entries in *Domesday Book* that the carucates mentioned above were administrative and not agricultural units. The normal pattern in the Bridlington area was a ratio of two carucates for taxation purposes to one ploughland for farming. The figures are useful only for showing whether a monastery acquired all or part of a large or small township. Five carucates in Fordon represented the whole township, three carucates in Reighton only three-eighths of the total. It is worth repeating the point made in the note on page 67. To translate grants such as the above into modern acreage figures without supporting evidence is a futile exercise.[2]

Bridlington Priory could not make a clean sweep of the churches in its area because, before it was founded, the Gant family had given to Bardney Abbey in Lincolnshire the church of Hunmanby, with its dependent chapels at Muston, Fordon, Wold Newton, Burton Fleming and Reighton. Hunmanby had clearly been a 'minster' church of the old kind (a team ministry), serving a wide area, and its dependent chapels had not yet evolved into independent parishes.[3]

By 1140 several donors, including the Percy family, Eustace FitzJohn and William le Gros, earl of Albemarle, had given eight more churches: Boynton, Scalby, Flamborough, Carnaby with its chapels, Atwick, Ottringham, Sproatley (all in eastern Yorkshire) and East Cowton, in the central North Riding. Ottringham was granted, together with some land and the tithe of the corn

A mid-Victorian view of the interior of Bridlington Priory church, looking west.

mill, by the family of the same name, on the understanding that the priory would put in as many canons as the tithe and other profits would support.[4]

A confirmation by Pope Eugenius III (1145-53) listed several additional churches in Lincolnshire, Derbyshire and Nottingham-shire granted by Walter de Gant's son Gilbert, earl of Lincoln. Most of these, given during the anarchy of Stephen's reign, were lost to the priory when normal feudal order was restored after the accession of Henry II in 1154. However, the confirmation issued by Henry in the period 1155-57 showed that Bridlington still held five churches, and a half interest in another, outside Yorkshire.[5]

It cost a lord virtually nothing to give a church to a house of canons, a process blessed by the bishops. Only in the case of Ottring-ham, about thirty miles from the priory, is the obligation to staff a church with canons mentioned. Otherwise the priory was free to decide whether to serve a church directly or to employ salaried chaplains. The canons probably acted as parish priests in some, if not all, of the churches within a radius of about ten miles — Bridlington, Filey, Flam-borough, Boynton, Carnaby and Atwick.[6]

King Henry I had given the priory free-dom from tolls, as well as authority over the manor of Bridlington. Stephen re-affirmed these rights in relation also to the borough of Bridlington. Four burgesses, ie borough-men, were living in the town at the time of *Domesday*; the borough probably existed before the Norman Conquest. In addition Stephen gave the prior control over the port of Bridlington. His confirmation charters included an extra carucate in Bridlington, giving the priory over three-quarters of the township, and more land in Hilderthorpe and Easton.[7]

Gilbert de Gant was very fond of Brid-lington Priory. He was born there and, in his own words, nourished from early child-hood by the community. He gave the priory most of the township of Burton Fleming, where an arable grange was established. Bridlington had permission from Henry II in the period 1154-58 to divert the highway there. Later in the century the priory re-ceived several small grants in the same town-ship. However, it suffered from the Gant connection during the worst phase of the civil war of Stephen's reign. Gilbert de Gant and William le Gros, earl of Albemarle, were on opposite sides in a private war which was fought within the main national struggle. In 1143-44 Albemarle seized Brid-lington Priory, expelled the canons, and fortified the buildings during a campaign in which he attacked and destroyed the Gant castle at Hunmanby. He later repented, and as a reparation gave the priory six parcels of land, one in Boynton, the rest in different parts of Holderness.[8]

Other grants of land and pasture rights came from donors great and humble. An estate of about 250 acres in Rudston was accumulated through eight separate gifts. One grant, of three bovates in Burton Fleming and two in Hornsea Burton, carried the condition that the donor's son was to be looked after by the priory until he reach-ed the age of twenty, when he would be made a canon. At least two other gifts, each of one bovate, were made by men joining the community.[9]

A substantial proportion of the priory lands lay within a radius of fifteen miles from Bridlington, an area which included the fertile valleys of the eastern Wolds, with their sheep and corn husbandry, and the heavier soils of northern Holderness. The

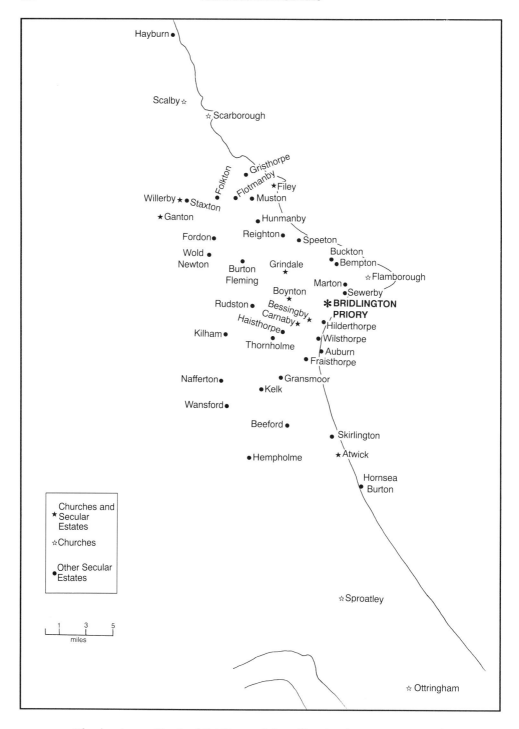

The churches and lands of Bridlington Priory. (See also the map on page 132.)

principal sheep stations were on the edge of the high Wolds, as at Gristhorpe and Willerby. Gilbert de Gant and Henry de Ganton allowed the priory to pasture five hundred and four hundred sheep respectively on the open arable fields of Hunmanby and Staxton, the donors benefiting from the sheep's manure. Hunmanby operated a two-field system, half of the arable being cropped in any one year, while the other half lay fallow. The sheep fed on the stubble, and on whatever grew naturally during the fallow year.[10]

Vaccaries were established at Hayburn, north of Cloughton, and in one of the most distant properties, the extensive township of Blubberhouses, north of Otley. Almost any gift could be put to good use. A grant of five 'holmes' (water meadows) in the area of Hempholme, in Leven parish, included two fisheries in the River Hull. Land acquired in Willerby township, at the foot of the Wolds escarpment, included rights in a marsh. The priory made agreements with other claimants to the marsh, whereby it provided one with 9,000 turves each summer, and allowed another to dig twenty cartloads of turf each year, presumably carting off the rest of the annual peat dig to use in the priory kitchen, infirmary and warming house.[11]

Bridlington spent very little money on the acquisition of land and rights in the twelfth century. Modest sums were paid in the following century for the extension of existing holdings, eg three bovates in Flotmanby bought in 1240 for £5 13s 4d. The priory's Swaledale estate was extended by a little trickery. It owned the village of Grinton and Harkerside, which extended two miles to the west. Beyond this it was allowed to have two vaccaries and pasture rights in

Whitaside. In the thirteenth century the priory claimed the full title, apart from the hunting rights, to Whitaside, described as 'a large pasture ... so clean and healthy that sheep there will always be free from scab, where dwell certain woodmen, tenants of the prior ...' The exploitation of the timber may have been the bone of contention. The priory's own records showed that its claim was false, but the archives of the lords concerned, the Gant family, were presumably less complete. The priory won the lawsuit.[12]

The priory's church at Grinton had an unwelcome visitor at about the beginning of the thirteenth century. The archdeacon of Richmond arrived on a visitation with a retinue consisting, according to the priory, of ninety-seven horses, twenty-one dogs and three hawks. The cleric must have secured permission to hunt in one of the local forests, Swaledale or Arkengarthdale, and was abusing his office to the advantage of himself and his friends. They consumed 'in a brief hour' what would have lasted the household 'for a long time'. Pope Innocent III (1198-1216) issued a stern admonition reminding the archdeacon that his maximum permitted retinue on a visitation consisted of seven horses, not ninety-seven.[13]

In 1120-21 Cecily de Rumilly, lady of the Honour of Skipton, and her first husband William Meschin founded an Augustinian priory at Embsay, near Skipton, with an initial endowment consisting of the church of Skipton, its dependent chapel at Carleton and the township of Embsay. By 1145 Cecily had added Kildwick township and church, and the corn mills of Silsden and Harewood. Other gifts from the same family included the manors of Sturton and Skibeden, and land in Weeton and Rawdon. The only other major donors at this period were Helto Mauleverer of Beamsley, who gave a quarter of the township of Malham and a large tract of woodland north and west of Beamsley, and Robert son of Malger, who granted a third of the township of Yeadon. The canons were also given the patronage of the churches of Broughton and Long Preston, but not at this stage the right to appropriate them.[14]

In 1155 Cecily's daughter Alice de Rumilly authorised the transfer of the priory to the manor of Bolton, which the canons received in exchange for the manors of Sturton and Skibeden. The new site by the River Wharfe was more sheltered and probably more fertile. In popular legend, expressed in Wordsworth's poem *The Force of Prayer*, Alice arranged the move out of sorrow at the death of her son William, 'the boy of Egremont', by drowning in the Strid, a turbulent section of the Wharfe just north of the new priory site. This cannot be so, as 'William my son of Egremont' was the first witness of Alice's charter. Her first husband William, son of King Duncan of Scotland, had recently died, and her son of the same name did not live to manhood. The legend emerged out of one or both of these events. The canons retained Embsay, and shortly after the move received a grant for a three-day September fair there, from Henry II.[15]

The estates of Bolton Priory grew slowly in the late twelfth century. The Mauleverer family gave more land in Beamsley, including Storiths, where the priory was allowed to station five men to staff the grange. Walter le Fleming gave twelve bovates in Cononley, to which smaller areas were added by other donors. The priory acquired the patronage of the churches of Keighley and Marton-in-Craven, but continued for some time to present secular priests to the livings. The priory gained only small annual

The west front of Bolton Priory in the mid-nineteenth century. (Walbran, *Guide to Ripon*)

pensions, but it may have found it useful to do favours to powerful people by presenting one of their nominees to a benefice.[16]

At the beginning of the fourteenth century Bolton Priory made some shrewd investments in land, especially the manors of Appletreewick and Holmpton in Holderness. The first of these gave the priory extensive pastures on which five pastoral granges were established, together with the leadmines on the west side of Greenhow Hill. The farming of the demesne of Holmpton proved profitable, and it supplied the priory with a good deal of its wheat. In 1304 the church of Long Preston was appropriated. The costs of fees, buying out the rector, and repairs to neglected property came to £300, but the investment was recovered within five years. The vicar received twenty marks a year and a bovate of land. The remaining income from glebe land and tithe went to Bolton.[17]

A detailed picture of the economic affairs of Bolton Priory is provided by the accounts for 1286-1325, which form the subject of Ian Kershaw's book *Bolton Priory: The Economy of a Northern Monastery*. Lay brothers managed the more important granges in Craven. Over three-quarters of the corn crop consisted of oats, because climatic conditions were unsuitable for the other grains, but it was a low-yielding crop, typically returning between two and three bushels for every one sown. The corn of all kinds was grown mainly for consumption within the priory or on the granges. As a source of cash, pastoral farming, and especially wool production, loomed much larger. In the ten years to 1314-15, the sheep flock averaged 3,200, modest by comparison with the leading Cistercian producers, but important to Bolton. The priory also marketed tithe wool, and *collecta*, fleeces bought from small producers. The sheep were managed separately from the granges, the shepherds being responsible to a head stockman, a lay brother, who also oversaw the cattle and other livestock. In 1310 these jobs were separated, under the control of two laymen.[18]

The accounts for 1298-99 show four vaccaries, with between seventeen and twenty-six cows of priory stock, let to laymen. Three of them were required to deliver annually four stones of cheese and two stones of butter from each cow, the fourth a little less. These production figures are much higher per cow than on the Fountains granges described on pages 106-8. The supply of stirks is not mentioned. Perhaps the calves were fed elsewhere.[19]

Although Bolton had only four parish churches from which it drew the bulk of the tithe and other income — Bolton, Skipton with Carleton, Kildwick and Long Preston — they gave the priory a substantial part of its cash revenues. The parishes of Skipton and Kildwick were very large, each containing ten or more townships. In the 1291 valuation for ecclesiastical taxation, the four churches were assessed at £111, compared with £57 from the estates. The comparable figures for Bridlington were: churches £261, estates £216. As mentioned above, these valuations were erratic, and should be used only for broad-brush comparisons. In fact the parishes of Kildwick and Skipton, assessed together at £65, were worth over £160 a year to Bolton Priory in the period 1295-1315.[20]

Before the canons of Embsay had made their move to Bolton, the better-endowed priory at Bridlington had become established as a centre of learning. The leading figure was the fourth prior, Robert, known as 'the Scribe', who was a contemporary of St Ailred of

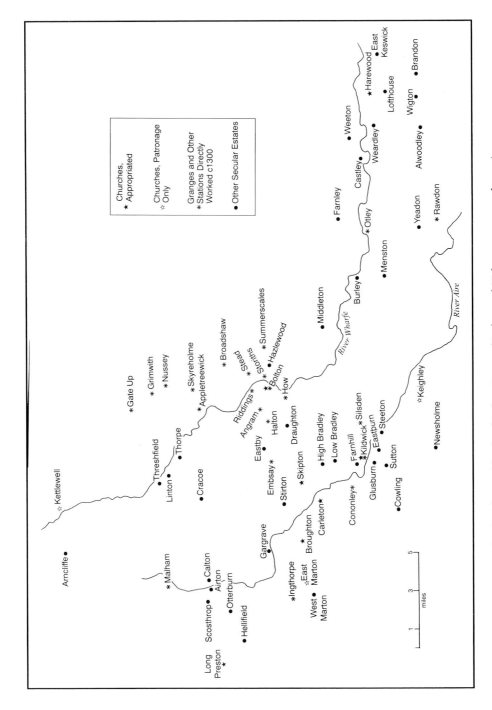

The churches and lands of Bolton Priory. (Ryther and Holmpton are not shown.)

Rievaulx. He wrote several commentaries on scripture, three of which have survived in manuscript form. The priory had a busy scriptorium, where books were copied and illustrated. Robert listed some of the forms of work suitable for canons: preparing parchment for the scribes, writing books (presumably meaning copying rather than composition), illuminating, ruling lines, writing musical notation, making corrections and binding books.

Robert is best known for the *Bridlington Dialogue*, written about 1150, which takes the form of exchanges between a 'master', Robert himself, and a 'disciple'. It is a practical treatise on the monastic life, based as might be expected on the Rule of St Augustine. The disciple asks why Augustine began his rule with love rather than faith. The gist of a long reply is:

> ... no one loves who does not believe. Whoever does not love can hope for pardon after a fashion. but he hopes in vain. But no one who does love can despair. Therefore where love is, there of necessity are faith and hope.

The master mentions in passing the daily mass celebrated in the priory, but deals in detail with the proper conduct of the eight offices, prayer services, held each day in the church. He explains, quoting Augustine, that the custom of singing in church 'was instituted not for spiritual persons but for the carnal and imperfect, so that the sweetness of the chanting might melt the hearts of those whom the words left unmoved'.

No doubt drawing on his own experience as head of the community, the Master argues that allowances should be made for different talents and temperaments:

> It is necessary therefore both that the quiet mind be not distracted by overmuch work, and that the restless one should not force itself to the practice of contemplation. For often those who were able to contemplate God when they were at repose have failed when pressed by work; and often those who might have lived well while they were busy with human occupations have been slain by the sword of their own repose.

Fortunately there was plenty of work to be done in and about the priory, apart from the scriptorium: indoor pursuits such as sewing new clothes for the brethren and mending old ones, making wooden spoons and candlesticks, fashioning baskets and nets, weaving mats, and the whole range of farming and gardening tasks, including 'planting, trimming, pruning, grafting and transplanting trees'.[21]

Of all the major orders of monks and canons, the Augustinians placed the highest value on scholarship. Bridlington stands well in this company. William of Newburgh, a canon of the Augustinian priory of that name and a leading twelfth-century historian, was by tradition born in Bridlington, although there is no evidence that he was ever a canon there. Two Bridlington canons of the fourteenth century were important literary figures. Peter of Langtoft wrote, in French and in verse, a history of the country from the ancient Britons to 1307, when Edward I died. The name of the second author is unknown. He wrote a chronicle of the reign of Edward II (1307-27), which was continued, possibly by the same pen, until 1339. One of his sources was a book in the priory library, *Incidentia Chronicorum*, consisting of transcripts or summaries of documents relating to the affairs of Church and state. Whether this work had been compiled in the priory, or simply copied in the scriptorium, is not known.[22]

The black canons, like the black monks, were subject to inspection by the archbishop of York. After a visit in January 1280, Archbishop William Wickwane issued a list of 'corrections made at Bridlington', which suggests that he was dealing with observed faults as well as providing the usual 'common form' list of virtues. The alms of the monastery were to go to the poor. Only those who were really sick were to be admitted to the infirmary. The prior should exercise due caution in giving canons leave to visit family or friends. Chests were not to be locked — this was part of the struggle to prevent the holding of private property. No canon was to live alone on a manor, especially at Blubberhouses where bad behaviour was suspected. The roof of the dormitory was to be repaired without delay. A worthy and industrious sub-prior should be appointed, and the performance of the sacrist (responsible for church supplies and equipment) needed to improve. Soon afterwards one of the canons, Reginald of Thornholme, apparently because of idleness, was sent to Nostell Priory to undergo penance. In September 1280 the archbishop told Bridlington not to admit any more canons or lay brothers, or grant any corrodies, without his permission. He cited the financial difficulties of the priory, and the smallness of the dormitory.[23]

When Archbishop John le Romeyn visited the priory in 1287 he found more rather than less evidence of slackness. Amongst those he ordered to be excluded from the cloister were nuns, women unless they were great ladies, persons of mean station, unnecessary servants, Jews (to be expelled from England three years later), and buffoons from the town who raised laughter which was inimical to the rule of silence. No canon or lay brother was to have the use of a horse without the permission of the prior, who was in turn ordered to play his proper part in the life of the community and sleep in the dormitory. The sub-prior was urged to be more diligent. John of Swaledale was to be removed from the office of sacrist. Several canons were to be confined to the precincts for periods ranging from a month to a year, with bread and water on one day a week for the worst of them. The miscreants included Reginald of Thornholme, Walter of Spaunton, and two Geoffreys of Kilham, known by the colour of their hair as 'black' and 'red' respectively. The surnames show that many of the canons came from the neighbourhood of Bridlington, or from the more distant estates such as Swaledale.[24]

Later visitations in 1314 and 1318 produced mainly routine injunctions, although one of the archbishops concerned, William Greenfield, found that the cult of the Blessed Virgin was getting out of hand. Reverence was permitted, but not adoration, and he condemned those who adored the image of the Virgin in the priory church. An inspection in 1321 was followed by the resignation of the prior and the removal from office of the sub-prior and cellarer. They may have been held responsible for the debts incurred by the priory.[25]

The new prior, Robert of Scarborough, had not been long in office when the Scots under Robert Bruce arrived in the area. In October 1322 Edward II narrowly escaped capture during a skirmish near Byland Abbey, and with some of his nobles beat a hasty retreat to Bridlington Priory. The royal party left the next day for the greater safety of Burstwick in south Holderness. Prior Robert thought it prudent to move, with

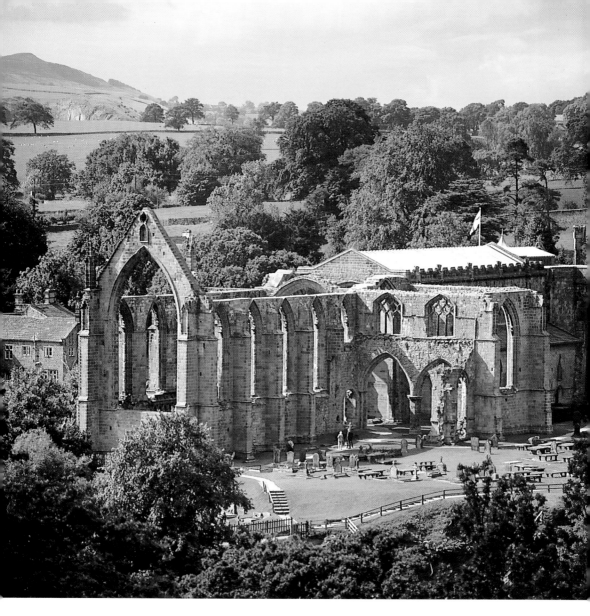

Bolton Priory from the north-east, with the ruined east end and north transept in the foreground.

most of his canons and the priory valuables, to the church of Goxhill, on the south side of the Humber, which belonged to the priory.

A poisoned chalice was handed to the senior canon remaining at Bridlington, Robert of Bainton. The Scots plundered the villages around Bridlington and threatened the priory. Canon Robert rode to Malton, where Robert Bruce had established his headquarters, and agreed to provide bread, wine and meat in return for a promise not to burn down the priory and its manors. The Scots sent eighteen horses to the priory to collect the provisions. After the raiders left the district a few days later, Robert of Bainton and the other canons who had stayed at Bridlington were accused of aiding the king's enemies. They were excommunicated by Archbishop William de Melton of York, a move which has all the hallmarks of a pre-emptive strike to avoid more serious action by Edward II. The canons petitioned for absolution, and in December 1322 the archbishop empowered Prior Robert to grant this.[26]

A hospital associated with Bridlington Priory was in operation in the middle of the twelfth century. In 1342 the widow of a physician, Master John of Brimham, petitioned the pope to be appointed as a sister in 'the hospital founded by the alms of the prioress and Augustinian convent of St Mary the Virgin, Bridelyngton'. 'Prioress' is presumably a clerical error.[27]

Four visitations of Bolton Priory in the period 1267-86 showed the house to be badly managed and torn by factional struggles. In 1267 Archbishop Giffard found that the cellarer was incompetent, and that he and the sub-cellarer neglected their spiritual duties and abused their position. The sub-prior was old and feeble, and agreed to resign. Prior William of Tanfield, in office for only a few months, told the archbishop that he had excommunicated two trouble-makers, William Hog and Hugh of York, and then confessed that he had not. The prior was not immediately deposed, but he had gone by 1270. His successor had a bumpy ride, with 'complaints and back-biting' according to the archbishop, and in 1275 he was pensioned off with £20 a year and accommodation in the priory's property at Ryther, near Selby, a safe distance away.

The new prior was none other than William Hog, whose faction must have gained the upper hand. He quarrelled with, and defied, the archbishop. Giffard came to Bolton, held an inquiry and deposed Hog.

John of Lund was unanimously elected to succeed him. John's conduct of affairs was much better than that of his three predecessors, although it did not measure up to the exacting standards of Archbishop Wickwane. The latter criticised, in 1280, the payment of a clothing allowance in money, drinking after compline (the last service of the day), eating meals 'which tend to luxury and wantonness', and the practice of canons 'roaming about the moors and woods'.[28]

When John le Romeyn visited Bolton in 1286 he found the house heavily in debt. He ordered that John of Lund, described as a former prior still living in the priory, should have an annual pension of 20s, in addition to normal subsistence, in recognition of his 'heavy labours'. In the following year John became prior of Marton in the North Riding. What is not clear is when he actually resigned his office at Bolton. His successor was John of Laund — not surprisingly the two Johns are confused in some accounts. The new John was highly regarded by Archbishop le Romeyn, and apparently accompanied the latter on a visit to Rome. He ruled Bolton for forty-five years or more, until 1331, and must therefore have been a relatively young man when appointed.

John of Laund's qualities as a spiritual father are unknown, but he was an excellent manager. When he took over, the priory was heavily in debt, and had a cash income of about £300 a year. By about 1310 the debt had been reduced considerably, and the cash income had reached about £460 a year. This had been achieved partly through the purchase of Appletreewick and Holmpton, and the appropriation of the church of Long Preston. Repairs were carried out to the grange and other farm buildings, and the sheep flock was expanded. In John's time, the number of canons ranged between twelve and nineteen, and the number of lay brothers between two and five.[29]

Bolton Priory suffered grievously from the disasters of 1314-22, the rain, the animal diseases and the Scots. In fact Ian Kershaw's analysis of the priory accounts forms one of the main sources for the first two of these events. In 1315 and 1316 the arable crops were ruined except on the limestone soils at Malham, where yields were normal. The loss of the hay crop and the sodden ground wiped out two-thirds of the 3,000 sheep. The Scots caused great damage on the granges in the spring of 1318 and the late summer of 1319, although whether the priory itself was attacked is uncertain. What would have been a good harvest in 1319 was generally lost to the Scots. The barn at Halton Grange,

rebuilt after its destruction in the previous year, was wrecked again, and the herd of forty-three oxen driven off. Soon afterwards the cattle plague arrived. The numbers of priory cattle fell from 496 in 1314-15, to 225 in 1318-19, and 31 in 1320-21. It was necessary in 1320 to move eight of the thirteen canons temporarily to other Augustinian houses. There was a slow recovery from this succession of disasters, but the economy of the priory never again reached the level of 1314.[30]

Before his retirement John of Laund began a new phase of building at the priory. The initial building programme had, by about 1200, produced a church which had a nave, transepts and a short eastern arm, with the choir stalls in the crossing. The eastern range of buildings included, as usual, a chapter house on the ground floor with a

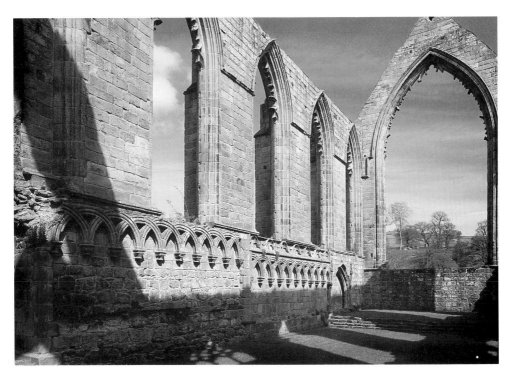

Bolton Priory: the choir and presbytery, looking east.

Bolton Priory: the west front, which is the face of the west tower, begun in 1520 but never completed.
'A beautiful example of late Gothic work at its best' (A Hamilton Thompson).

Bolton Priory from the south-west. In the priory church are, from the left: the unfinished west tower; the nave (now the parish church); and the ruined transepts and east end. On the south side of the cloister was the refectory; on the west (left) stood the original prior's lodging. To the right of the south transept can be seen part of the octagonal chapter house, built c1370. The rectory house in the foreground is post-suppression; the priory infirmary stood to the right of it.
(Cambridge University)

dormitory above. The prior's lodging was in the western range, and the frater (refectory) was parallel to the church on the south side of the cloister. About 1240 the nave was enlarged by the building of a north aisle, perhaps to accommodate an increased number of parishioners. Because at Bolton and Bridlington the priory church was also the parish church, the nave of each was preserved at the dissolution. The Bolton nave, apart from some internal re-ordering, is still as it was in the middle of the thirteenth century.

The work begun by John of Laund involved enlarging the transepts and building a major extension to the eastern arm, including a large Decorated-style east window. Also in the fourteenth century the eastern range was extended to provide a new lodging for the prior, and a new octagonal chapter house was built, the date of the latter being 'not earlier than 1370', according to Professor Hamilton Thompson. There was a tower over the crossing, of unknown date. The strengthening of the crossing piers during the fourteenth century suggests that the tower was either causing problems or was heightened at that stage. A new tower was begun at the west end of the church in 1520 by Richard Mone, prior

from 1513 to 1540. It was still incomplete, having reached only as high as the roof of the nave, at the suppression.[31]

At Bolton the layout of the church and cloister can be seen from the ruins or foundations of the buildings pulled down or allowed to decay after the priory was closed. Only the nave of Bridlington Church survives, although the marks of the cloister can be seen on the south side, and excavation has revealed some details of the overall plan. By way of compensation, one of Henry VIII's surveyors, Richard Pollard, recorded shortly after the suppression of the priory in 1537 a description of the conventual buildings and the church, apart from the nave. From the survey and archaeological evidence, Mr John Earnshaw of Bridlington has drawn a plan of the layout, shown opposite. He has also made a reconstruction drawing of the interior of the church, seen below. The section to the east of the nave is partly conjectural, but it makes use of Pollard's description of the windows, choir stalls and shrines. *(The plan and drawing are reproduced here by kind permission of Mr Earnshaw.)*[32]

The first stone church of the priory, which would have been built in Norman style, has left traces in the form of re-used

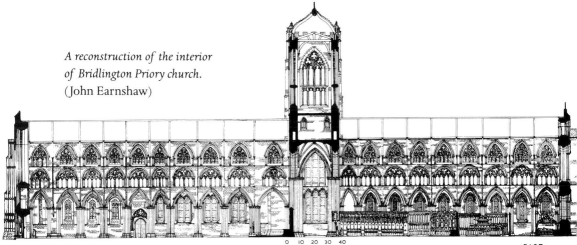

A reconstruction of the interior
of Bridlington Priory church.
(John Earnshaw)

WEST

SCALE

0 10 20 30 40
⊢⊢⊣ ⊢⊣ ⊢⊣ ⊢⊣ FEET
⊢⊣ ⊢⊣ METRES
0   3   6   9 12

EAST

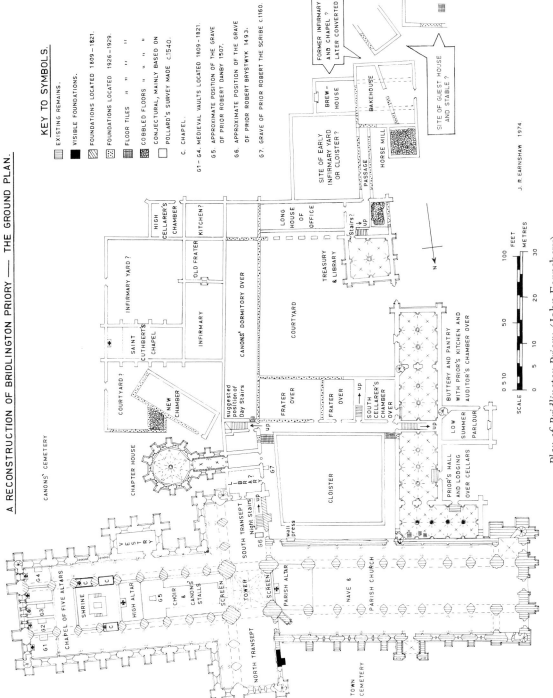

Plan of Bridlington Priory. (John Earnshaw)

Bridlington Priory church from the south west in the early nineteenth century.
(Prickett, *Priory Church of Bridlington*)

masonry — a carved scalloped capital, segments from an arch and part of a small column — incorporated in the footings of the north aisle on either side of the porch. The north side of the nave and the lower part of the north-west tower are Early English, dating from the thirteenth century. The north porch is a splendid example of the same style. The south-side windows are mainly early Decorated, indicating a reconstruction in the early fourteenth century. The financial difficulties of the priory at this period may have been due in part to an ambitious building programme. It is not clear why the alignment of the transepts and east end deviated from that of the nave. The rebuilding of these great churches was always a piecemeal process, and some problem may have arisen through building up to, or round, an existing structure.

The central tower was causing problems in the fifteenth century, when a large buttress was inserted on the nave side of the north-west pillar to provide additional support. Pollard described the tower as being high, containing seven bells, and 'daungerously in decaye'.

The west front, as it appeared in the early nineteenth century, is shown in the engraving above. Apart from the north-west tower, it is in Perpendicular style, dating from the end of the fifteenth century. The illustration shows that the two towers did not reach the arch of the great west window, apart from a small octagonal belfry on top of the south-west tower. The upper sections of the two towers were added in a Victorian restorat-ion. The whole priory church was about 330 feet long, about the same as Beverley Minster, and twice as long as Bolton Priory Church excluding the west tower.[33]

The gatehouse of the priory has surviv-ed, although with some modifications since the suppression. Pollard explains that the three-weekly court of the prior's manor of Bridlington was held in an upstairs room, with on the ground floor, north side, 'a Prison for offenders within the Towne called the Kydcott'. The most striking feature to

be described by Pollard has gone, because it stood in the chancel behind the high altar. This was the 'Saynt John of Brydlyngton Shryne, in a fayre Chappel on hygh, having on ayther syde a stayre of Stone for to goo and cume by'.[34]

The saint concerned, the last member of a religious order to be canonised before the Reformation, was John of Thwing, born in the Wolds village, eight miles from the priory, about 1320. He attended the village school, which would have been taught by a local priest, and at the age of fourteen became a novice at Bridlington Priory. His scholarly ability must have been noticed, because he was sent to Oxford for two years, before being professed as a canon at the age of twenty. After ordination as a priest he climbed the ladder of authority, becoming

Bridlington Priory gatehouse. (Prickett, *Priory Church of Bridlington*)

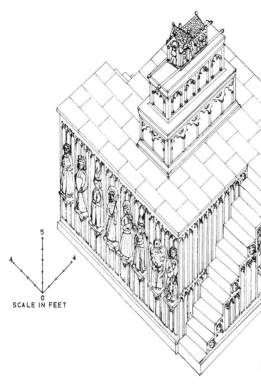

Reconstruction of the Shrine of St John of Bridlington by John Earnshaw.

ed an inquiry into the matter. Some of the miracles had occurred during John's lifetime. Typical of these was the story of five sailors from Hartlepool who were in danger of drowning in a storm. They prayed to be rescued by the merits of the holy prior of Bridlington, whom they had never met. An Augustinian canon came across the water, took the boat in hand, and guided it to safety in Bridlington harbour. They rushed round to the priory to offer thanks, and when they saw Prior John they recognised the canon who had walked upon the water. They fell on their knees before him, but John rebuked them, saying that he had been in the priory all the time, and that their thanks should be offered to God alone.

The posthumous miracles included raising the dead to life (some of them drowned fishermen), curing the seriously ill, and restoring the sight of the blind. In 1391, at the request of Richard II, the pope ordered an inquiry into the miracles, and in 1401 the bright and pious boy from a Wolds village was canonised as St John of Bridlington.[36]

The reputation of John brought considerable material benefits to the priory. In 1388 Richard II, 'out of regard for John of Thweng, late Prior', licensed the priory to crenellate its buildings, ie construct battlements or a battlemented wall. This was apparently never done. In 1390 the pope granted a remission of penance to pilgrims who visited the priory and/or gave money for the fabric of the church.

In 1403 Henry IV assigned an annual payment of 110 marks — a very large sum — out of the revenues of Scarborough Church,

successively master of the novices, cellarer and sub-prior. He was asked to become prior in 1356, but refused, saying that he was unfitted for the task. When the prior then elected, Peter of Cotes, died in the second wave of bubonic plague in 1362, John was prevailed upon to accept the post, which he held until his death in 1379.[35]

John had a reputation as a considerate leader, a benefactor to the poor, and a man who glowed with holiness. There was no shortage of recruits in his time. In 1380-81 there were twenty-four canons apart from the prior, and one lay brother. After John's death on the 10th October 1379, stories accumulated about miracles attributable to him, and in 1386 Archbishop Neville institut-

Bridlington Priory: the present church (the monastic nave) from the south-east. The cloister abutted on to the eastern (nearer) half of the nave.

which had been confiscated from Citeaux Abbey because of the French wars, 'for making a new shrine in honour of the body of St John of Thweng, late Prior'. Two years later the king went one better, and gave Scarborough Church to the priory, to become its most valuable possession. In 1409 the pope granted to the prior and his successors the right to wear the mitre, ring and other episcopal insignia within the priory and in its churches. Taxes due were waived by both Henry VI and Edward IV, the latter proclaiming in 1468 'the special devotion of the King to the glorious Confessor St John'.

In 1448 Henry VI clearly had the saint in mind when he issued a charter for the priory to have three fairs, lasting for three days each, at the Nativity of the Blessed Virgin (8th September) and the two feasts of St John.[37]

So Bridlington Priory gained the remission of taxes, one of the richest parish churches in Yorkshire, extra profits from commerce at the fairs, and enhanced dignity for the priors, on the reputation of a saintly prior who placed no value on material possessions and scorned the pomp of power. Where the material and spiritual worlds meet is a land of paradox.

7

THE WHITE CANONS
The Premonstratensians, especially Easby

Of the three Premonstratensian abbeys established in Yorkshire — Easby, Coverham and Egglestone — the first, and the best endowed, was the abbey of St Agatha at Easby (1151).

The name of its patron saint was adopted from the minster church already in existence at Easby. The principal founder was Roald, constable of Richmond Castle, supported by his son Alan, and later his grandson Roald. They gave the church of St Agatha, two carucates of land in Easby (one-third of the township), and a carucate at 'Warth' (Wath Cote, between Richmond and Skeeby). Another major contributor was Richard de Rollos, who gave land in Easby and Brompton-on-Swale, and confirmed the gifts of his subordinates, which included land in Brompton, Skeeby and Hesselton, near Hunton. Pigot de Lasceles gave a carucate in Carperby in Wensleydale. The overlord of all the above donors, Duke Conan of Brittany, earl of Richmond, confirmed their gifts, with the valuable bonus of exemption from the knight's service due to him. Conan added gifts of his own, including 'all the land of Scales, which belonged to Warin the archer', now represented by High and Low Scales, just north of Richmond. He also gave a tithe of Richmond Fair, which was worth £2 13s 4d in 1200. Lesser landowners contributed grants of between two and twelve acres

in Easby and Brompton-on-Swale, and both land and pasture rights on the moor of Middleton Tyas. All of the above grants had been made by 1162, when they were listed in a papal confirmation. In material terms, Easby Abbey had made a good start.[1]

The son and daughter of Roald gave to the abbey the churches of Great Langton and Stanwick St John. Early in the thirteenth century Easby acquired the advowson (the right to appoint the priest) of Manfield, the nearby chapel of Cleasby, and Warcop in Westmorland, the latter transferred later to Shap Abbey. In the late twelfth century, Thomas de Burgh (Brough, near Catterick) confessed that he had cheated the canons, to the peril of his soul, by persuading them to take only 20s a year out of Great Langton Church. He restored the patronage to Easby, and the archdeacon of Richmond negotiated an arrangement whereby the abbey was to receive £5 a year, the rest of the benefice income going to the vicar. A vicarage was also instituted at Stanwick.[2]

In the later years of the twelfth century, further grants consolidated the abbey's estates in Easby and Brompton-on-Swale, in both of which sheep stations were established. The corn mill of Easby was also acquired. North of Richmond the abbey developed a grange on Middleton Tyas Moor, and was given land and pasture rights in Skeeby,

The guests' solar at Easby Abbey.

Dalton, Barton and Croft. For example, the gift of Warin son of Peter de Dalton in the township of the same name included the site of a sheepfold, pasture for twenty cows and a hundred ewes with their lambs, plus annually thirty waggon-loads of peat and the same of brushwood. The family of Stapleton gave nearly half of the township of Stapleton (total assessment eight carucates) early in the thirteenth century.[3]

The abbey had to pay for a few of its acquisitions, for example £20 for half a carucate in Skeeby, but in most cases its only financial obligation was the discharge of services due to a superior lord. For a carucate of land in

Bellerby it had to pay an annual sum equivalent to one-twelfth of the service of one knight, plus one pound of pepper at Richmond Fair. The charge for the land at Stapleton was the proportion of the knight's service and 6s 8d a year in lieu of castle-guard at Richmond Castle. When feudal service obligations were split into small units, they were commuted to money payments. The most homely arrangement was made by Ralph de Scall, who was about to depart on the Crusades in 1188. He had already given a small plot of land in Carperby to Easby, and now leased two bovates there for three years. The abbey was to

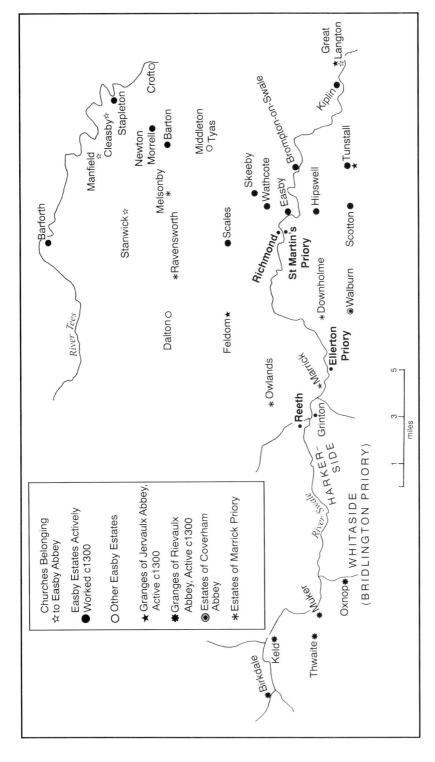

The estates of Easby Abbey and monastic Swaledale. (See also the map on page 85.)

supply his wife daily with three 'household loaves' and yearly with half a quarter of flour. If he failed to return within three years, Easby was to give his wife her share of the land as dower (normally one third), and use the rest for the maintenance of his only daughter.[4]

All of the lands mentioned above were within nine miles of the abbey, except for Carperby, thirteen miles away. At the end of the thirteenth century Easby had other properties further west, including a substantial grange, possibly leased, in the Forest of Bainbridge, and a grange, corn mill and chapel at Garsdale. The estates had a good balance of arable and pastoral lands.On the other hand, the financial benefit from the

patronage of churches was small. The Premonstratensian order discouraged the exploitation of parish revenues, and the only church staffed by the canons in the early Middle Ages was at Easby itself. At a later period, when the office of vicar had been established at both Easby and Manfield, the abbey improved its finances by appointing one of its canons to each of these two posts. The profits of parish churches were therefore much less important to the white canons than to the black (Augustinian) canons. The economy of a Premonstratensian abbey such as Easby was much closer in style to that of the Cistercians.[5]

Because so little has survived of the abbey church, it is difficult to trace the early

The south wall of the frater and adjacent parish church, Easby Abbey. (Bernard Jennings)

stages of the building programme. Nothing remains of the nave except for the base of part of the north wall of the north aisle. It seems that the church was built in the 1180s and 1190s, with an aisled nave, transepts with chapels, and an eastern arm consisting of a short, aisleless presbytery. This is the plan found in several other Premonstratensian churches of the same period in England and France. St John Hope considered that the presbytery and south transept were built about 1180, in the style called 'Transitional', as the Norman was giving way to the Early English. The north transept, in the Early English style, is a little later.[6]

A gift of land in Brompton-on-Swale was made about 1180 or a little later, 'for the fabric of the new church'. This raises the question, where or what was the old church? There are two possibilities, that the canons managed with a temporary wooden structure for thirty years or more, or that they held their services in the parish church, which stood within the curtilage of the abbey.

Egglestone Abbey from the south-east.

A view of Easby Abbey c1800 showing the frater and its undercroft. Above the third arch of the undercroft can be seen the pulpit used by the lector, who gave spiritual readings during meals. The tracery of the east window was almost complete at this time. (Whitaker, *Richmondshire*)

Monastic communities developing a virgin site erected wooden buildings first, and then began their essay in stone with the part of the church which accommodated the choir stalls and high altar, ie the transepts and presbytery. If there was an existing parish church, this could be used, extended by new buildings and then replaced. Because of the lie of the land, the parish church of St Agatha could not be developed in this way. The abbey church — the 'new church' of c1180 — was built a short distance away. If the old church was used for abbey services until the 1180s, the canons may already have erected some stone buildings around the cloister.[7]

At the end of the thirteenth century a chapel was added in the angle between the north aisle of the nave and the north transept, and about 1340 the eastern arm was extended by the area marked 'presbytery' on the plan. During the thirteenth century the buildings around the cloister were replaced, according to an unusual plan. Monastic cloisters were nearly always rectangular, but the west side of the Easby cloister is fifty per cent longer than the east side. The site is to some extent constricted by the River Swale, but the main factor was the position of the parish church, preventing the construction of a long eastern range. As

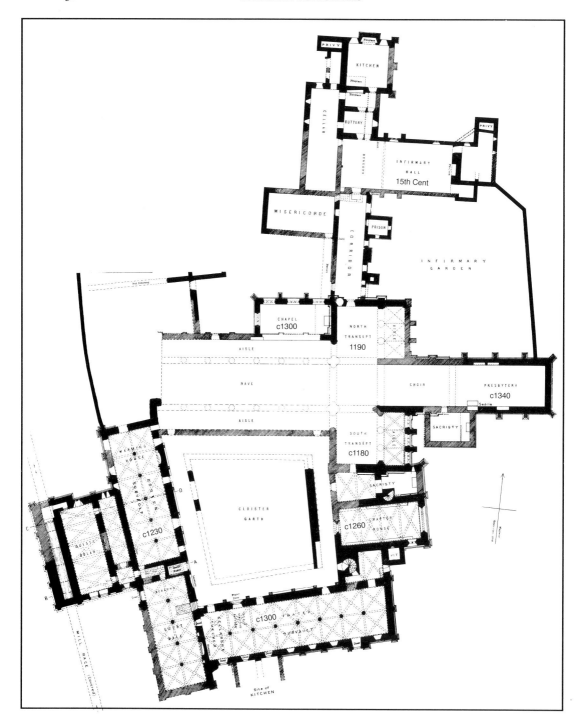

Easby Abbey. (St John Hope, *YAJ*, vol 10)

a result of the same constraints, the infirmary was built on the north side of the church instead of being adjacent to the cloister, the only example of this amongst the English abbeys of the order. The abbot's lodging appears to have occupied the upper floor of the wing linking the church to the infirmary.

The western range, built about 1230, contained the canons' dormitory on the first floor, and may have had accommodation for the lay brothers. The lavatories were built over the tail race of the corn mill. The eastern range, dating from about 1260, had the chapter house on the ground floor. In the middle of the fifteenth century the upper storey was rebuilt and extended, but for what purpose is uncertain.[8]

The geographical position of the three abbeys of white canons made them vulnerable to the Scottish raids during the reign of Edward II. After a brief foray through

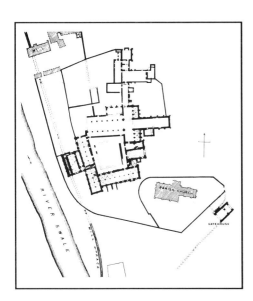

Easby Abbey and its position in relation to the parish church and other buildings.
(St John Hope, *YAJ,* vol 10)

Swaledale in 1314, the Scots came again in 1316, exacted a large ransom from the town of Richmond by threatening to burn it down, and, to quote the *Lanercost Chronicle,* 'marched some sixty miles to the west, laying waste everything as far as Furness'. Then followed the major attacks in 1318 and 1319, in which the Scots came down the Vale of York, returning by the Pennine valleys. In 1318 the tax assessment of Easby Abbey and its estates was cut from £162 to £40. The reduction for Coverham was from £33 to £13 6s 8d, and for Egglestone from £63 to £30. The latter abbey was also excused tax arrears of over £27. It was badly hit in later Scottish incursions.[9]

Easby had a stroke of good fortune about 1330, when Thomas de Burton, successor in title to Roald the Constable, sold an estate which included the patronage of the abbey to Sir Henry Scrope. Some 'founders' were indifferent to the monastery under their patronage; others were interested only in some free accommodation and provisions; but the Scropes were generous benefactors. In 1386, in the course of a legal dispute in which Sir Richard Scrope accused Sir Robert Grosvenor of carrying a shield bearing the Scrope arms, the abbot of Easby testified that the Scrope arms, 'azure a bend or' (a diagonal band of gold on a blue background), were to be seen 'throughout the church of St Agatha in glass windows, and on panels before the altar, on the vestments of the said abbey, and in glass windows in their refectory'. Sir Henry Scrope was buried in the choir, and his effigy and coat of arms were displayed in the presbytery, where his son Sir William lay in another tomb, decorated with the same arms. Other members of the family were buried in the church.[10]

The Scropes became founders about ten years before the east end of the church was

Easby Abbey: the east end of the frater and, to the right, the corner of the chapter house building.
(Bernard Jennings)

doubled in length. The two events can hard-ly have been unconnected. Henceforth the choir and presbytery had a dual role, for the services of the canons and as a splendid chapel for a proud family.

In February 1393 Sir Richard Scrope secur-ed a licence from the king to assign a rent of £150 from certain manors to establish a chantry of six chaplains in the chapel of Bolton Castle, and to support six additional priest-canons at Easby Abbey 'and for the support of twenty-two poor men therein'. More than two-thirds of the money was to go to Easby. The twelve priests would say masses daily for King Richard II, the mem-bers of the Scrope family, and their souls after death. In May of the same year Sir

Richard dropped the Bolton Castle part of the project, and raised the staffing at the abbey to ten priest-canons and two secular chaplains. 'Priest-canons' were specified because men who could say mass were re-quired, and recruits to the order were norm-ally professed as canons a few years before the normal age for ordination as priests. The May document made explicit what was normally implicit in such arrangements, that the 'twenty-two poor inmates of the abbey' were required to pray for the found-ers and the king.[11]

Something went wrong with the project. Perhaps the abbey could not recruit enough canons who were already priests or would be ready for ordination within a short time.

In March 1399 the abbey, 'being in full poss-ession of the said rent', agreed to release it to Sir Richard, who planned instead a new scheme centred on Wensley Church and Castle Bolton.

The abbey was clearly in financial diffic-ulties at this period. In 1400 the pope gave Easby permission to change the status of the churches of Easby and Manfield, where perpetual vicarages had been instituted. At the next vacancy the abbey could appoint one of its own canons as vicar, or employ secular chaplains, who were cheap and had no security of tenure. At the same time indulgences were granted to penitents who, at two specified periods in the year, should visit the abbey 'and give alms for the con-servation or repair of the Premonstratensian monastery of St Agatha by Richmond'. There is nothing to suggest that the abbey had fallen out with the Scropes. When Rich-ard, now Lord Scrope, died in 1402 he beq-ueathed a valuable collection of vestments, sacred vessels and other silver to Easby.[12]

The references in the May 1393 document to the twenty-two poor people at Easby show that they were already there. The stat-utes of the order laid down that each abbey was to provide hospitality and alms, includ-ing 'a guest house ... for the reception of the poor ...'. At Easby this formed part of the three-storey building projecting from the western ranges which is named on St John Hope's plan (see page 136) as the 'guests' solar'. We do not know how many poor people were accommodated, and over what period.[13]

In 1380-81, Easby Abbey had nineteen canons, Coverham sixteen and Egglestone eleven. There were only two lay brothers, one each at Easby and Coverham. There is no record of any lay brother at an English abbey of white canons in the fifteenth cent-ury. In the 1470s Easby had twenty canons, including two who were vicars of Easby and Manfield, and another who served the chapel at Garsdale. There were nineteen canons at Coverham and fifteen at Eggle-stone. There is no suggestion here of any difficulty with recruitment.[14]

The link between the English white can-ons and the mother house at Premontre was weakened by the long wars between the English and French kings, and the payment of dues became very erratic. In 1459 Richard Redman, abbot of Shap, obtained a comm-ission for life as the representative in Eng-land of the abbot of Premontre, a position recognised a few years later by both the king and the pope. Redman was made a bishop in 1471, ultimately progressing to the see of Ely. The abbeys of the order were exempt from inspection by the ordinary bishops, but the reports of Redman's regular visits to Easby fill this gap in our knowledge for the last quarter of the fifteenth century.[15]

In 1478 Easby, under Abbot William Ellerton, a former cellarer, was said to be in an excellent state, as it was in 1482 except that one canon had been excommunicated for apostasy. He had presumably left the abbey without permission. The same canon had reformed by 1488, when Ellerton had sixteen canons in priests' orders, three in deacons' orders and two novices. However, another canon was imprisoned in the abbey on Redman's orders for continual disobed-ience. Inspections during the 1490s found no more than minor faults, but in 1500 the canon who was vicar of Manfield was found to have made a will disposing of property which he regarded as his own, but which by the rules of the order belonged to the abbey.[16]

*Effigies from
Coverham Abbey.*

On the 2nd August 1534 Robert Bampton, abbot of Easby since 1511, issued a written declaration that on that day the abbey had received John Lord Scrope of Bolton, after the death of the previous Lord Scrope, 'as our veray trewe and undoubted founder of our said monasterye, with procession and ... other solemnities and ceremonies ...'. For two centuries the Scropes had been active patrons and supporters of the abbey, being rewarded in this life with many outward signs of their dignity, and after death with the masses and prayers of the canons. However, in the same year Parliament passed acts making Henry VIII the Supreme Head of the Church in England; confirming the king's marriage to Anne Boleyn and making the children of that marriage heirs to the throne; declaring any opposition to the marriage to be treason; and making the monasteries which were exempt from episcopal visitation subject to inspection by officers of the Crown. The year 1534 was not a good one for an abbey to promise that 'the sayde John Lord Scrope of Bolton and his heirs' would be 'partakers of our praers ... and other devoute and meritorious actes ... for ever.'[17]

THE ONLY ENGLISH MONASTIC ORDER
The Gilbertines, especially Malton and Watton

Of the four Gilbertine houses in York-shire, by far the most important were Watton, a double house of nuns and canons, and Malton, for canons only, both founded by Eustace FitzJohn and his wife Agnes in 1150.

Watton was thought to be the site of an Anglo-Saxon nunnery. Eustace held all of the township, assessed for taxation at sixteen carucates, with the exception of one caru-cate bought about fifty years earlier by St Mary's Abbey. According to *Domesday*, there was land for nine plough-teams, and there-fore on the conventional reckoning of 120 acres to the ploughland, an estimated 1,080 acres. With the support of their overlord William Fossard, Eustace and Agnes gave their Watton lands to the priory. The odd carucate was leased from St Mary's. There was later a dispute about the rent, settled by the arbitration of the archbishop of York, who fixed it at 10s a year.[1]

Eustace FitzJohn also gave eight caruc-ates in Hutton Cranswick, about two-thirds of the township, together with the advow-son (the right to appoint a priest) of the church there. A few years later William Foss-ard, as a substitute for a planned visit to Jeru-salem, gave to the priory three carucates in Hawold (total assessment six carucates), in the Wolds about seven miles from Watton. He had recovered this holding from a sub-ordinate by compensating him elsewhere,

which suggests that the priory particularly wanted this well-drained arable land, doubly valuable because of access to extensive sheep pastures.[2]

At about the same time a couple gave 195 acres of arable land in Etton, in return for the fraternity of the priory. Some gifts were made by the parents of Watton nuns, eg Walter de Boynton — two of whose daught-ers had taken the veil — gave four bovates of land in Burnby, near Pocklington. This was of limited value to Watton because of its small size and the distance involved, and the holding was later exchanged with Wart-er Priory, two miles from Burnby, for a ploughland at Hawold.[3]

The original grant of Eustace and Agnes had included a bondman in North Ferriby, holding three bovates of land and therefore a substantial peasant. Their son William de Vescy confirmed this part of the grant, and also arranged to resettle some of the bond-men of Watton. He made an agreement with the priory that it could either retain or remove any bondmen still left there on the 1st July 1178. William was also instrumental in securing for the priory the corn mill of Pouzthwaite, with one carucate of land, in the now depopulated township of Sunder-landwick.[4]

Other lands and pasture rights were acquired in Kilnwick, Huggate, North Dalton,

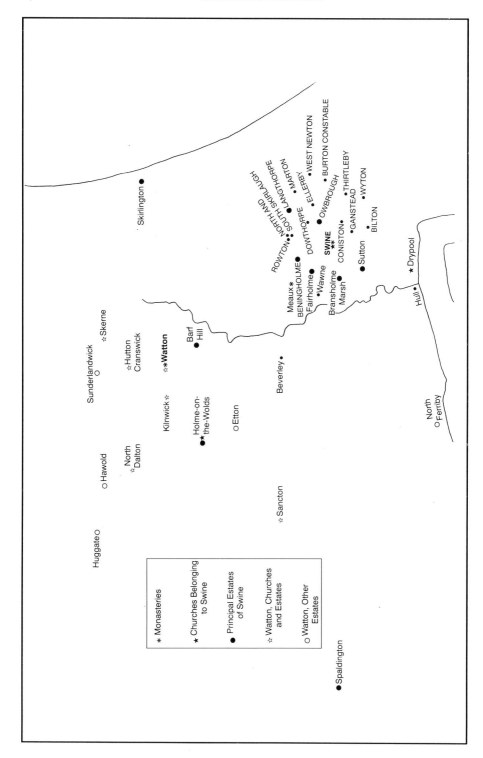

The estates of Watton and Swine priories. Townships in the parish of Swine in the twelfth century are in capitals.

Sancton, Birdsall, Tranby, and Hilderthorpe, on the south side of Bridlington. The priory was also allowed to collect 'fligheres' — curved timbers for a ship — within the township of Flamborough, for use in its own ship. The Watton estates were relatively compact, and had a good balance of lowland arable and Wolds pasture. The canons, although in office mainly to minister to the nuns, would have no difficulty in serving the parish churches of Watton (separate from the priory church, but within the precinct) and Hutton Cranswick. In due course the priory appropriated these two churches and four others — Sancton, North Dalton, Kilnwick and Skerne — installing vicars in each.[5]

Eustace FitzJohn endowed Malton Priory with the churches of Old Malton, Winteringham and Brompton (between Pickering and Scarborough), and the township of Linton, to the south-east of Winteringham. As explained on page 28, the canons were made responsible for three hospitals in the Malton area. William de Vescy gave the church of Ancaster in Lincolnshire and the chapel of Sowerby in Winteringham parish. The latter is apparently the same as St Helen's Chapel, which collected tithes separately from the parish church of St Peter. Later the priory was given by William and his wife Burga the churches of Langton and Norton. Walter Neville added the church of Walden in Hertfordshire. In the middle of the thirteenth century, the priory also owned the churches of Marton-in-Galtres and Winterton in Lincolnshire.[6]

It was probably because Malton Priory was founded for canons only, with an intended complement of thirty, that its early endowment was so heavily weighted towards churches, four of which were within a six-mile radius. Land for a balanced farming economy was, however, gradually acquired. Through many small gifts, holdings in Winteringham, Newton and Linton were built up into one large grange. The arable part of this needed eleven plough-teams in the middle of the thirteenth century, which suggests an acreage of about 1,300.[7]

Further south William Aguillon, in return for being received as a lay brother with the option of becoming a canon if he wished, granted forty-two acres of land, and pasture for sixteen oxen and three hundred sheep in Mowthorpe, together with all of Hornhow Wold, from the bounds of Thoralby to those of Sledmere and Towthorpe, and lands adjacent to the canons' existing property at 'Houstwald'. The village of Mowthorpe is represented by the farm of Low Mowthorpe, in a shallow valley between Duggleby and Kirkby Grindalythe. Thoralby, now lost, was on the west side of Mowthorpe. William's family made other grants of land and pasture for what became the grange of Mowthorpe, described as such in a papal confirmation in 1178. The priory was not responsible for all of the depopulation in this Wolds area. In the 1297 tax lists, Newton and Mowthorpe were comparable in population to several neighbouring villages which have survived.[8]

Another string of properties was acquired in the Swinton-Amotherby-Easthorpe area, where the land of the townships extended from the marshes along the River Rye, south to the eastern end of the Howardian Hills. A grange was established at Swinton. (Other acquisitions are shown on the map on page 146.) The economy of Malton was therefore based mainly upon churches and Cistercian-style granges, the number of which grew from three in 1178 to eleven in 1244. The granges and sheep

The prior's lodging, Watton Priory.

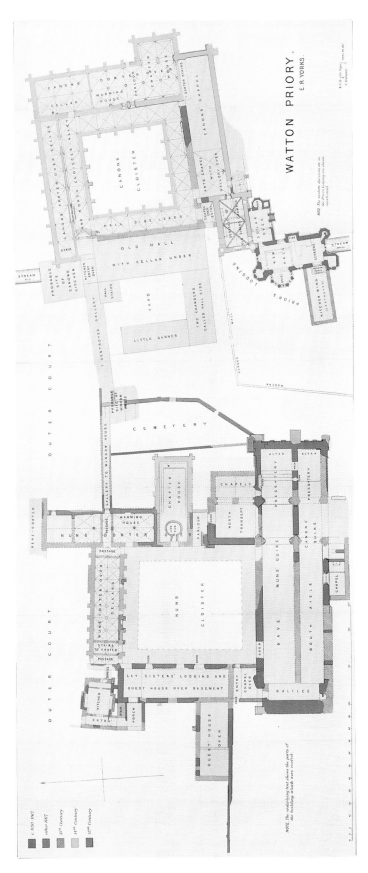

Plan of Watton Priory. (St John Hope, *Trans East Riding Antiq Soc vol VIII*)

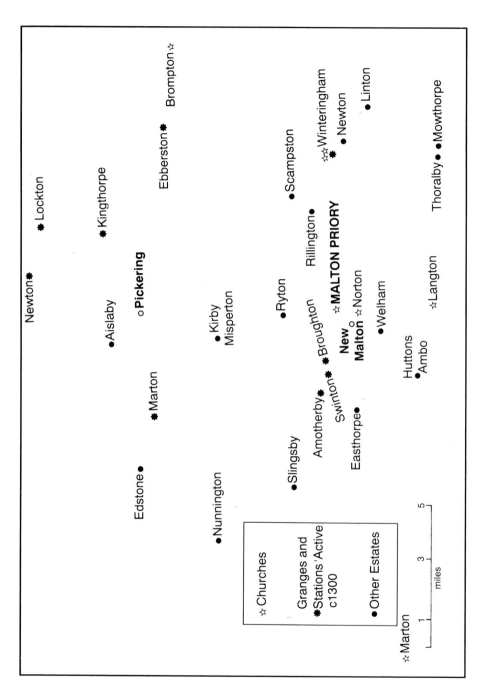

The estates of Malton Priory.

stations were managed by lay brothers, assisted by paid labourers. The rules of the order allowed Malton a maximum of thirty-five lay brothers, but whether this number was reached is not known. In 1164 the Gilbertine and Cistercian orders made a 'no poaching' agreement, whereby hired servants could not be recruited from a house of the other order until their time of service had expired. Malton Priory had some bondmen; their possession was not forbidden by the order. In the mid-thirteenth century the prior gave four bondmen their freedom, commuting their services into a money rent.[9]

The double houses of the Gilbertine order, such as Watton, contained nuns, lay sisters, canons and lay brothers. Malton had only the two groups of men. The rules of the order provided that boys could be admitted on probation at the age of fifteen, be professed as a canon at the age of twenty, and ordained as priest a few years later. The minimum age for girls intending to be nuns was twelve. They moved to the novitiate at fifteen and professed at eighteen. Lay sisters professed at twenty after one year's probation, but lay brothers had to be twenty-four before they could be admitted as novices.[10]

Following the Rule of Sempringham, the business affairs of Watton Priory were the responsibility of four 'proctors', the prior (who was head of the house), the cellarer, and two lay brothers, one of them the granger, who supervised the monastic farms. Accounting was done by means of tallies — marked sticks split in two to form a duplicate record — so that it was not necessary for the lay brothers to be literate. According to the Rule, the lay brothers had the same voting power as the prior and cellarer, although whether this operated in

practice is another matter. Once a month the four men submitted their accounts to the *scrutator*, a canon who held the office for one year, and two or three times a year a financial inspection was carried out by 'general *scrutators*' of the order. Large purchases or sales required the consent of both the nuns' and canons' chapters, and the approval of the head of the order, the Master of Sempringham. The money and financial records were kept in the nuns' quarters, in one or more chests with triple locks. Three mature and reliable nuns had one key each. The nuns, who were usually five times as numerous as the canons, were governed by three prioresses, each presiding for one week in turn, but none of these could serve as a keyholder. At Malton three canons kept the treasury, and three lay brothers checked the receipt of money.[11]

The emphasis on the passage in the Lord's Prayer, 'lead us not into temptation', did not apply only to financial matters. Watton Priory was constructed and organised so as to place strict limits on oral communication, and virtually prevent visual contact, between the two sexes. The church was partitioned lengthways by a wall five feet thick, which prevented the nuns and lay sisters in the broader north side, and the canons and lay brothers in the narrower southern section, seeing each other. The wall did not reach to the roof, so that the women could hear the mass celebrated daily by canons, and the sermon preached on feast days. For the distribution of Holy Communion, the sacred vessels were passed through a turntable opening, close to the door near the east end which was opened for processions on the fourteen main feasts of the Gilbertine year.

During processions round the church and the nuns' cloister, doors and curtains were opened and closed so that the men and women never saw each other. When a canon heard the confession of a nun or lay sister, through an opaque screen, other nuns and canons had to be present so that nothing unseemly could happen in the privacy of the confessional. However, the penitents would normally have been sent by the presiding prioress, who had already heard the faults confessed in the chapter house, and decided that priestly absolution was required. There was, therefore, nothing unusual in having an audience for the recital of sins.[12]

The food for the whole community was cooked by lay sisters in a kitchen in the nuns' enclosure. The meals for the canons and lay brothers were delivered through a turntable-window in the wall separating the women's and men's areas. Each day 'the brother of the window', accompanied by a canon, told the two 'sisters of the window' how much food was required, and whether there were guests or the sick for whom a special diet would be appropriate. The cellaress then put out from her store fish, eggs, cheese, bread, beans, flour, etc, for the cooks to use.[13]

The fears of impropriety which lay behind these physical arrangements and rules of conduct were graphically illustrated by a scandal at Watton, recounted by Abbot Ailred of Rievaulx. He prefaced his account by describing the heights of spiritual rapture reached by the nuns, who continued to pray for a deceased sister until an apparition assured them of her salvation. Archbishop Henry Murdac had asked Watton to take in a girl of four, to bring her up, the assumption being that at the appropriate age she would become a novice. The girl may have been an orphan, or illegitimate. Murdac died in 1153, and therefore the child was handed over between 1150 and 1153. As she

grew up, despite verbal corrections and beatings, she showed no enthusiasm for the religious life. When a group of brothers, presumably lay brothers, came into the nuns' cloister to do some work, the girl caught the eye of one of them, they arranged to meet, and, to quote Ailred, she 'went out a virgin of Christ [and] returned an adulteress'. The latest date for the writing of Ailred's account is 1166; he described the events as taking place some years earlier; and the earliest date at which the girl could have reached the age of eighteen was 1164. It is probable, therefore, that she was still a novice.

The affair was discovered, the girl confessed her pregnancy and was beaten and chained up by the nuns, and the young man, who had fled, was captured. Some of the nuns asked for him to be handed over to them — in modern police parlance, to assist them in their enquiries — but in fact with a different purpose. The erring girl was given a knife and forced to castrate her lover. He was returned to the brothers, and fades from the story. The girl was chained up again. When she was due to give birth, Archbishop Henry appeared twice to her in a vision, on the second occasion accompanied by two women, who took away the baby. The nuns examined the girl, and found no trace of pregnancy or childbirth. The chains and one of two fetters holding the girl had fallen off, apparently by a miracle. In a less credulous age the observers would have recognised an hysterical pregnancy.

At this point St Ailred was asked by St Gilbert, the Master of Sempringham, to investigate the matter. He visited the imprisoned girl, and concluded that the chains and fetter had been removed by divine intervention, a view which was confirmed by a letter which Ailred received on his return to Riev-aulx, stating that the remaining fetter had fallen off. In his account, written to a 'dearest friend who is far removed from these parts' (identity unknown), Ailred explains that he made some forceful criticisms, in charitable language, of Gilbertine security. As for the behaviour of the vengeful nuns, he commented, 'I praise not the deed but the zeal'. He did not criticise the practice of taking in young girls, but the order subsequently tightened up its rules on this.[14]

There was unrest at Sempringham in the mid-1160s, when lay brothers revolted against the rule of Gilbert. Questions were raised about the conduct of double houses, but the prior of Bridlington, fifteen miles from Watton, wrote that he had heard nothing to the discredit of the Gilbertines. Archbishop Roger of York described Watton as the only religious house in his diocese in which 'canons and lay brothers live together honourably with nuns ... but separately ...'[15]

The history of the buildings of Watton Priory has not been easy to trace. The fifteenth century prior's lodging has survived, now as part of a private house, but the remaining structures have disappeared above ground level. Chalk was used extensively in the construction, for internal walls and in external walls faced with sandstone. After the suppression, as the district lacks good building stone, the ashlar blocks were quarried, some taken in 1613 for the repair of Beverley Minster. The exposed chalk would soon weather. Some of it was burned in a limekiln.[16]

The site was excavated in the years 1893-98 by William St John Hope and Rev Dr Cox. It proved possible to trace the plan of the church, with the exception of the north transept, inaccessible under some large

trees. The church was seriously damaged by fire in 1167. This is known from the chronicle of Meaux Abbey, which records that in 1160 the first abbot, Adam, resigned as a result of the financial difficulties of the house, and retired as an anchorite to Watton, 'then a new monastery of virgins'. After seven years he had to be rescued from the fire, as his cell was under the church, and decided to return to Meaux. St John Hope concluded that, apart from the west end of the church which might have survived from the first building, the church was all built in one process, beginning after the fire.

The only other documentary evidence of the priory buildings is a survey of the canons' cloister made at the suppression for the purpose of calculating the amount of lead on the roofs. It includes a dormitory, the adjoining 'Jakis house' (toilet block), and a kitchen, which suggests that at some stage the canons had meals prepared in their own sector. Because of the nature of the physical evidence, the dates assigned to different parts of the buildings by St John Hope are inevitably more tentative than usual.[17]

As the parish church of Watton was a separate building (the earliest part dating from the thirteenth century), there was no case at the suppression for preserving the priory church. The situation at Malton was different, as the nave of the priory church was used by the parishioners of Old Malton. New Malton was a separate township, with a larger population, served by two chapels belonging to the priory. The central part of the priory nave, ie without the aisles, now serves as the nave and chancel of the parish church.[18]

The priory church was built, as usual, from the east end, in a process which appears to have been continuous but slow.

The west front is thought to date from about 1200-10. In the fifteenth century a large window was inserted over the doorway in this wall. Originally there were, in addition to a central tower, two towers at the west end. The southern one of these, of early twelfth century date, survives. After a fire in the late fifteenth century, the north aisle was demolished and a solid wall built along the north arcade of the nave. The north-western tower was probably pulled down in the same process. The community may have lacked the resources for a full restoration. At the suppression the lead was removed from the central tower, transepts and east end, leaving the buildings to decay. By 1636 the central

The south wall of Malton Priory church, inserted after the demolition of the south aisle of the monastic nave.

The west front of Malton Priory.

Malton Priory: the west doorway.

tower had become unsafe and was demolished. The remains of the eastern arm were finally cleared in 1734.[19]

The accounts of Malton Priory for the years 1244-57 have been preserved. The priory was still acquiring land, £500 being spent for this purpose in fourteen years. Some of the land had been mortgaged to the Jews. Part of the new land was farmed

directly, part let off, increasing the annual rental income from £48 in 1244 to £61 in 1257. The priory also spent an average of £15 a year renting land and pastures.

The priory had 49 plough teams in use, 3 on the home farms and the rest on the granges, with 11 at Winteringham, 8 at Swinton (probably covering the grange of Broughton) and 7 at Mowthorpe. The house was not, however, self-sufficient in corn, spending about £75 a year on wheat, barley, rye and malt. The main source of cash income was wool. In the Italian merchant's list of c1300, discussed in relation to the Cistercian abbeys on pages 99-100, both Malton and Walton were put down for forty sacks of wool, equivalent in each case to nearly 10,000 fleeces annually. This figure, even if it is reliable, includes both tithe wool and *collecta*, ie wool bought from other producers, so the size of the priory flock is not known.

The Gilbertines had been exempted from all taxation by Henry II and later monarchs, but this privilege was invalidated as a result of their liability to contribute to papal finances. On the pretext of funding a Cru-

sade, Henry III obtained from the pope a grant of one tenth of the revenues of the Church in England for three years. A valuation was made for this purpose in 1254. The income of Malton was assessed at £281 3s 4d, of which the profits of churches accounted for £150 18s. The other main items were £60 13s 4d rent of tenants, and £55 6s 8d profits from the granges and other lands farmed directly. The income from wool was not taxed, as this would have taken the form of a customs duty, from which the priory was exempt.[20]

The Lay Subsidy return for 1301, a tax which included the produce of land farmed directly by monasteries, but not money rents or the profits of churches, shows that Malton Priory was still actively engaged in

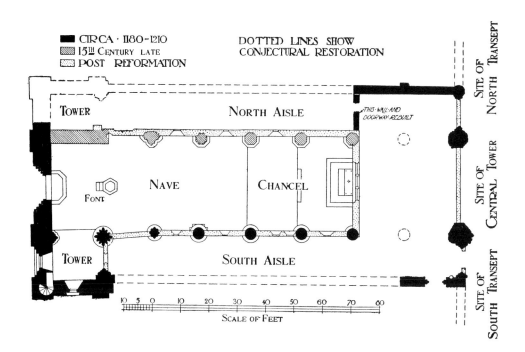

Plan of Old Malton Church, which occupies the nave of the priory church.
(Courtesy general editor of VCH, from *VCH YNR I*)

arable and pastoral farming on its North Riding lands. The return from the East Riding, including the Winteringham/Mow-thorpe area, has been lost. East of Malton were the main granges of Broughton, Swinton and Amotherby. In the Vale of Pickering, Ebberston was the largest operation, follow-ed by the grange of 'Sutermarton' (Marton in Sinnington parish). The priory had a line of pastoral stations north of Pickering, at Kingthorpe, Lockton, Newton and Goath-land.[21]

The Gilbertines were exempt from episc-opal visitation, so that we are denied the insights into the internal life of the priories which would have been provided by the archbishop's reports. More is known about the relationship of Watton and Malton with the outside world. In 1272 Henry III told the sheriff of York that Agnes de Vescy, who as widow of William de Vescy had inherited the position of 'founder' of both Watton and Malton, had descended on Watton Priory 'with a great number of women and dogs and other things which have interfered with the devotion of the nuns and sisters'. She was ordered to stay away, unless given special permission by the Master of Semp-ringham.[22]

At Watton, Agnes may just have been sponging off the community, as founders sometimes did. Towards Malton she showed clear hostility. She disputed the right of the priory to present parsons to the churches of Brompton and Langton, but lost both claims. She used her position as lady of the manor of New Malton, and her control of the market there, to harass the priory. In 1278 Edward I ordered his sheriffs to uphold the rights of the Gilbertines, not just in York-shire. In 1283 the king commissioned two judges to hear accusations that Agnes de Vescy and the townspeople of New Malton had assaulted the canons and lay brothers of the priory and seized their goods.[23]

In the early fourteenth century Malton Priory was involved in a dispute with John de Bordesden, about the alleged over-stocking of pastures in the Swinton/Apple-ton-le-Street area. Each party took the law into its own hands, seizing cattle and causing damage. In 1316 justices were appointed to hear the complaint of Watton Priory against Peter de Maulay, lord of Mulgrave Castle and of the manor of Birdsall, and others, about the seizure of livestock and corn in several places, including Birdsall, Hawold and Kilnwick. The famine conditions following the torrential rains of 1315-16 may have been a factor. Maulay and company were accused of breaking open a cart 'in which seven nuns were shut up' at Kilnwick — the nuns always travelled enclosed in this way — and of seizing other carts containing some of the charters of the priory. The prior seems to have won the case, as in 1319 Peter de Maulay was recorded as owing £400 to Watton.[24]

In 1317 Edward II sent two members of his staff in retirement, one to Malton and the other to Watton. Whether they became canons or corrodians is not clear, but mon-asteries had to put up with this kind of intrusion, which cannot have been good for discipline.[25]

Both priories were affected by the Scottish wars. In 1305, Margery, daughter of Robert Bruce and a captive of Edward I, was lodged at Watton with an allowance of 3d a day for subsistence and 13s 4d yearly for clothing. In 1310-11 and again in 1314 corn and livestock were taken from the Watton granges by purveyors authorised to make compulsory purchases for the army. During the 1322 Scottish raid, Robert Bruce seized Malton and its castle, and held them for several weeks while his men pillaged the surrounding country. The damage to Malton Priory and its estates is not recorded, but must have been considerable.[26]

In the 1330s both Malton and Watton were in debt, and were helped by loans from William de Melton, archbishop of York. In 1335 Malton owed Thomas de Holm of Beverley, a wool merchant, 127 sacks of wool worth £929, plus £446 10s in money. English wool merchants had inherited the former Italian practice of signing up monasteries for contracts with payments in advance.[27]

There were at least 53 nuns at Watton in 1326, when Archbishop Melton blessed that number, and 64 in 1378-79. The number of canons at Watton and Malton in the fourteenth century is not recorded. There is no mention of any lay brothers after the Black Death (1349), and their work was presumably taken over by lay servants. In 1370 the prior of Watton prosecuted five men for leaving his service without leave or good cause before the end of their term.[28]

There are only fragments of evidence about the affairs of the two priories in the fifteenth century. A lawsuit in 1423 showed that Watton had a fishery attached to the pond of its corn mill at Skerne. Because of the importance of fish in the monastic diet — even those communities which ate meat freely would avoid it on prescribed days of abstinence — fisheries might be kept going when a monastery had let most of its lands to tenants. In 1444 Henry VI granted Watton exemption from taxation because of poverty caused by floods.[29]

The other two Gilbertine houses remained small and poor. In 1380-81, St Andrew's, York, had four canons and Ellerton five. A few years later the latter priory received the gift of 160 acres in nearby Spalding Moor from Sir James Pickering. In the *Valor Ecclesiasticus* of 1535, Ellerton had a net annual value of £62 and St Andrew's £48. The corresponding figures for Watton and Malton were £361 and £198. There were therefore sharp contrasts amongst the Gilbertine houses of Yorkshire: two struggling priories, too small for a viable communal life; a moderately endowed house of canons at Malton; and a relatively wealthy double house at Watton, which had far more nuns than any of the independent nunneries in the county.[30]

THE SMALLER MONASTIC ORDERS
Grosmont, Knaresborough and Mount Grace

Three orders had between them only four houses in Yorkshire, the Grandmontines and Trinitarians with one each, and the Carthusians with two. The first and third of these were products of the same reform movement as the Cistercians.

The first Grandmontine house in England was established about 1204, when Joan Fossard gave to Grandmont Priory, near Limoges, a house in the Forest of Egton, on the River Esk, with 200 acres of woods, pasture for forty cows and their calves, fifty sheep, and horses and pigs, together with the right to take timber for building. A corn mill at Egton and the services of a peasant there were also included. The same donor gave other property in Goldsborough, Doncaster and York.

Joan Fossard was the granddaughter of William Fossard, a co-founder of Watton Priory, and had inherited the family's Yorkshire estates. She was married to Robert de Turnham, King John's seneschal (high steward) in Poitou and Gascony. Robert later added another 100 acres in the Forest of Egton. Joan and Robert gave to Grandmont the advowson of the church of Lockington, a grant confirmed by Archbishop Gray in 1228. The church was not appropriated, and it is unclear what benefit was derived from the advowson.[1]

The Grandmontine house at Grosmont,

known as Eskdale in the records of the order, was a cell until 1317 when, with the re-designation of Grandmont Priory as an abbey, it became a priory. The main motive of the French lord and lady in giving away a slice of Yorkshire was to support Grandmont. It was not a very successful scheme. Eskdale/Grosmont remained poor. The resources were barely sufficient to maintain a small community, and the remittances to Grandmont were apparently small. When Edward III seized control of the alien priories after the outbreak of the Hundred Years War with France in 1337, Eskdale turned out to be too poor to bother with. An investigation in 1344 reported that all of the nine brethren were English. They included priests and lay brothers, but the respective numbers of each are not given. In addition there were four servants and some farm labourers. The priory had twenty-four oxen, enough for three plough teams. In store they had a hundred quarters of oats and twenty of wheat. The scale of pastoral farming was small — a hundred sheep and forty lambs, four cows and their calves, and three horses. The outgoings included a yearly pension of 30s paid to Grandmont, and five corrodies costing 30s a year. The brethren gave hospitality to passers-by, but the resources were inadequate for reasonable subsistence, and the priory had to rely on alms from the people of the district.[2]

The priory buildings were very small in scale. A survey made at the suppression has survived, which makes a reconstruction possible. The east end of the church ended in an apse, part of which survived until the early nineteenth century. In 1360, because nearly all of the priory buildings including the church, bell-tower, cloister, refectory and dormitory had been destroyed by fire, the pope granted remissions of penance to penitents who gave alms and visited the priory church on certain feast days.[3]

The suppression survey described the church as being seventy feet long and twenty-four feet wide, with sixteen choir stalls. A local historian writing in 1817 gave the dimensions of the church ruins as a hundred feet by forty. As far as the length is concerned, an original dimension of a hundred feet

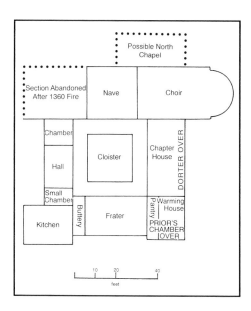

A conjectural reconstruction of Grosmont Priory.

would fit in well with the measurements of the buildings around the cloister. Architectural historian A W Clapham concluded that when the church was rebuilt after the fire, the nave was shortened by thirty feet. If there were no lay brothers left, a longer nave would not be needed. The difference in width would be explained if Grosmont had a north chapel, as did the other two English houses of the order, but this part of the plan reproduced below is, of course, more speculative.[4]

In 1394 Grandmont gave up its claim to Eskdale, the independence of which was recognised by Richard II, on condition that during the war the annual pension of 30s should be paid to the Exchequer. As the Grandmontine order was exempt from episcopal visitation, there are no reports on the standards and lifestyle of the community.

Eskdale / Grosmont remained a small and poor house until the suppression of the smaller monasteries in 1536, when there were five monks. The oldest was aged sixty-eight, the youngest thirty-one. The surnames included Egton, Skelton and Seamer. A prior recorded in 1469 was called William Whitby. It is probable that the brethren were recruited locally, and that the numbers were determined by the resources of the priory.[5]

The full title of the Trinitarians was the Order of the Holy Trinity and of the Redemption of Captives in the Holy Land. The order was founded in 1197 with the object of collecting money to ransom captive crusaders. Their habit was white, with a red and blue cross on the front, and the head of the house was called the minister. Although they were called friars, and begged for alms for the ransom fund, they had little in common with the preaching friars such as the Dominicans. In both their rule and their economic organisation they were close to the Augustinian canons. Their communities were relatively small. The Knaresborough house had six friars in 1360, when the number may have been reduced by the Black Death, but by 1375 it had recovered to a more normal eleven.[6]

The Trinitarians had lands around Knaresborough and in lower Nidderdale, and five churches. As a result of the Scottish raid in 1318, when 140 of the 160 houses in Knaresborough were burned down, the tax assessment of the friary was reduced from £26 13s 4d to £5. In the later Middle Ages it received regular remissions of half the taxation due, on the grounds of poverty, one statement referring to 'their notorious poverty'. The rules of the order required that one-third of friary revenues were to be used for the redemption of captives, but in 1402 the pope legalised the practice — already long-standing — of assigning a smaller quota.

The most interesting aspect of the history of the Knaresborough friary is its connection with the cult of St Robert. In the late twelfth century Robert Flower, the son of a mayor of York, became a hermit. He spent brief periods with the Cistercians at Newminster in Northumberland and with the Benedictines at Headley, a cell of Holy Trinity, York, but settled in a cave by the river at Knaresborough. For the details of his life, we are dependent in the main upon an account written by a Trinitarian friar in the early fifteenth century.

According to this account, Robert was harassed by William de Stuteville, lord of the Honour of Knaresborough from 1173 to 1203. The hermit used his spiritual power to send demons to torment and threaten William in his sleep. A repentant lord endowed the hermitage with land and gave Robert some livestock. Robert's brother Walter built a little stone chapel, in honour of the Holy Cross, with a house where Robert might receive pilgrims and minister to the poor. The hermit was joined by a colleague, Ivo, who was eventually to succeed him. Brian de l'Isle, constable of Knaresborough Castle and keeper of the Honour under King John, brought the king to see Robert, who, far from showing any worldly respect, held out an ear of corn and told the king that he had no power 'to create such a thing out of nothing'. Whatever the truth of this particular anecdote, King John certainly gave the hermitage half a carucate of land.

One of the stories about Robert was so persistent in local tradition that it is depicted in a fifteenth-century window in Knaresborough Parish Church. While collecting alms, Robert asked a man of rank for the gift of a cow. He was given a beast which had been living wild in the Forest of Knaresborough and was too vicious to handle. The hermit tamed her with a touch. One of the donor's men posed as a cripple to beg the cow back, but Robert made his feigned disability real until he confessed his deceit.

Robert died on the 24th September 1218. Fountains Abbey tried to claim his body, which would have attracted pilgrims and donations, but, according to another account of his life, Robert had foretold and forbidden this. He was buried by his own wish in the Chapel of the Holy Cross. His tomb became a place of pilgrimage where miracles were worked. The chronicler Matthew Paris, writing about the events of 1235, described how 'medicinal oil' had flowed from the tomb. It was probably to cash in on the cult of St Robert, and to acquire the endowment of the hermitage, that the Trinitarians came to Knaresborough

St Robert's Cave and Chapel, Knaresborough.

at the invitation of Richard, earl of Cornwall and lord of the Honour of Knaresborough, in 1252. In that year the pope granted an indulgence to those who 'help in completing the monastery of St Robert of Knaresborough where that saint's body is buried'. This is the earliest official reference to Robert as a saint.

Thirty years later, according to the *Lanercost Chronicle*, the friars were engaged in building a new church over the chapel 'where lies the body of that just man', ie St Robert. The old chapel, where pilgrims came 'in order to perform vigils and burn candles' would therefore have been left as a crypt. 'The spirit of the just man resented

this, and a tremendous flood, such as no man there remembers, carried the waters of the Nidd into the upper part and middle of the church, destroying the vaulted work in the night', and bringing the friars back to the level of St Robert. Once again we have a saint, like St German in Selby, jealously guarding his own domain.

The friary, named of course after St Robert, was still attracting large numbers of pilgrims at the beginning of the fifteenth century, when the pope authorised the minister and six other priests to hear the confessions of the crowds of people coming to the church on Trinity Sunday and the feast of SS Peter and Paul (29th June). Only a few fragments of stone from the friary buildings have survived. Assuming that the friary church was built over the chapel of the Holy Cross, there is no trace of the latter. The cave-chapel known as St Giles's or St Robert's cave, about a quarter of a mile from the friary, is shown in Stephen Good's drawing on the previous page. A cave-chapel by the Nidd near Low Bridge, which has on the outside the figure of a knight holding a sword, has been described by some topographical writers as 'St Robert's Chapel'. It was, however, made in the early fifteenth century in honour of the Blessed Virgin, and has nothing to do with Robert or the friary.

Two Carthusian priories were founded in Yorkshire, at Hull in 1377 and Mount Grace, the last medieval religious house to be established in the county, in 1398. Nothing remains of the Hull Charterhouse, but Mount Grace has the best preserved Carthusian buildings in England. They are of particular interest, because for no other order does the layout of the monastery tell us so much about the way of life of the brethren. A Carthusian priory could be described as a community of hermits. The Mount Grace monk spent most of his time in his 'cell', actually a two-storey building, twenty-seven feet square externally. Water was piped to it, and a lavatory (in the modern sense) was built at the end of the garden over a stream. The ground floor contained a living room, measuring about sixteen feet by ten feet six inches, with a fireplace, a bedroom / oratory, and a small study equipped with a desk. The upper floor consisted apparently of only one room, used probably as a workshop. The equipment of a monk, Thomas Golwyne, who moved from the London Charterhouse to Mount Grace in 1520, included 'a complete frame for to wefe

wt corsys'. This probably meant the key parts of a loom for weaving the narrow woollen cloth known as kersey. Despite the use of the word 'complete', it would be extraordinary if the heavy wooden frame had been transported from London.[7]

In the original Carthusian scheme, the monk prepared his own meals, living partly from the produce of his garden. By the mid-thirteenth century it had become the practice for meals to be cooked centrally. No meat of any kind was eaten, the diet consisting of fish, eggs, vegetables, fruit, bread and cheese. On Sundays and feast days the monks ate together in the refectory, listening in silence to a reader. All other meals were delivered to the cell via an L-shaped hatch which prevented visual contact. General conversation was allowed for one hour on Sundays and feast days, and on the weekly walk which the monks took outside the priory. Otherwise there was a strict rule of silence.

The monk wore a sleeveless hair-shirt, reaching to the waist, under coarse, heavy garments which would suit the climate of Mount Grace. The discomfort of the hair shirt would be increased by the fleas which were invariably present when clothes and bodies were washed infrequently. New statutes issued by the Carthusian order in 1368 forebade luxuries which had crept in, including bed sheets, carpets and cushions. Thomas Golwyne had four pillows and 'a kosshyn to knele on', together with a 'chafyng dysshe' for keeping food warm, evidence of some relaxation in the austerities by the sixteenth century.[8]

Although the church was used for the daily high mass and the private masses of the priests — it was the normal practice for the monks to proceed to ordination — the

Mount Grace Priory from the west. To the left of the church is the great cloister, round which most of the cells were built. (Cambridge University)

centre of the Carthusian life of prayer and contemplation was the cell. The monks had no pastoral role; they did not preach or teach, except indirectly through the books which they wrote; their service to the community was prayer.

The Carthusians used lay brothers, who, as in the case of other orders of monks, used the nave for services. There were still six lay brothers at Mount Grace when it was suppressed. The principal officers were the prior; the vicar, who corresponded to the sub-prior in a house of black canons; the sacrist, who looked after the church and its equipment; and the procurator, who managed the material affairs of the house, and supervised the lay brothers and servants.[9]

The original design of Mount Grace included fifteen cells round the cloister on the north side of the church, together with the cells of the prior and sacrist, and two other cells which may have been occupied by the vicar and procurator. In 1412 Henry IV, in return for confirming the gift of the alien priory of Hinckley, Leicestershire, at the request of his uncle Thomas Beaufort, required Mount Grace to support five additional priest-monks, who would say masses and pray for the souls of the king and his uncle. In response the priory built a set of five cells on the eastern and southern sides of the church. This suggests that the cells around the cloister were fully occupied, or nearly so. A possible sixth cell seems to be too narrow for the function. The range of buildings on either side of the gatehouse, marked by St John Hope on his plan (reproduced overleaf) as '?guest house', may have

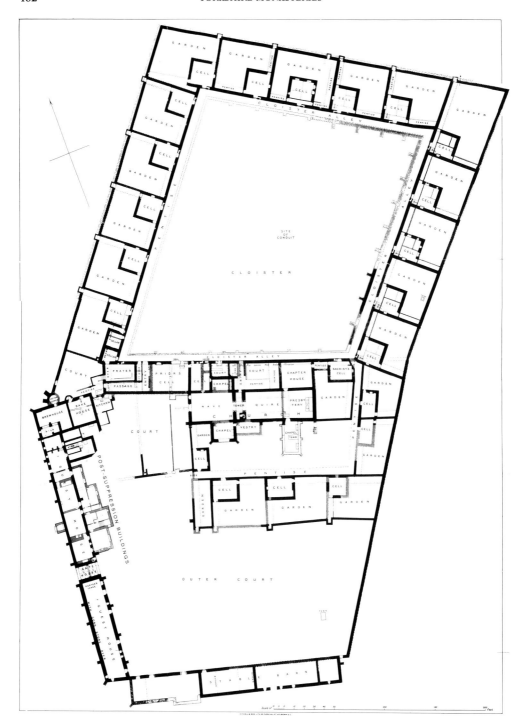

Plan of Mount Grace Priory. (St John Hope, *YAJ* vol 18)

included the accommodation of the lay brothers.[10]

The church was originally built without aisles, eighty-eight feet long internally, with an average width of twenty-six feet. The north wall and west end survive almost to their full height. In the 1420s or a little later the presbytery was extended by thirty feet to the end of the chapter house, and chapels were built on the north and south sides of the nave. The addition of these chapels was connected with the recruitment of five more priest-monks, but the longer eastern arm may have been part of the original plan. In 1439 the prior and monks stated in a petition that because of the uncertainty of their title to some alien priories, they had been unable to complete the monastery.

The next development was the erection of a little tower, nine feet three inches by six feet six inches internally, over the space between the monks' choir stalls and the lay brothers' choir in the nave. To support it, two strong walls with high pointed arches were built across the church. At some time after c1450 another chapel was built on the south side of the presbytery. If the plan of the priory church is looked at in isolation from the other buildings, it gives the impression of having been designed by a lay brother whose expertise was in the care of livestock. In fact, when chapels were needed

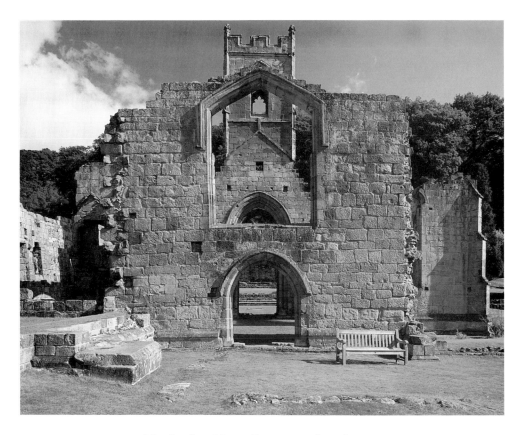

The church at Mount Grace Priory from the west.

Alan Sorrell's reconstruction of Mount Grace Priory as it would have appeared in the early sixteenth century: on the left is the great cloister, round which most of the cells (cottages and gardens) of the monks were grouped; beyond and to the right of the church are the additional five cells built in the early fifteenth century; and in the right foreground are the buildings which probably accommodated guests and lay brothers. (English Heritage)

they were added wherever there was space available adjacent to the church, within what had become a very complex layout.

A chapel, known both as the Lady Chapel and as the Chapel of the Mount, was built early in the sixteenth century on the top of the steep bank to the east of the priory. It was apparently a chantry chapel, but it was

treated at the suppression as belonging to Mount Grace Priory.

The financial instability of Mount Grace in its early days had two causes. First, its principal founder, Thomas Holland, duke of Surrey, and his uncle Richard II had both been killed within two years of the foundation. Secondly, the endowment consisted

Mount Grace Priory church from the south-east. The south chapel is in the left foreground; the choir is to the right of the tower.

mainly of the confiscated property of alien priories, the title to which was in some cases insecure. It is, incidentally, not certain that Thomas Holland actually owned the manor of Bordelby, in which the priory was located. John Ingilby had a licence in 1397 or 1398 to have mass said in a chapel in his manor of Bordelby; prayers for his family are mentioned in the foundation charter; and from 1438 the Ingilbys were recorded as patrons of Mount Grace. Gradually the finances became more secure, and new grants of land, tithes and other resources were made. At the suppression the net revenues amounted to £323, compared to £279 for Rievaulx Abbey. The properties were scattered across several counties, and the only lands directly cultivated were in the vicinity of the priory.[11]

According to the historian of the order in England, E M Thompson, the Carthusians were interested in learning only to the extent that it would assist the monk in his search for personal holiness through contemplation: 'the cell to him was heaven, where at any time he might be favoured with the Beatific Vision and the sense of intimate union with God'. If, however, this is taken to mean that the Carthusians were not an intellectual order, Mount Grace was an exception. The priory had a substantial library, specialising, appropriately, in books about the search for spiritual union with God through individual prayer and contemplation. Many works in this field were copied and/or translated at Mount Grace. Richard Methley, a monk at the priory from the 1470s, wrote five mystical works in Latin, and John Norton, who joined the community in 1482 and was prior from 1509 to 1522, gave accounts of his spiritual visions in three treatises.

The most famous of the Mount Grace scholars was Nicholas Love, apparently the third prior, who produced in 1410 *The Mirror of the Blessed Life of Jesus Christ*, written in English. The *Mirror* was in part a translation of *Meditationes Vitae Christi*, thought at the time to be the work of the great Franciscan St Bonaventure, and consisting of a series of devotions based upon the gospels. Love omitted a good deal of the original, substituting his own material as more relevant to the interests of the laity. He declared that he was writing 'to the confusion of all false Lollards and heretics'. 'Lollard' was the label pinned on a loose and shadowy grouping of rebels against certain Church doctrines, especially relating to the Eucharist, who had been influenced by the writings of John Wycliffe (c1328-84). The Church authorities were suspicious of theological works written in English, and in 1409 the archbishop of Canterbury, Thomas Arundel (who had previously been archbishop of York), set up a system for their inspection. Nicholas Love was prudent enough to secure the approval of Arundel before issuing his book.[12]

The *Mirror of the Blessed Life of Jesus Christ* was printed by Caxton in 1484, and frequently reprinted between that date and 1530. In addition, more than fifty manuscript copies have survived. One of these belongs to Wasada University in Japan, which in 1995 hosted an international conference on Nicholas Love and *The Mirror*. The prior of a monastery in a remote corner of Yorkshire has therefore been 'canonised', not by the pope, but by the international academic community.[13]

IO

THE HOLY WOMEN

The Nunneries, especially Marrick, Nun Monkton,
Swine and Wilberfoss

At each of the nunneries chosen here for detailed consideration, part of the church has survived because of parochial use.

The nave at Nun Monkton and Wilberfoss, and part of the east end at Swine, are still in use as parish churches. The church at Marrick is now a Church of England youth centre. The physical survivals of the other twenty Yorkshire nunneries are not extensive. A mile below Marrick, the fifteenth century tower of Ellerton Priory stands alongside fragments of the church. At Yedingham and Wykeham, parts of the church wall can still be seen. An east-west range of buildings at Sinningthwaite Priory, probably containing the refectory, is now a farmhouse. A fragment of a stair turret is all that remains of the nunnery at Rosedale. Some of the outer buildings of Kirklees Priory are part of a farm, but it is not certain that all of the gatehouse, the most prominent feature, dates back to before the suppression. There are no other significant survivals.

It is not possible anywhere in Yorkshire to stand in the middle of a nuns' cloister, as one can in some of the monks' and canons' houses, and use a little imagination to restore the buildings and visualise the members of the community going about their

spiritual and secular tasks. By way of compensation, the buildings of eleven nunneries were surveyed at the suppression, partly for the purpose of identifying re-usable materials, especially lead and glass. They are Arthington, Basedale, Esholt, Handale, Kirklees, Nunkeeling, Swine, Thicket, Wilberfoss, Wykeham and Yedingham. A sixteenth century drawing of Marrick Priory, and the distinctive nave at Nun Monkton, bring the number about which we have some useful architectural information to thirteen, out of

The fifteenth century tower of Ellerton Priory in Swaledale. (Courtesy general editor VCH, from VCH YNRI)

The remains of four nunneries: (top left) the exterior doorway in the south wall of Yedingham Priory nave, now inside a farm building; (above right) the north wall of Wykeham Priory church from the south; (below left) adapted buildings of the south range of Sinningthwaite Priory's cloister; (below right) the remains of a spiral staircase from Rosedale Priory.

a total of twenty-three nunneries which survived until the sixteenth century. The twenty-fourth, Foukeholme or Thimbleby, was last recorded in 1349, the year of the Black Death.

There is one problem in the use of the suppression surveys. In no case are transepts mentioned, but a drawing of Swine Church made in 1784 *(see below)* clearly shows the remains of north and south transepts. The survey of Swine describes the 'hole church' as measuring internally seventy-six feet by twenty-one feet, with no reference to the tower or transepts. The reconstruction drawings shown here assume that all the other descriptions are accurate.[1]

At two of the nunneries described in the surveys, the parish church and the nuns' church formed distinct units, although under the same roof. At Wilberfoss the parish church was at the west end of the nuns' church, but at Nunkeeling the nuns' church, forty-six feet long and twenty feet wide:

> *stondith at the nether ende* [ie the west end] *of the parish churche of Nonne-kelynge and the walles and the roofe are alle hole of one story ... and there are ii doorys by the hygh altar for to go and come into the parish churche.*

The steeple at the west end of the nuns' church contained the parish bells. There was a similar arrangement at Marrick Priory. Presumably at Swine and Nun Monkton the nave was used for parochial services. The parish church at Nunkeeling continued in use after the suppression. It was rebuilt about 1810, but is now a ruin.

The remains of the nunnery at Swine in 1784. (Poulson, *Holderness*)

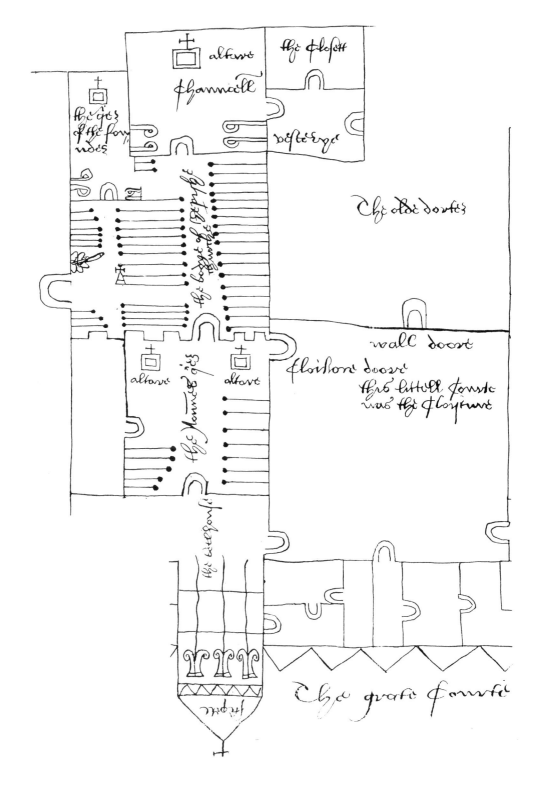

A plan of Marrick Priory made after the conversion of the residential buildings into a house. The labels in the church (abbreviations extended) read: the choir of the founder (the Aske family chapel); chancel; the body of the parish church; the nuns' choir; the bellhouse; steeple. To the right of the church are: closet; vestry; the old dorter; wall door; cloister door; this little court was the cloister; the great court.

Nunkeeling Priory church from the north-east in 1784. (Poulson, *Holderness*)

In the most common arrangement, the main domestic buildings were grouped around a cloister on the south side of the church, a layout found in most houses of monks and canons. The dormitory was over the chapter house in the eastern range, with the refectory on the south side of the cloister. A mirror image of this plan was found at Arthington, Thicket and Wilberfoss, where the cloister was on the north side of the church.

Seven of the churches surveyed were roofed with lead, the other four with slate-stone, thin sandstone slabs. The latter was commonly used for domestic and farm buildings where it was available locally, as at Arthington, Esholt and Kirklees. In other parts of the county we find a mixture of lead and thatch. Nearly all of the buildings of Basedale Priory, apart from the church, were thatched.

Accommodation for chaplains was described at seven of the eleven nunneries, usually as 'the priest's chamber'. Swine had a 'vicar's mansion' under the same roof as four priest's chambers. At the other four priories, there were unlabelled houses or rooms which could have accommodated chaplains. Kirklees and Nunkeeling had almshouses.

The domestic buildings which could not be fitted into the cloister area, including guest houses, were grouped around the 'inner court', the location of which, in relation to the cloister, was not uniform. In the outer yards were the farm buildings: animal houses; corn and hay barns; cart houses. About half of the nunneries had dovecotes. Basedale and Handale had water corn-mills, both described as 'overshot', ie the water ran over the top of the wheel to turn it in the

The interior of Nun Monkton Priory church, looking east.

direction of the flow. The mill house at Basedale was, however, in decay 'so that the seid mylne goith not'. Swine Priory ground its corn by using a horse mill.

The Yorkshire nunneries were, on the whole, poorly endowed. In the *Valor Ecclesiasticus* of 1535, only five nunneries had a higher net annual value than the four poorest houses of monks and canons. The latter were, with values to the nearest pound:

North Ferriby £60; St Andrew's, York, £48; Egglestone £36; and Grosmont £12. The five wealthiest nunneries were: Swine £83; Nun Monkton £76; Nun Appleton £73; Hampole £63; and Sinningthwaite £60. Marrick was valued at £49 and Wilberfoss £22. Nunburnholme was the poorest nunnery, with a net value of just over £8.[2]

The endowment of a nunnery normally consisted of lands for farming; rents and

Nun Monkton Priory from the south-west.

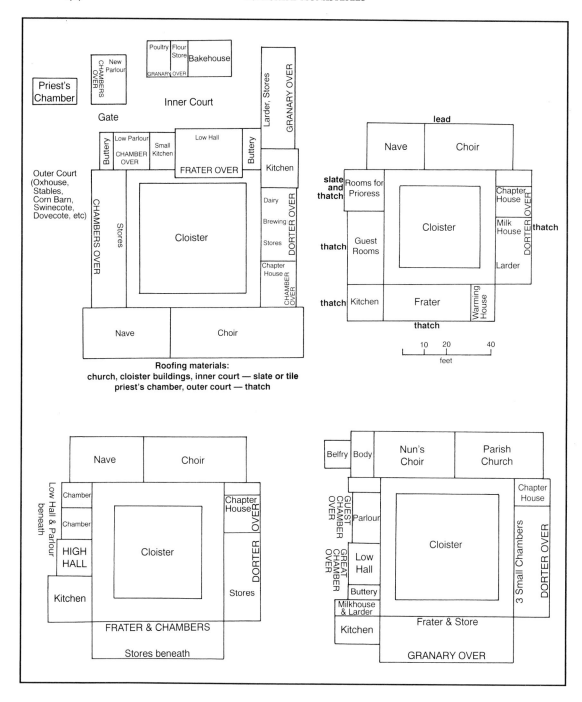

Plans of four priories, all to the same scale and all aligned north. Roofing materials are shown in bold type.
Clockwise from top left: Wilberfoss, Basedale, Nunkeeling and Yedingham.

other sources of money income, eg corn mills; and one or more churches. The most valuable possession of Swine Priory was the initial grant by the Verli family of the church of St Mary, Swine, with the tithes, offerings and other income derived from the extensive parish of Swine. There were larger parishes in the sparsely-populated upland areas of Yorkshire, but Swine parish contained twelve townships which in 1066 had between them fifty ploughlands, and therefore upwards of 6,000 acres of arable land. The priory acquired a second church at Holme on the Wolds.[3]

Some of the land given to the priory was in the parish of Swine. A grange was established, for example, at Fairholme in Benningholme. Across the River Hull the nunnery had a grange at Belaga (Bealey), with a vaccary (cattle station) at Akenberg ('the hill by Aike', now Barf Hill), both of which had apparently belonged at one time to Meaux Abbey. From successive generations of the lords of Sutton, the priory received substantial grants of arable and meadow land within Sutton, together with a sheepfold and common pasture in the marshes along the River Hull.[4]

Further afield, the priory was given upwards of 100 acres of arable land and extensive woodlands in Spaldington, north of Howden, on which to develop one or more granges. The associated pasture rights were for twenty mares with their foals, four hundred sheep, a hundred cows and a hundred pigs. These were probably 'long hundreds' of six score, which would make the actual figures 480, 120 and 120 respectively. A carucate of land in Long Preston, eighty miles away, was too far for convenience, and was exchanged with the donor for the corn mill of Thorpe le Street, near Market Weighton. Swine did not normally have to pay for its acquisitions, but Walter le Nair received £3 6s 8d towards his expenses on the Crusades when he handed over a toft (the plot on which a farmhouse stood) and two bovates in Skirlington, between Atwick and Skipsea. The above transactions took place about 1190.[5]

Between 1155 and 1170 the priory was given a carucate of land in Fraisthorpe, south of Bridlington. Through further gifts the property had grown to ten bovates and eight tofts by about 1240, when it was exchanged with Bridlington Priory for land in Holme on the Wolds, where Swine already held a carucate of land in addition to the church. The policy of the priory was to concentrate its major holdings within a convenient radius for direct working by its lay brothers. In this respect it may have been consciously following the practice of the male Cistercian houses. However, the Cistercian nunnery of Swine differed from Cistercian abbeys in one important respect — its dependence upon tithes. In the 1291 valuation for ecclesiastical taxation, the income from lands, rents and mills was assessed at £48, the profits from the parish of Swine at over £53.[6]

The yield from tithes would have been even greater but for the occupation of some land within the parish of Swine by Meaux Abbey, which, like Swine Priory, enjoyed exemption from tithe on land directly farmed. The two religious houses were just over three miles apart, and proximity did not lend enchantment. The Meaux chronicle records a series of disputes in the early thirteenth century, including conflict about the digging of peat in the marsh between Wawne (belonging to Meaux) and Swine, and an allegation of body-snatching by the nuns when the two houses were arguing about the burial of a benefactor, Amand the Butler.[7]

A friend of Swine Priory at this period, and also on bad terms with Meaux, was Saer of Sutton. In 1226 he gave to Helewise, prioress of Swine, and her successors the advowson of Drypool Church, in return for the provision by the priory, at its own cost, of a chaplain to celebrate divine service, in perpetuity, for Saer and his family in the chapel of St George at Ganstead. It was clearly the intention that the priory would receive the tithes of Drypool, less the costs of employing chaplains there. In 1236 the arrangement was confirmed by Saer and Prioress Sybil, with the additional provision that Saer could maintain a chapel and

chantry in his manor of Southcoates within the parish of Drypool. In return he gave to Swine eighty acres of Bransholme Marsh, on the south side of a thirty-acre plot previously given. The eighty acres were to be measured by the perch of twenty feet, and therefore equalled 118 statute acres. The priory was allowed to enclose and drain both plots of marsh. At the same time Saer confirmed to the priory exclusive rights in the watercourse which stretched from the grange of Fairholme to the moor of Swine, together with the fisheries within it. There was plenty of work for the lay brothers of Swine.[8]

Soon after this agreement was made, Swine demanded the payment by Meaux of tithes on animals pastured in Southcoates

The Norman west door of Nun Monkton Priory.

and Drypool. The monks produced their papal exemption, but Swine pressed on, and the result was a long and expensive lawsuit won by Meaux. According to the chronicle of the abbey — not, of course, an unbiased source — the total bill for costs and damages incurred by Swine was 700 marks (£467). The chronicle claimed that Swine was forced to hand over the advowson of Drypool Church to Meaux, but the nunnery still had an interest in the parish in 1535.[9]

Nun Monkton was another nunnery which drew the greater part of its income from the profits of churches. It was endowed initially with four: Thorp Arch, Kirk Hammerton, Askham Richard and Kirkby Wharfe. The church of Nun Monkton was shared with the parish, but whether the nuns enjoyed the tithe income is not certain. They had, however, about three-quarters of the land of the village, as well as estates in Askham Richard, Kirk Hammerton and Appletreewick. About 1235, after a dispute, the nunnery agreed to surrender its right to the church of Thorp Arch in return for the advowson and tithes of the chapel which served the township of Walton, in the parish of Thorp Arch, and some land and tithes in Thorp.[10]

The economy of Marrick Priory was quite different in structure. The initial grant (1154-58) by Roger de Aske included the church of Marrick, and the priory later acquired the tithes of Kirkandrews near Carlisle. The profits of these churches made up only a small part of the income of the house. In 1456 the tithes of Kirkandrews were replaced by a pension of 40s a year.[11]

In Marrick itself the priory received about a third of the township from Roger de Aske, whose daughters (number unspecified) were becoming nuns there. About 1200

Conan de Aske gave the vaccary of Owlands on Marrick Moor, where the nuns were allowed to have five hundred ewes with their lambs, eighty cows with their young to the age of three years, and horses and pigs without limit. Two meadows were included in the grant. Another grant made soon after the foundation came from Hervey son of Acaris, whose wife and daughter became nuns. He gave sixty acres of land in Kirkby Ravensworth, together with common pasture on the moor there.[12]

In the 1160s Alan de Lyng gave about 100 acres of land in Melsonby, together with pasture for a plough team of oxen (usually eight), four cows and a hundred sheep. At about the end of the century, five grants in Downholme, totalling nearly 100 acres, were made, two of them earmarked for 'charity at the nuns' gate and the weak and sick in the infirmary', and one for the maintenance of a light before the altar in Marrick Church. In the process, the sister of one of the grantors became a nun. Within its first fifty years the nunnery received a large number of grants of land and pasture rights, nearly all within a radius of fifteen miles from Marrick. Most were too small or scattered for direct exploitation, and were let off for money rents. Some were consolidated into units large enough to be worth working by the lay brothers. For example, in Harmby, near Leyburn, eight grants were made, ranging from half a carucate given for charity at the gate and for the infirmary, to half an acre.[13]

The modest possessions of Wilberfoss Priory are not well documented. The early grants included the local parish church and the chapel of Newton-on-Derwent, together with land in Wilberfoss and Catton. In the 1170s Ralph de Meltonby gave half a

carucate of land in Meltonby near Pocklington (about four miles from Wilberfoss)
when his daughter became a nun. At about
the end of the century the nunnery received
two grants of land in Youlthorpe, each of
two bovates, one of them made in connection with the burial of a local man in the
parish church. Otherwise the largest holding
consisted of four bovates in Yapham.[14]

If the Italian merchant's list of wool production at the beginning of the fourteenth
century is reliable (its use and limitations
have been discussed on pages 99-100 and
153), sheep farming was just as important to
some of the nunneries, in proportion to the
modest scale of their economies, as it was
to Cistercian abbeys such as Fountains and
Rievaulx. Swine and Marrick are each put
down for eight sacks, equivalent to about
2,000 fleeces. The Swine figure could include a considerable quantity of tithe wool.
At the top of the list is Keldholme with
twelve sacks, followed by Arden, Rosedale
and Ellerton-in-Swaledale, with ten each.
Nun Monkton is named, without any figure,
and Wilberfoss does not appear in the list.
Most of the nunnery sheep were pastured
on the North York Moors or the Pennines,
but the main grazing for Swine was on the
marshes of south Holderness.[15]

The nunneries needed men for two
functions, to act as chaplains, and to do the
heavy work around the priory and on the
land. For the latter purpose *conversi*, lay
brothers, were recruited. There is definite
evidence of their use at ten nunneries, and
indications of their presence at seven more.
For example, 'Brother William, *conversus* of
Marrick', witnessed a transaction in the
years 1197-1208. Some of the archbishops of
York were strongly of the opinion that nuns
needed men to manage their business

affairs. Four patterns emerged: the employ-
ment of chaplains; the appointment, on a
long-term or short-term basis, of a priest as
'master', in overall charge; a similar appointment for business matters only; and in two
cases the formation of a double house of
nuns and canons.[16]

The double house at Marton, established
about 1150, did not last long. By 1167 the nuns
had moved to a separate convent at nearby
Moxby. The foundation charters of Swine
Priory, c1150, were issued in favour of nuns,
and a confirmation charter of Henry II,
dated between 1163 and 1172, also mentions
nuns only. However, another grant dated
between 1155 and 1170, which could be later
than the royal confirmation, was made to
'the brothers and sisters' of Swine. In 1181
Henry II declared that he had taken into his
protection, and conferred a range of privileges on, 'the house of Swine and the master
... and canons and brothers and nuns serving
God there ...'[17]

The community of Swine was made up
of four elements: nuns, lay sisters, canons
and lay brothers. The male and female areas
of the priory were separated, on the same
lines as at Watton. Communication took
place through two windows, which were
supposed to be under strict regulation. The
meals for all four groups were prepared in
the women's section, and the canons and
conversi received their food and drink
through the windows.

The arrangements for the overall management are uncertain. The 1226 agreement
with Saer of Sutton was negotiated on
behalf of Prioress Helewise by 'Brother
Robert Malger, her attorney', who could
have been either a canon or a lay brother.
Prioress Sybil was the only representative
mentioned in the transaction with Saer in

Swine Priory: the church from the south-east.

1236, and she also conducted a lawsuit about Owsthorpe corn mill in 1251. However, in the tithe dispute with Meaux Abbey, at some time in the period 1236-49, the senior priory figure was Canon Hamo, 'master of the ... nuns of Swine'. He was described as an Augustinian canon from Healaugh Park Priory.[18]

It is clear that Swine did not have a permanent office of master, and that normally the prioress was in overall charge. Whereas

formidable Anglo-Saxon ladies of high rank, such as St Hilda, had no difficulty in ruling a double house of monks and nuns, in the culture of the thirteenth century it would have been difficult for a prioress to exercise unquestioned authority over a group of canons, as distinct from a chaplain or two whom she could hire and fire at will. At the only other double house operating in Yorkshire in the thirteenth century, Watton

Priory, the canons and lay brothers were ultimately answerable to the prior.

This management problem may have been a cause of the sorry state of affairs found by Archbishop Giffard when he visited Swine in 1268. The communicating windows, which should have been carefully guarded by two nuns appointed as 'janatrices', were used for frequent conversations of a suspect nature between canons and lay brothers on one side, and nuns and lay sisters on the other. More seriously, the door leading into the church, which should have been the responsibility of a trustworthy lay brother, was kept by a careless secular boy, who allowed the canons and *conversi* to slip into the church at dusk to chat with the nuns and lay sisters. The household of Sir Robert de Hilton (lord of the manor of Swine and successor in title to the original founder) wandered dissolutely through the cloister and parlour, holding suspect conversations with the nuns and sisters. Robert himself was troublesome and threatening, and out of fear of his oppression, the canons, with-

The Hilton family monuments in the north chapel of Swine Church.

out the consent of the community, had given him a barn full of corn, which ought to have supplied the priory.

That was not the only crime of the canons. They and the *conversi* were supposed to take good care of the material resources of the priory, which were sufficient to maintain everyone, but instead had used them wastefully. The diet of the nuns was reduced to bread, cheese and ale — on two days a week, water instead of ale. Meanwhile the canons 'and their accomplices' enjoyed the best of everything. The nuns were given only one pair of shoes a year, and their tunics had to last for three years, unless parents or friends came to their aid. The sick nuns in the infirmary were neglected, and had little more to eat than the fit nuns in the refectory, even though Saer of Sutton had given land specifically to support the infirmary. The sin of simony had been committed, by accepting money from women who wanted to take the veil.

The prioress was weak and vindictive, and had lost control of her community. The nuns, some of whom were named as malicious or troublemakers, had formed factions. There were bad relations between the nuns and lay sisters, the latter claiming equality of status and demanding the right to wear the black veil, the distinguishing mark of the professed nun, instead of the regulation white veil.

Archbishop Giffard forbade the admission of any more nuns or lay sisters without his permission, because the priory was nearly £100 in debt. He warned that, if the failings of both canons and nuns were not quickly corrected, he would take action himself. Two months later he issued instructions for the proper conduct of affairs. The nuns were to obey the prioress, who was to treat them all fairly. Silence was to be kept according to the rule. For the proper management of provisions, forty marks were to be entrusted to a reliable lay brother. Although the archbishop's letter was addressed 'to the prioress and canons of Swine', nothing in it was said about the future behaviour of the canons. It may have been Giffard's intention to phase them out, and replace them with chaplains.[19]

In 1287 Archbishop John le Romeyn visited Swine, and found the community in difficulties through poverty. He arranged with the abbot of the Premonstratensian house at Croxton, Leicestershire, for one of his canons, Robert of Spalding, to be appointed 'master of the monastery of the nuns of Swine'. He ordered the prioress, nuns, canons and lay brothers to obey Robert, who continued in office until 1290. This is the last reference to canons at Swine.[20]

Prioress Gundreda, who had not been in office in 1268, resigned in November 1288 and one of the nuns, Cecily of Walkingham, was elected in her place. She did not last long, resigning in 1290 to be replaced by Josiana of Anlaby. Meanwhile the archbishop had borrowed John Bustard from St Robert's Friary, Knaresborough, to act as master. John and Josiana had to deal with rebellious nuns, and the archbishop intervened to transfer some of them to Rosedale and Nunburnholme. Bustard's performance was deemed unsatisfactory, and St Robert's was asked to recall him. Robert of Spalding returned for another spell, after which William Darains, a secular priest who was rector of Londesborough, was appointed master. The archbishop arranged for the transfer of a nun called Helewise Darains to Wykeham Priory, to be exchanged for a virtuous nun of that house. Helewise must

have been a relative of the new master, who was being moved out of prudence to avoid accusations of favouritism.[21]

Archbishop le Romeyn appointed Robert, rector of Sutton-on-Derwent, as *custos* (guardian or warden) of Wilberfoss Priory. His predecessor Archbishop Wickwane (1279-85) had forbidden the prioress to admit any more nuns or lay sisters without his permission. He had been informed that the priory had become overstrained economically by accepting nuns at the behest of powerful people, and under the same pressure had taken secular women and girls as boarders.[22]

Archbishop Greenfield sent commissioners to inspect Wilberfoss in 1308. They did not find any major faults, but the archbishop ordered the nuns to stop gathering in the guest house after compline to chat with visitors. They were also forbidden to wear unauthorised clothes, including red garments and 'supertunics too long', following current female fashions. There were twenty nuns in 1310, including eight office-holders: prioress, sub-prioress, two cellarers, two sacrists, cantrix and guest mistress, together with one 'senior nun'. No infirmarian was listed.[23]

Nun Monkton and Marrick were, together with Ellerton-in-Swaledale, within the archdeaconry of Richmond, which had a high degree of independence of the archbishops. The visitation of monasteries was normally left to the archdeacon. As the records of the latter are fragmentary compared to the registers of the archbishops, there are fewer glimpses of life in these two nunneries. Marrick was visited in 1252. The priory's lay brothers were responsible to a *custos*, called alternatively the 'master', who dealt with the granges and external business.

In addition to nuns and lay sisters, the priory had women servants, whom it was allowed to employ 'for such work as it was not decorous for the nuns or sisters to do'. 'Sisters' in this context always means lay sisters, and those at Marrick were comforted by the presence of women of an even lower status.

In the same report the prioress was forbidden to sell wool or livestock without the consent of the master, a wording which suggests that the latter was not permanently in residence. The master or *custos* at some nunneries functioned like an auditor who made periodic visits. As the resources of the nunnery were limited, guests were to stay for no more than one night. No nuns, sisters or lay brothers were to be recruited without the permission of the archbishop; and no girls or women were to be taken in as pupils or boarders without similar authority. Restrictions were placed on the sale of corrodies.[24]

There was no indication of any grave lapses at Marrick, but Archdeacon Dalby found a very different situation on his visit to Nun Monkton in 1397. The prioress was Margaret Fairfax, the sister of John Fairfax, rector of Prescot in Lancashire, who had died in 1393. He was a wealthy man, and used some of his money to secure masses, eg from the four orders of friars in York. He left to Nun Monkton Priory an embroidered vestment, a silver-gilt chalice and 13s 4d in money, together with 6s 8d for each nun and 3s 4d for each sister. Three nuns, Elizabeth Fairfax, Margaret of Pickering and Margaret of Cottam (later the prioress), received respectively 26s 8d; 20s plus a piece of silver; and 13s 4d. He also left money to Sinningthwaite Priory and its nuns and sisters; a cow each to two nuns at Marrick and Nun Appleton; and £5 between two of his own sisters who were Gilbertine nuns at Sempringham.

The prohibition of private property, although routinely re-asserted, had become a dead letter.[25]

To his sister Margaret, the prioress, John Fairfax left ten marks, three silver or silver-gilt bowls or cups, a silver basin, a silver box for 'spice' (sweetmeats), six silver spoons, and one cloak trimmed with grey fur. It is not surprising to find in the archdeacon's report that she wore silk veils, several different kinds of fur, and other unapproved outfits. Her faults, however, went beyond vanity and luxury. She had abused her authority by holding the post of bursar as well as prioress, and had sold timber to the value of 100 marks. She was on familiar terms with John Monkton, invited him to parties (*convivia*) in her chamber, plied him with drink and played at 'tabulas', a kind of backgammon. A chaplain and two laymen had caused scandal by their relationship with the nuns, and nuns guilty of fornication had been treated too leniently.

Strict orders were issued, forbidding the four men to speak to a nun except in the presence of two senior and honest nuns. Priests were not to frequent the priory without good cause. A list of banned clothing and ornaments was drawn up, including silks, firs, rings, broaches and gowns fashionable with secular ladies.[26]

No comparable scandals were recorded at Wilberfoss Priory at this period, but it was chronically short of money. In 1389 the pope granted indulgences to those who visited the priory on certain days and gave alms for the upkeep of the church and buildings. Another appeal was made eight years later.[27]

Not all *convivia* at nunneries were surreptitious affairs. In 1268 Ellen, prioress of Ellerton, sued the principal freeholder in her local manor, Adam of Ellerton, claiming that, in return for the land which he held, he had to attend her manor court every three weeks, make certain annual payments including 4d for castle-guard at Richmond Castle, ride with her as steward or provide her with a horse whenever she journeyed, and 'make for the said Prioress and Convent and her household one *convivium* yearly for one day'. Adam agreed that he should attend the court and make the payments, but denied the other obligations. He offered the annual provision of three pounds of wax as an extra, and his terms were accepted.[28]

Swine Priory had its share of troubles in the early fourteenth century. After a visitation, the record of which has not survived, Archbishop Corbridge appointed one of the senior canons of York Minster to investigate further, and if necessary arrange for the election of a new prioress. This was apparently the occasion on which Josiana of Anlaby was replaced by Joan Mowbray. A few years later, one of the nuns was accused of fornication with a local blacksmith, and there was some criticism of the management of the estates. In 1309 Joan Mowbray resigned and Josiana resumed office, remaining until she retired on account of old age in 1320. During her second term a nun became sexually involved with two monks of Meaux Abbey, and the instructions issued after a visitation imply that some of the nuns neglected their duties in church, wore forbidden garments and were too casual about their contacts with lay brothers and other men.[29]

One familiar theme in the reports of the archbishop's visitations was the poverty of many of the nunneries. Sometimes there were specific causes, eg the weather, the animal diseases and the Scots in the early fourteenth century. In 1318 Marrick was excused the payment of £83 in arrears of taxes because of poverty. The Scottish raids of 1314-18 must have been a major factor. Archbishop Melton found in 1319 that the nuns of Sinningthwaite who had no help from their family or friends did not have enough clothing to keep out the cold. The nuns of Rosedale and Moxby had to be dispersed after the Scottish attack in 1322. When Arden Priory was assessed for taxation in 1331, it was reported that the total income from its property exceeded the barest subsistence level for the community by only 20s a year.[30]

Because of the limitation of resources, most nunneries were forbidden to recruit nuns, sisters or lay brothers without the licence of the archbishop. Aspirants had to wait for a vacancy. The numbers in all but a few relatively prosperous houses, such as Swine, reflect not the popularity of the vocation but the economic situation of the nunnery. Permission was also required to take women, or girls over the age of twelve, as boarders, a wording which suggests that the nunneries provided care, and some kind of education, for younger girls.[31]

Financial constraints tempted the nunneries to commit the sin of simony, ie admission to a religious office in return for a payment. Voluntary offerings were acceptable. Robert de Playce, rector of Brompton-by-Sawdon, left £5 in 1345 to cover the costs of making his niece a nun. In 1430 Richard Fairfax provided nineteen marks for the expenses of making his daughter a nun at Nun Monkton, and endowed the priory with an annual income of £2 for the term of her life as a nun. Elizabeth Sewerby spent lavishly on making her niece a nun in the same convent in 1470, providing a new habit, other clothing, an 'adequate bed', and £3 as 'a certain fee which the said prioress and convent claimed to have by custom'.[32]

The largest recorded bequest to any Yorkshire nunnery was made by Walter Skirlaw, bishop of Durham, in 1403-4. He was born, in modest circumstances, in the village of Skirlaugh (to use the modern spelling) in the parish of Swine. To Swine Priory he left £100 to create a perpetual obit, ie a memorial service on the anniversary of his death. Each nun and sister attending his funeral was to receive 4d, and the prioress, chaplains and parish priests 6s 8d (apparently between them) for the same service. The prioress was his sister Joan, who was given a silver-gilt cup with a lid and £40 in money.[33]

That the bishop's legacy was exceptional is shown by a survey of Yorkshire wills for the period 1322-1429, taken from three volumes of the Surtees Society. The record is incomplete, because Yorkshire had several independent probate jurisdictions, including the archdeaconry of Richmond, the Honour of Knaresborough and the Peculiar of Masham, for which few, or no, medieval wills have survived. It will still suffice, however, for a broad-brush treatment. Fourteen of the twenty-three nunneries received no more than £5 during this period, seven of them being given only £2 each. The smallest gain for a friary during the same years was £14. The nuns could pray, but not say mass, which was a limitation in the competition for legacies. Swine came top of the list with £11 6s 8d, and an unspecified sum for repairs, in addition to the bishop's £100. Marrick, thanks mainly to the Scrope family, received nearly £20, and two other houses between £15 and £18. Bequests to Nun Monkton totalled £9 13s 4d plus £2 a year for the life of Ellen Fairfax, and Wilberfoss received nearly £9.[34]

At thirteen of the priories, bequests were made to individual nuns, ranging from 1s each at three houses to the £40 received by Prioress Joan Skirlaw. Gifts in kind included robes, beds and bedding, the two cows already mentioned, and a fat pig. Roger Morton, a York merchant, in 1390 left 20s to Clementhorpe Priory, 13s 4d to his sister Ellen who was a nun there, and to his daughter Isabel, a nun in the same house, £2 13s 4d 'to mend her black flannel'. Some at least of the personal legacies supplied deficiencies in the household economies of the nunneries.[35]

A place in a nunnery offered a convenient solution to the problem of an illegitimate girl born to a gentry family, for whom a suitable marriage would be difficult to arrange. A dispensation was required for a man or woman born out of wedlock to become a priest or a nun. John Tillotson has pointed out that of fourteen Yorkshire nuns given such a dispensation in the fifteenth century, nine reached the rank of prioress. Although a few dispensations were granted to young nuns, it seems that convents often did not bother about the issue until the nun concerned was a candidate for some office. Alice Ravensworth, who was prioress of Marrick in the 1430s and 1440s, received a dispensation in 1419, but Margaret Easingwold was given hers on the eve of becoming prioress of Wilberfoss in 1479.[36]

Marrick is one of only two Yorkshire nunneries — the other being Esholt — for which any accounts have survived. The records for 1415-16 show that the economy of the priory was managed by three nuns, Cecily Blakeston the bursar, Agnes Gower the sacrist and Agnes Wensley the granger. There was no male *custos*. The priory was still working its 'home farms' within Marrick township and on Stainmoor. Nearly two-thirds of the grain used was home-grown, with a small surplus of barley and oats for sale. As the climate was much less suited to the growing of wheat, nearly all of the wheat and maslin (a mixture of wheat and rye) consumed in the priory was bought in. The sales of wool were only about one fifth of the level implied by the Italian merchant's table of c1300 mentioned on pages 99-100. Items of expenditure included butter bought for sheep salve and repairs to the wall of the cabbage garden.

Most of the priory's land was let off for money rents. Some land was difficult to let, despite reductions in rent, and many tenants were in arrears. Several ended the year owing more than at the beginning. A rent of 2s a year from two properties in Cumberland had been unpaid for five years. At such a distance it was probably not worth the trouble to try to pursue the defaulters. Total rent receipts for the year, including some back payments, came to nearly £32, with outstanding arrears at the year end of nearly £38. Land values and rents in the Pennine dales were generally depressed at this period. The Black Death of 1349 had been followed by a succession of less calamitous but still serious outbreaks of plague, which had held back the recovery of the population. It was not until about 1480 that there were clear signs of a recovery in the agrarian economy.

The main item in the sacrist's account was £5 6s 8d for one year's stipend to the parish priest. There is a separate reference to the prioress's chaplain. The sacrist also paid 17s for thirty pounds of wax, 5s for tallow and 1s 1d for candlewick, all for making candles. Oil bought for 12s 4d was presumably used for liturgical lamps in the church.

There is no indication in the Marrick accounts of any extravagance or luxurious living. Half of the bursar's income went on food for the house, most of it on cereals. Seventeen beasts were killed for the larder. Only £2 3s 9d was spent on fish, but the priory may have had its own fisheries. The basic element in the diet on most days was bread, supplemented by cheese, eggs and home-grown vegetables. Beer was brewed, but no payments for wine are recorded. There is a striking contrast between this situation and the conspicuous consumption at Selby Abbey in the fifteenth century. Marrick was far from being the poorest nunnery in Yorkshire in the later Middle Ages. The motives for joining such a community can hardly have included a yearning for the fleshpots.[37]

It is clear from a survey of all the Yorkshire nunneries that a great deal depended upon the qualities of the prioress. A good one might have some trouble from spiteful or lax nuns, but could usually cope. Weakness and favouritism undermined discipline and morale. A bad prioress dragged the whole community down. Rapid action by the archbishops could stop the rot, but it is not clear how good their intelligence was. Prioress Isabella Westerdale of Wykeham was deprived of office in 1444 for immorality and sent to Nun Appleton Priory to do penance. Her affairs 'with many men both within and outside the monastery' must have been going on for some time.[38]

There is, of course, the danger of taking the sensational cases out of context. Most Yorkshire nunneries avoided both scandal and gross mismanagement for long periods. Furthermore, examples of both disgraceful behaviour, and lapses which were less serious and more frequent, seem to be spread

Above: a drawing from Whitaker's Richmondshire *of Marrick Church and the ruined east end of the nunnery church, made before the reconstruction of the church around 1811; and (below) the same view today, showing a different east window in the church.*

The ruins of Rosedale Priory. (George Young, *History of Whitby*, 1817)

at random throughout the period from the thirteenth to the sixteenth centuries. The idea that there was a golden age around the year 1200, followed by a decline into moral decay by 1500, can be dismissed.

We may reach a better understanding of community life within the nunneries by looking at the opposite end of the scale of offences from the sinful prioress. In the early fourteenth century Archbishop Greenfield told the nuns of Keldholme and Rosedale to stop taking their puppies into church. His injunctions to three Yorkshire nunneries in 1314 included the requirement that no nun should miss any of the divine offices 'on account of occupation with silk work', ie embroidery. There is no evidence of any serious academic study, in theology or other fields, in the nunneries. Books bequeathed to nuns by relatives or friends were usually psalters. From 1489 the archbishops issued injunctions intended to be

read out in nunneries in English. They continued to address houses of men, and write personally to prioresses, in Latin. The implication is that at least some of the nuns had an inadequate grasp of Latin.[39]

If the Latin of the church services was imperfectly understood, if the chants were learned parrot-fashion, much of the meaning would be lost to the participants. There is no way of knowing how many nuns took part without enthusiasm in activities which had become monotonous. Those who fell into this category were in danger of what Eileen Power described as 'the peculiar menace of the cloister', a condition called in Latin *accidia*. The medieval Latin dictionary translates this as 'spiritual sloth', but it is more accurately rendered as a mixture of boredom and melancholy. It is at the very opposite end of the spiritual scale from the blissful contemplation of the Beatific Vision.[40]

THE PREACHING FRIARS

Austins, Carmelites, Dominicans and Franciscans

For a book concerned with 'exploring', with relating the historical record to what can be seen on the ground, the four main orders of friars — Franciscan, Dominican, Carmelite and Austin — present a particular difficulty. Their mission took them to the towns, and therefore after the suppression of the monasteries their buildings lacked the degree of protection which remoteness gave to sites such as Rievaulx or Mount Grace. The friaries were quarried for building stone by local people. Only three of the eighteen Yorkshire houses have any significant remains, the Franciscan church at Richmond, and parts of the domestic buildings of the Beverley Dominicans and the Austins of Tickhill. This chapter concentrates on those three, together with the Carmelite house at York, chosen to represent the white friars.

The house of the Friars Preachers — the Dominicans — of Beverley was founded before 1240 by Master Stephen Goldsmith, a cleric. Building work was still in progress in 1263, when Henry III made a present of fifteen oak trees. The friars enjoyed the support of later monarchs and successive archbishops of York. In 1281-82 Archbishop Wickwane twice made gifts of ten marks (£6 13s 4d). In November 1314, when corn prices were high because of a poor harvest, Archbishop Greenfield gave three quarters

of corn. During three royal visits to the town between 1299 and 1310, the first two Edwards gave sums of money for food for the friars for one to three days. The conventional allowance on these occasions was 4d; on that basis there were about forty friars.[1]

The question may be asked, what did forty Dominican friars do in Beverley, a town which also had about thirty-six Franciscans and a great number of secular clergy, in the Minster and elsewhere? (In 1525-26 there were sixty-six secular priests in Beverley.) The internal life of a friary absorbed some man-hours — the masses and services, much simpler in form than in houses of monks; theological study; the training of novices. There were, however, no estates to manage, and therefore few managerial posts. A friary was not an enclosed, self-contained community concentrating on an inner life of prayer, but a base for operations. The friary's mission was to the community, and its core activity was preaching. This way of life attracted some men who would not have been so readily drawn to a vocation in an enclosed monastery.

Sermons were preached, not only in the friary church, but also in the open air, and on visits to such parish churches as would extend a welcome. When in 1291 Archbishop John le Romeyn organised a preaching programme in support of the Crusades, he asked the Beverley Dominicans to deliver sermons at either Preston or Hedon, Ravenser near Spurn Point, and Wyke, shortly to be renamed Kingston-upon-Hull. The Beverley Franciscans were sent to South Cave, Driffield and Malton, the York Dominicans to Leeds, Otley and Skipton; and other houses of both orders to other specified towns. The Carmelites and Austins were not involved in this campaign. The Franciscans and Dominicans may have had established circuits for their preaching missions.[2]

Itinerant preaching had a dual purpose. Most of the income of the friaries, in money and in kind, came from begging. Some seventy-six friars begging in Beverley would soon have exhausted the charitable possibilities. They therefore had to take to the road, relying upon overnight hospitality and free meals, and also soliciting gifts of money to take back to the friary.

From time to time the archbishops licensed named Dominican friars in Beverley to preach and/or hear confessions. The former function created few problems, as preaching was not the strong point of the parochial clergy. The friars, although much better educated than the majority of secular priests, at least in the early Middle Ages, did not deliver abstruse academic discourses. Their sermons were stimulating and entertaining, spiced with moral tales taken from books of stories compiled for this purpose, or drawn from their own experiences on the road. The joys of salvation and, especially, the horrors of damnation, were painted in bold colours.

The secular clergy were much more concerned about the activities which affected their pastoral and financial relationship with their parishioners, ie hearing confessions, administering the last rites, and burying the dead. In 1269 Archbishop Giffard wrote to the Beverley Dominicans about the licence he had issued to them, and to the Franciscans of the same town, to hear confessions from time to time in their churches. He had been informed that the Dominicans had been freely admitting the parishioners of St Martin and St Mary in Beverley to confession 'and certain other sacraments', with the result that tithes and other income had been diverted from the parishes to the friary. The 'tithes' in this case were the offerings which the faithful were required to give, not produce tithes. The 'other sacraments' would have been Holy Communion, which people were obliged to receive once a year about Easter time, and/or the last rites.[3]

On Easter Sunday 1309 some parishioners of the altar of St Martin in Beverley Minster were given Holy Communion in the Dominican church. This was elevated from a minor grievance into a major one because one of the recipients had previously been excommunicated. Some ecclesiastics handed out excommunications like parking tickets, but it was a serious matter nevertheless. The Dominican responsible, Friar John of Lockington, was ordered by his prior, Walter of Grimsby, to ask for pardon on bended knee from the canons of Beverley Minster. Walter promised that the rules would in future be followed, but to make sure the minster canons resolved to issue an annual warning that the parishioners must attend only at St Martin's altar on Easter Sunday, under pain of excommunication.[4]

St Martin's parish was unusual in that its spiritual centre was one of the eight altars in Beverley Minster, until St Martin's Chapel was built on the outside of the minster near to the south-west tower. The earliest reference to 'St Martin's altar in the chapel ... in the Minster Yard' occurs in the borough minutes for 1425.[5]

Walter of Grimsby's successor as prior, Hugh of Leicester, was deposed in 1314 by the Dominican General Chapter meeting in London. His fault is not recorded. In 1328, Archbishop Melton gave the friars 20s to pray for the new king, Edward III, who was campaigning in Scotland. Edward visited Beverley in the following January, and gave

10s 8d for one day's food, indicating a complement of thirty-two. When the Provincial Chapter met at Beverley in 1342, the king gave £15 to feed the assembled dignitaries for three days. The Dominican friar Roger of Querndon, who had been confessor to Edward III, retired to the Beverley friary in 1352 with a pension of £5 a year.[6]

In 1449 the dormitory and library of the friary were destroyed by fire. Henry VI,

The restored medieval buildings of Beverley Friary, with a modern extension to the left.

describing the house as a royal foundation, no doubt on the basis of the early support given by Henry III, gave ten marks 'for the relief of their great poverty and for the rebuilding of the said house'. The medieval buildings which have survived to the present day are thought to consist mainly of the rebuilt library and dormitory. Together with some post-Reformation additions, they have now been restored and adapted for use as a youth hostel. The railway line from Hull to Beverley runs over the central part of the friary church. Excavations undertaken by Ken MacMahon revealed the foundations of the western end of the church and part of the cloister on the west side of the railway (ie the same side as the surviving buildings). The east end of the church is thought to lie beneath gardens on the other side of the line.[7]

From the early fourteenth century the friary received bequests, some of them substantial, given to secure masses and prayers. Sir William Vavasour left 40s in 1311, and a Beverley tanner gave 12d in 1347 to provide a 'pittance', an extra dish of food, for the friars. In 1351 Sir Henry Percy left 40s each to the Dominican friaries of Scarborough and Beverley. Some bequests were made to secure burial in the friary precinct. John of Hessle was buried in the cloister in 1349, the year of the Black Death. In 1428 Thomas Hilton, a priest, asked to be buried within the south door of the friary church, near the holy water font, and arranged that, on the day of his funeral, clothes should be given to twelve poor men and food to forty. Some testators specified the spiritual service they required. Sir John St Quintin left 20s in 1397 for the friars to say eight trentals (a trental was thirty) of masses for his soul, and another 13s 4d for a pittance. Wealthy men

commonly bequeathed money to a large number of friaries, sometimes to all of the eighteen in Yorkshire.[8]

During the fifteenth century, bequests to individual friars became more frequent, suggesting that they, like the monks and canons at the same period, were allowed to keep small sums of money for personal expenses. For example, Robert Manfield, provost of Beverley Minster, left 1s in 1419 to every friar of the house who was a priest, and could therefore say masses for him. Most legacies still went into the general fund. The gentry and priests made up the majority of testators, but there were some merchants and tradesmen. In 1477 Robert Fisher, a Beverley mercer, left 3s 4d to each of the two friaries in the town, as well as 30s in other religious bequests, mainly to secure masses. He was the father of Cardinal John Fisher, bishop of Rochester, who, with Sir Thomas More, was executed in 1535 for opposition to the policies of Henry VIII.[9]

In an attempt to solve the problem of disputes between friars and parish clergy about burials, Pope Boniface VIII had decreed in 1300 that one quarter of all burial fees and legacies should be given to the parish priest. This provision was revoked in 1474 by Sixtus IV, whose bull gave the friars the right to conduct funerals even without the permission of the parish priest, and to keep all the fees and legacies. He confirmed these privileges five years later, adding indulgences to those who visited friars' churches and gave them alms. Sixtus was a Franciscan, who had been Master General of the order.[10]

A list of burials in the Dominican precincts was drawn up about 1500. It does not include Thomas Hilton, so it presumably does not go back to 1428. Fourteen knights

The remains of Richmond Friary from the south-west, showing the lower part of the fifteenth century tower and the east wall of the south aisle.

A double arch from Tickhill Friary, now inside a private house,

were buried in the church. Lady Helen Wake, daughter and heiress of Lord Wake, was buried in the choir before the high altar. Sixteen other ladies are named, but their resting place is not given. Fifteen males and two females are listed in the third section, headed 'esquires', the next rank down below a knight. They were apparently buried in the cemetery.

At the end of the list the number of friars is given, fourteen. The numbers of the mendicant orders had been in decline for some time. The days of fervour and self-sacrifice were distant memories for all except a reform group within the Franciscans, the Observants, who had no houses in Yorkshire. The alternative concept of an interesting religious career did not fit the friars, still living by begging and without the resources to provide the discreet comforts of the well-endowed houses of monks or canons.

Amongst the distinguished people represented in the list of burials were members of the Darcy family. Thomas Lord Darcy was a generous supporter of the friary in the early sixteenth century. In 1524, in recognition of the 'greate benifices and manifold Almus' (alms) which he had bestowed upon the house, the prior and friars made a solemn covenant in writing that after Lord Darcy and his wife Lady Edith departed 'oute of this miserable Worlde unto the mercy of Godde', they would have the spiritual benefits of the friars. After the death of either of them, the *de profundis* would be recited every Sunday for a year, with a trental of masses annually thereafter. Thomas Lord Darcy departed out of this miserable world on the 20th June 1537, when he was beheaded for his involvement in the Pilgrimage of Grace, a rebellious movement provoked in part by the suppression of the smaller monasteries. The Beverley Dominicans did not have long in which to fulfil the covenant, as their house was suppressed eighteen months later.[11]

In one respect the mendicant friars upheld the values of their pioneers. They acquired very little property. Apart from a few acres in Great Cowden near Hornsea, the Beverley friars owned only their church, buildings, gardens and orchards, totalling four and a half acres.[12]

The Franciscan friary in Richmond was founded in 1258 by Ralph FitzRandal, lord of Middleham. He provided a site just outside the walls of the town, not far from the market place, and probably paid for the erection of the first buildings. When he died in 1270, his heart was buried in the chancel of the friary church, his body in Coverham Abbey. Apart from the founder, the greatest benefactors were the families of Neville (one of whom married the daughter and co-heiress of Ralph FitzRandal) and Scrope. They donated five and a half acres of land adjacent to the friary in the second half of the fourteenth century.

In 1387, during the course of the Scrope-Grosvenor dispute mentioned on page 137 in connection with Easby Abbey, evidence was given of all the places in the friary precinct where the Scrope arms were displayed. This information, supplemented by the results of excavations carried out by Edwin Bush, throws light on the building plan.

The church was at first a simple aisle-less structure 120 feet long and 22 feet wide internally. About fifty years before the Scrope-Grosvenor affair, a south aisle, nearly 18 feet wide internally, was added to the nave. In the Franciscan plan, the friars used the chancel for their own services, and the lay people gathered in the nave to hear sermons.

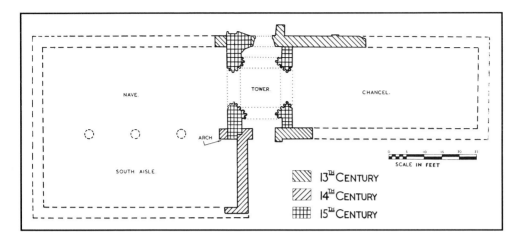

A ground plan of Richmond Friary.

The accommodation for the latter purpose was nearly doubled by the addition of the south aisle. Compared to churches of the older monastic orders and the larger parish churches, a Franciscan church was a very simple building, and its nave could be thought of as a medieval version of an early Methodist chapel.

The domestic buildings were grouped around a cloister on the north side of the church, as the access to the town was on the south side. The rooms mentioned in the Scrope record included a dormitory, refectory, parlour, 'the studies', and 'a certain room where the friars in the said house wash themselves together when they come to the said room tired and weary'. A guest house had been added at about the same time as the south aisle. There were presumably a

Richmond Friary from the south-west showing, to the left of the tower, the east wall of the south aisle, and to the right the north wall of the chancel.
(Whitaker, *Richmondshire*)

chapter house and infirmary, but they are not mentioned in the Scrope document.

According to John Leland, writing around 1540, the friary had the only piped water supply in the town. The room called 'the studies' relates to the work done by the Franciscans and Dominicans in the field of theological education. Nearly every Franciscan friary, and all the Dominican houses, had a lecturer in theology, part of whose time was devoted to providing instruction for the under-educated secular clergy.

In their main role as preachers, the Richmond grey friars took part in Archbishop le Romeyn's campaign in support of the Crusades in 1291. Archbishop Greenfield, in 1315, called on all the friars in Yorkshire, and particularly the Richmond friars and the Dominicans of Yarm, to rouse the people to resist the incursions of the Scots after Bannockburn.[13]

Apart from the produce of their gardens and orchards, the Richmond Franciscans depended on what they begged from the faithful. St Bonaventure, who became Minister General of the order in the year before the foundation of the Richmond house, criticised aggressive begging, arguing that people were as fearful of meeting a friar as a robber, and accused some friars of luxurious living. He did not, however, try to return to the literal observance of the precepts of St Francis, restating them as 'simplicity rather than poverty … austerity rather than asceticism … wisdom rather than humility'. In 1354 the General Chapter of the order allowed friars to accept presents from friends.[14]

Amongst the recorded gifts in kind received by the Richmond brethren were quantities of wheat, including one from Fountains Abbey. The present of a ferocious sow by Ralph Rokeby is commemorated in a comic poem *The Felone Sowe of Rokeby*, dating probably from the fifteenth century:

She was more than other three
The grizzliest beast that ere might be

which, after a violent resistance, was carried off triumphantly to Richmond in:

Two panniers made of a tree.[15]

The Scropes and Nevilles were generous in bequests to the friary, the highest sum being £10 from Richard Lord Scrope in 1402. One of his sons, Sir Stephen, left 6s 8d to each friar of the house attending his funeral. Bequests to individual friars usually treated them all equally, but Dame Jane Strangeways (1500) gave £2 to one friar. She also provided 10s for a trental of masses, and another 10s towards the maintenance of the friary and to say 'Placebo and Dirige and Mass of Requiem for my soul'. *Dirige*, from which the word dirge is derived, and *Placebo* are the opening words of the matins and vespers respectively in the Office of the Dead.

In 1484 Richard III (1483-85), who was familiar with the Richmond area because of his association with Middleham, gave £8 6s 8d to the friary to say a thousand masses for the soul of King Edward IV.

William Burgh, of Brough near Catterick, made an agreement with the friars in 1474 whereby one of them was to celebrate mass each Wednesday and Saturday except in Holy Week, 'in the Chapel of St Anne standing on the bridge at Catterick'. Burgh undertook to provide 'the chalice, missal, vestments and all altar furnishings' and to pay the friary an annual fee of 26s 8d.[16]

Later in the century a dispute, described as 'a greate travers', arose between Abbot William Ellerton of Easby and Friar William Billyngham, warden of the friary, about the goods of Margaret Richmond, an anchoress who had died. Her cell was apparently attached to the chapel of St Edmund on Anchorage Hill in Richmond. The disputants and the officials of the borough of Richmond agreed that the conflict should be settled by the arbitration of two senior officials of the Honour of Richmond and a canon of York Minster — a heavyweight force for so small a matter. The arbitrators decreed, in April 1490, that after Margaret's debts had been paid and her cell repaired (under the supervision of four Richmond priests!), the remaining goods should go to the Franciscans 'for cause that the said Ancores tooke hir habbet of the said Frers'. For a similar reason, the goods of Margaret's successor Alison Comeston were to be at the disposal of Easby Abbey, and so in future according to the 'habbet of religion' of the recluse. The nomination of the anchoress, who received a small endowment for her support as well as occasional legacies, was to remain with the borough of Richmond, as it had 'withouten tyme of mynde'. The abbey, the friary and the borough solemnly attached their seals to the agreement.[17]

This unedifying squabble showed that not even the 'lesser brothers' were immune from the disease of monastic litigation. It could be argued, however, that a more decisive rejection of the ideals of St Francis was signalled by the building of the tall bell-tower in the late fifteenth century. Towers were in fashion, and it is possible that wealthy patrons pressed the amount of money required on the friary. Otherwise the cost must have been met out of the legacies and the income from begging. Tall and graceful, the tower is one of the most cherished features of the Richmond scene. It is one of only three bell-towers to survive out of sixty-one Franciscan friaries in the country.

But it had no function except to house the three bells, which weighed together 2,000 pounds. The contrast with the rest of the church, which was simple and functional, is striking.

It was usual in Franciscan churches to have a passageway between the nave and the chancel, with double doors on either side, which could be closed to make the chancel into a chapel for the friars. The passage allowed access from the cloister to the outside of the church on the opposite side, in the Richmond case from the cloister on the north to the path leading through the town wall, by Friars' Wynd, on the south. The design of the tower preserved this arrangement. It was built over the passageway, within the older walls of the church with buttresses resting on part of the latter. When the other friary buildings were quarried by the townspeople, the tower was saved by its height and the elaborate pattern of battlements and pinnacles on the top. It was worth no-one's while to mount the major operation which would have been required to demolish it safely.[18]

Clarkson in his *History of Richmond* (1821) wrote: 'The present tower ... was erected not long before the Dissolution and is said not to have been finished.' This is untrue. Later writers have distorted Clarkson's statement to mean that the tower was the beginning of a new church which was never finished. That is equally untrue, and quite absurd. No one would demolish an existing church and begin its replacement with a tower. All this confusion has arisen out of the visual contrast between the robust appearance of the tower and the crumbling fragments of the rest of the church.[19]

When the friary was suppressed in January 1539 there were fifteen friars. There is

no earlier record of their numbers. In England as a whole there were about 600 grey
friars at this time, compared with an estimated maximum, about the year 1300, of
1,500.[20]

Yorkshire had three houses of Austin
friars, in order of their foundation, Tickhill,
York and Hull. In the middle of the fourteenth century, Friar John Waldeby gave up
the attempt to compose his tract on the
Creed in the York friary, because the place
was so busy and unsuitable for contemplation. He sought instead the peace of 'our
solitary place, Tickhill', where he wrote the
greater part of his treatise. The friary was
'solitary' not because Tickhill was a place
of no account — it had a castle, which was
the headquarters of a great lordship — but
because the friary was built a few hundred
yards outside the town, in a secluded valley.[21]

The reason for the location of the friary
was its connection with the nearby manor
house of Clarel Hall. It is said to have been
founded by John Clarel, dean of St Paul's,
London. There was no dean of St Paul's of
that name, but in 1256 a John Clarel was a
canon of Southwell Minster and rector of
East Bridgeford, both in Nottinghamshire.
If we can rely upon the tradition that the
York friary, documented from 1272, was
founded from Tickhill, the latter house must
have been in existence in the 1260s. As will
be explained, the date 1263 comes into the
story. The earliest definite reference occurs,
however, in 1274, when four friars were
ordained (three priests, one deacon) in nearby Blyth Church.[22]

In 1276 the friars were granted a licence
to enclose a way outside the town on the
north side of the church, between the friary
and the land of William Clarel, amounting
to a quarter of an acre, provided that an

alternative road of equal dimension was
made out of the adjacent Clarel land. Three
years later Edward I provided 'four oaks fit
for timber' from a woodland in Sherwood
Forest. The friars were planning a further
extension to their property in 1284, when
they applied for a licence to enclose an adjacent piece of waste ground 30 feet wide and
over 200 feet in length. Two local men complained that this would inconvenience them
in taking their beasts to water, and permission was apparently denied.[23]

In November 1274 the king issued an
order to all sheriffs and other officials to
arrest 'all Austin Friars found at large, as the
king understands that some have left their
order in contempt of their profession'. In
the following June he renewed the mandate
for one year, referring to 'vagabond friars
of the order of St Augustine'. Presumably
friars out on legitimate preaching and/or
begging missions would carry credentials
issued by their prior.[24]

Queen Eleanor, wife of Edward I, left 40s
to the friary at her death in 1290. The castle
of Tickhill had been part of the property
assigned to her as dower on the occasion of
her marriage. In 1300 King Edward provided
6s for one day's food, which suggests that
there were eighteen brethren at the time.
The York house had thirty-five friars in 1300.
When a Provincial Chapter was held at Tickhill in 1319, Edward II contributed £10 towards the expenses. Edward III gave 4d a
head for the twenty-four friars at Tickhill in
1335. At about the same time Robert Clarel
gave them two acres of land in Tickhill, and
they paid 6s 8d for a licence to enclose a lane
on the west side of their house.[25]

The Austin friars, although dependent
mainly on alms, had a more relaxed attitude
to property than did the Franciscans or

Dominicans. At the suppression the Tickhill friary owned about sixty acres of land in and around the town, let for nearly £3 a year, and a substantial estate at Newton-on-Derwent, which produced £5 8s a year. The York house had a rental income of £7 10s 8d, most of it from houses in the city. The Hull friars had no property except for the church and conventual buildings.

The commitment to the common life was also weaker. Originally the dormitory of an Austin house was made up of a series of cubicles, each with a clear window in the door. Only the prior and masters of theology had separate rooms. The practice developed during the fifteenth century of allowing friars who could afford it to construct private rooms, within the dormitory or elsewhere in the precinct, in which they could, if they wished, take their meals.[26]

The achievements of a few Tickhill friars are recorded. In the first half of the fourteenth century Robert of Worksop was known for his treatises on theological topics. His namesake in the next generation became a suffragan bishop, latterly in the archdiocese of York. He was buried at Tickhill about 1375. The York friary was a major centre for theological study for the whole English province. A catalogue of its library, made in 1372, lists 656 volumes, containing over 2,100 works of theology, philosophy and science.[27]

In common with other friaries, Tickhill benefited from legacies in return for masses said for the souls of the deceased. They received sums of £1 or £2 from wealthy benefactors who left money to all the Yorkshire friaries, the names including Percy, Neville and Scrope. Other testators made Tickhill their special concern, eg Robert Morton of Bawtry who bequeathed £3 6s 8d in 1396.

The extent of the continued support of the Clarel family is unknown, but Thomas Clarel (1441) and one of his sons, Robert, were buried in the friary.[28]

Sir Richard Fitzwilliam of Aldwark, near Rotherham, married Elizabeth Clarel, the heiress to the family estates. In his will (1479) he asked to be buried in the friary, and left £2 for masses. His son Sir Thomas (1497) requested burial near the tomb of his father. His body was eventually interred in a richly-decorated alabaster tomb, topped by effigies of himself and his wife Lucy Neville. The family had the good sense, at the suppression, to move the tomb into the parish church. The paint has faded away, and the effigies are damaged, but it still stands as a reminder that the plundering of the monasteries destroyed much more than the buildings.[29]

The remains of the Tickhill friary, incorporated with post-suppression work and re-used medieval material in two adjacent houses, are easier to admire than to interpret. The building runs east-west, and was therefore parallel to the vanished friary church. In most orders this range would contain the refectory, but the Austins did not necessarily follow this arrangement. Furthermore the practice of creating private rooms would have involved the internal remodelling of some buildings in the last monastic century. From a study of the site it seems probable that the church lay to the north of the surviving buildings, accessible to the main road leading out of Tickhill towards Maltby. Some large stones found in ground clearance work on the presumed site of the church may have come from the foundations of the west end, and beyond its east end was a cemetery.

The houses contain some thirteenth and fourteenth century features. The most striking detail is the double arch with ornate

The tomb of Sir Thomas Fitzwilliam (died 1497), with effigies of him and his wife Lucy, which was moved at the suppression from Tickhill Friary into the parish church. (Bernard Jennings)

carving, pictured on page 193. Above the capital in the centre of the arch is the figure of an Austin friar, and above that the date '1263'. The style of the arcade, which is not necessarily in its original position, indicates that it dates from the late fifteenth or early sixteenth century. Whoever instructed the carver may have known the date of the foundation from the records of the friary, or may have been relying upon an oral tradition. In either case the date 1263 cannot be far wrong.[30]

There are no physical remains of any of the five Carmelite friaries of Yorkshire, located in Northallerton, Scarborough, York, Hull and Doncaster. A brief account of the York house is given here, to avoid neglecting the white friars altogether. The building of

the second Carmelite church in York, about the year 1300, has been described on page 35. The site, given by William de Vescy, lay between Stonebow Lane and the River Foss. In 1314 Edward II gave the friary some houses and land in Mersk Lane, which bounded the site on the west, and he added other properties during the next two years. The king also allowed the friars to construct a quay, giving them access to the River Foss, and to keep a boat there. In the years 1335-37 the number of friars averaged forty.

The white friars experienced the negative side of their location in York. The city had a surfeit of churches, and it was divided up into a series of small parishes, each jealously guarding its rights. The Carmelite site fell into two parishes: St Saviour's, appropriated to St Mary's Abbey; and Holy Cross, otherwise St Crux, in Fossgate. St Mary's Abbey protested against the building of the friary in Stonebow Lane, and was bought off with a payment of 30s a year as compensation for any loss of income at St Saviour's. In 1320 Archbishop Melton ordered the friars to compensate the rector of St Crux as well. However, the Carmelites provoked the rector by building a chapel near the gateway, on the east side of the friary, which opened into Fossgate. In 1350 they were forced to stop holding services in the chapel, remove an image of the Blessed Virgin there, and refrain from ringing the bell or accepting offerings in the chapel.[31]

The Carmelites were given several more properties in the vicinity of the friary in the period 1331-50. At the end of the century, Henry Lord Percy was instrumental in securing sites at either end of the friary church, which prepared the way for its rebuilding, to which Bishop Walter Skirlaw contributed £40. The Vescy interest had descended to the Percys, who became thereby the 'founders' of the Carmelite houses in York and Doncaster. When Henry Percy, earl of Northumberland, made his will in 1485 he left £20 each to the two friaries, on condition that each said two trentals of masses within a month of his death, and also kept an *obit*, a service of remembrance on the anniversary of his death. The next Percy earl gave £8 for repairs in 1515, and also provided an annuity of 40s for the prior.[32]

The white friars of York had a reputation for learning. Prior John Bate (died 1429) was a noted Greek scholar. Friar Richard Misyn translated into English some of the works of Richard Rolle, a fourteenth century hermit and mystic of Hampole, near Doncaster, who was one of the most widely read authors in medieval England. The friars also engaged in more humdrum activities. The records of monasteries of all kinds are sprinkled with references to lawsuits against defaulting craftsmen. The prior sued a stonemason in 1362 for breaking his contract for work at Tadcaster, and won damages of £2. In 1385 a later prior claimed 20 marks damages from a plasterer for building an oven so badly that it fell apart.[33]

The community numbered thirteen at the suppression in 1538. The church — like the Carmelite church in Northallerton — had a belfry with two bells. The rental income from property in York was £3 19s, with no record of any property in Tadcaster. Doncaster had the highest rental income, nearly £11 a year, part of which came from the Lion Inn in Hallgate.[34]

It is impossible to determine what proportion of the income of the eighteen Yorkshire friaries came from legacies, because in no case have any accounts survived. However, a rough indication of their relative gains from legacies is provided by an analysis of the wills for the period 1322-1429, the use of which is discussed on page 184.

In these years, nine of the friaries, disregarding gifts in kind and bequests to individual friars, had legacies totalling between £14 and £18 6s 8d. Tickhill came in the middle of this list with £16. The Scarborough Dominicans received £17 plus £2 a year, and the Franciscans of the same town £30 3s 4d. The grey friars of Richmond received £30 10s, more than half of it in two bequests from the Scrope family. The Carmelites of Northallerton had the largest sum of all, £122 6s 8d, thanks to two gifts from the Neville family. John Lord Neville provided 100 marks in 1389 for the repair of the friary buildings and for spiritual benefits for his

*Part of the domestic
buildings of
Tickhill Friary.*

family. Ralph Neville, earl of Westmorland, bequeathed £40 in 1425 for the rebuilding of the kitchen and other repairs to the friary buildings.

The four friaries in the city of York were in a different league from the rest of the county, Northallerton excepted. It was by far the largest town in Yorkshire, with a substantial business class, and also contained the town houses of aristocracy and gentry whose principal seats were outside the city. Many wealthy benefactors of the friars were buried in their churches, especially the Dominican and Franciscan. Their receipts to the nearest pound were: Dominicans £83, Franciscans £72, Austins £62, and Carmelites £59 plus the gift of £40 from Bishop Skirlaw, which was to be paid before his death if the rebuilding of the white friars' church had been completed, otherwise as a legacy. If it were possible to calculate the total amounts paid to individual friars, the relative dominance of York would be increased. Walter Skirlaw left £2 to each priest-friar in York to say a trental of masses for him within a year. There were fifty-nine friars, including some novices, in the four York houses at the suppression. There were probably at least seventy priest-friars at the beginning of the fifteenth century. If that figure is accurate, the bishop paid £140 to secure 2,100 masses.[35]

Legacies to friaries to secure masses and prayers remained a common feature of wills until the suppression. Inevitably, given the nature of the evidence, much more is known about the social bond between the friars and the small minority of people who made wills than about their relationship with the rest of the population. The records throw much less light on the mission of the friars to the living poor than on the consolations which they offered to the dying rich.

12

THE LAST DAYS

Charting the history of religious move ments is rather like climbing a York-shire escarpment, as at Sutton Bank or Garr-owby Hill, and then following the gentle dip-slope downwards. A burst of spiritual fervour gives way to a gradual period of adjustment, in which the standards of the pioneers come to be regarded as unattain-able, and indeed as unreasonable. Move-ments since the Reformation have trod a similar path. For example, in his last years John Wesley warned that the success of Methodism carried the seeds of its own spir-itual decay. The moral discipline of Method-ism led to success in business; success brought wealth; and wealth bred pride and complacency.

As it is usual in writing history to begin at the beginning, it is difficult to avoid port-raying the later years of medieval monastic-ism as a period of decline. Certainly some common features — the relaxation of diet-ary rules, the holding of personal property, the lordly lifestyle of the heads of the wealthier houses — would have been roundly condemned by the abbots and priors who had set the standards in the early days of their orders, men such as St Ailred of Rievaulx, Abbot Hugh of Selby and Prior Robert the Scribe of Bridlington. On the other hand the scandals, eg factionalism, the misuse of resources and immorality, seem

to be distributed almost at random through the period from c1200 to the suppression. In terms of these failings, the Yorkshire monasteries, taken as a whole, were in no worse a condition in the early sixteenth century than two or three centuries earlier.

Post-Conquest monasticism in Yorkshire had a long history, from the foundation of Selby Abbey in 1070 to the closure of the religious houses in 1536-40. In fact the date of the suppression of Selby Abbey is nearer in time to the present day than to the year of its opening. During this period, changes in social attitudes and in monastic practices were to some extent interactive. The people of the early sixteenth century saw the mon-asteries as long-established institutions which provided a range of social and spirit-ual services. Hospitality, charity, the care and education of children, the provision of retirement homes through corrodies, and the safe keeping of both money and prop-erty deeds were amongst the social services. The most important spiritual provisions were prayers and masses, especially for the souls of the departed, although the mainten-ance of shrines and relics, as points of con-tact with the saints, was also valued.

If these services were delivered in a con-scientious manner, the lay recipients were content. Although serious moral faults were viewed with disfavour, there is no reason to believe that people were upset by meat-eating in the abbeys and priories, or the payment of money allowances for clothes and personal expenses, or even the spectacle of abbots out hunting. A spirituality which was rather tepid, by comparison with the self-sacrificing fervour of the pioneering years, was the acceptable norm. Similarly, although the educational standards of the beneficed clergy (rectors and vicars) were higher in 1500 than two or three centuries earlier, the people were satisfied if their priests were conscientious sacramental functionaries.

At the centre of the elaborate salvation apparatus of the pre-Reformation Church was the priest saying mass. At the centre of the concerns of the laity was purgatory. Most people, seeing themselves as neither the saints, pure and undefiled, who would go straight to heaven, nor as irretrievably lost souls, expected to find themselves in purgatory. They would enter the afterlife carrying the spiritual debt of non-mortal sins unconfessed and inadequate penance for pardoned faults. These debts were settled in the pains of purgatory. The suffering souls had two consolations, the certainty of an ultimate place in heaven, and the knowledge that masses and prayers were being offered up, to be weighed in the judgment scales against the burden of sin.[1]

To the medieval mind, the hard road to salvation was not travelled alone. The pilgrims on earth helped the souls in purgatory and were in turn succoured by the saints in heaven, not only the canonised saints but all of those enjoying their eternal reward who were commemorated in the feast of All Saints. The pilgrims accumulated spiritual credit by good works, such as helping the poor or repairing religious buildings. The saints known by name were asked for prayers of intercession, and especially for help in the case of illness or other misfortunes. Particular value was placed upon devotions at the shrine of a saint, eg St Hilda at Whitby Abbey or St John of Bridlington in the priory church. Some relics of the saints, held by monasteries or other churches, were regarded as helpful in the relief of particular conditions, eg the large numbers of 'girdles of the Blessed Virgin' for childbirth.

This structure of organisation and belief was attacked at key points by the thinkers of the Protestant Reformation. Salvation was achieved through a personal relationship with Jesus Christ, who was accessible to everyone who studied the gospels. No intermediaries were needed. The cult of saints, shrines and relics was usually superstitious, always useless. The central sacramental role of the priest was downgraded. He no longer changed the bread and wine into the body and blood of Christ in a re-enactment of the sacrifice of Calvary on an altar, but presided at a communion service which was a commemorative meal, on a table. Good works did not earn merit; they were a consequence, an outward sign, of merit. The sacrifice of Christ on the cross was powerful enough to ensure the salvation of all those with sufficient faith and trust. Purgatory did not exist. In the communication system, the picture — frescoes on church walls, pictures in stained glass, images and the moving picture of the rituals — yielded place to the word, made available through the translation of the scriptures into English and the invention of printing.

In theory there was no incompatibility between the beliefs of the reformers and the idea of a life of self-denial, prayer and contemplation, although the 'protestant work

Fountains Abbey from the south. Contrasting symbols are the 300 foot long lay brothers' wing (left foreground), the base for the creation of the economic empire of the abbey; and the grandiose tower built at the end of the north transept by Abbot Huby (1494-1526). (Cambridge University)

ethic' which emerged had no time for such wasteful pursuits, or for the thirty or so holy days in the year which interfered with economic progress. If the sacramental priest was to be replaced by the preaching minister, the friars offered a ready-made model. Some friaries nurtured and spread reform ideas — Martin Luther himself was an Austin friar. Taken as a whole, however, monasticism was so closely integrated with religious beliefs and practices which were anathema to the reformers that the possibility of an accommodation was very slight.

Rev Marmaduke Prickett, writing his history of the priory church of Bridlington in 1831, attributed the suppression of the monasteries in part to the eyes of the people being opened 'to the absurdity of the miracles pretended to be performed by the monks, the inefficacy of masses for the souls of the dead, and of adoring saints and relics'. In fact the monasteries were struck down before the 'new learning' had become either government policy — Henry VIII persecuted Lutherans and other protestants — or widely accepted by the common people. In the early sixteenth century Yorkshire had some Lollards, whose beliefs were rooted in the ideas of John Wycliffe (c1328-84), and newer reform ideas were being disseminated by professional or trade contacts with London or the continent. For example, in the mid-1530s Robert Plompton, of Plompton Hall near Knaresborough, who was studying law in London, sent to his mother 'a godly New Testament', presumably Tyndale's translation which, to quote Bishop Moorman, included 'glosses and notes of a strongly protestant flavour'. Robert declared that 'the gospell of Christe was never so truly preached as it is nowe ... God will give ... knowledg of the Scriptures as soon to a

shepperd as to a priest, yf he ask knowledg of God faithfully'.[2]

It was, however, to be some years before the wording of the will of Edward Hoppay, a yeoman from the Halifax area (1548), became common form:

> ... I comitt me unto God and to his mercy, trustyng undoubtedly that by ... the merites of Jesus Christe I ... shall have remission of my synnes ... theire is but one ... mediator betwixt God and man, whiche is Jesus Christe.

In the 1530s the preamble used by Sir William Bulmer of Wilton in Cleveland (1531) was still normal:

> I gyve and bequeith my soull unto Almyghty God, and to His blissid Moder our Lady Sanct Marie, and to all the celestiall compeny of hevyn ...

Sir William left money to several friaries, 2s to each monk at Mount Grace, and £10 to Guisborough Priory plus 6s 8d to the prior and 2s to each canon. He made provision for the hire of a priest for seven years, at seven marks a year, to sing masses for his soul, those of his family, and 'all Christen saullis'. He also arranged for the continuation of a payment of £4 a year to Easby Abbey to secure masses in Easby parish church for the Aske family, to whom Sir William was related. This annual sum was funded for seventeen years. The wills of this period give no indication of any shift in religious sentiment. The friars were the main beneficiaries, but quite large sums were left to favourite abbeys or priories. Requests for burial in monastic churches were still quite common.[3]

In 1534-5 Edward Lee, archbishop of York, visited personally, or through his officials, at least eight religious houses in Yorkshire, including five nunneries. Lee had supported

Henry VIII in his divorce of Catherine of Aragon and his marriage to Anne Boleyn, and had accepted the Act of Supremacy of 1534, which declared that the king was 'the only Supreme Head in earth of the Church of England'. Opposition to these provisions was treason, and Bishop John Fisher and Sir Thomas More paid for it with their lives. Lee encouraged the reading of the Bible in English, and urged his clergy to pay more attention to preaching, but he was generally conservative in matters of doctrine.

Lee's visitations revealed that at neither Healaugh Park nor Warter was the Augustinian Rule properly observed. The canons at Warter were ordered to sleep in the dormitory and eat together. They were not to wear gold or silver ornaments. No women were to be received at Healaugh Park by the prior or a canon unless two other canons were present. The infirmary at this priory was in a ruinous condition. There were irregularities of dress, too, at St Mary's Abbey, a bad example being set by the abbot with his velvet garments and gilt spurs. The archbishop ordered that no wine was to be sold within the precincts. The most serious charge against the abbot was suspect conversations with a married woman.

A nun of Esholt who had borne a child was to be imprisoned, and given strict penances and beatings for up to two years. The prioress was told not to allow an alehouse within the precincts. The prioress of Nun Appleton was ordered to give her nuns the same quality of bread and ale as she enjoyed, provide them with enough spoons, and employ a laundress to wash their clothes. The nuns at Sinningthwaite seem to have been inadequately fed.

The Esholt nun apart, the visitations revealed more slackness than scandal. The archbishop dealt by correspondence with one case which indicated two organisational weaknesses of the monastic system, the inadequate testing of vocations, and the virtual impossibility of a dignified withdrawal for someone found to be unsuited to the religious life. A long and strict novitiate would have filtered out many of the people whose inability to accept cheerfully the disciplines of the religious life made them a nuisance to their more dedicated fellows. Once professed, a man or woman who left the monastery was labelled an apostate and a lost soul. For this reason every effort was made to keep backsliders within the system in the hope of reform.

Such a delinquent was Joan Fletcher, originally a nun at Rosedale Priory, who was elected prioress of Basedale in 1524. She resigned three years later to avoid being deprived for bad behaviour, and 'lived indecently and irreligiously, wandering and talking amongst seculars'. She expressed regret for her apostasy, and was sent to Rosedale to do penance. There, according to Archbishop Lee, her penitence was shown to be a sham, and in 1534 she was returned to Basedale in the hope that, in the nunnery of which she had been prioress, she would face up to her faults.[4]

There was plenty of work for a conscientious archbishop to do, and Lee may have planned to stamp out slackness, or worse, in order to protect the monasteries from attack from outside. If so, he was unsuccessful. On the 18th September 1535 Lee was forbidden by Henry VIII to make any further visitations of religious houses. The new Supreme Head of the Church had other plans. As far as the religious institutions were concerned, the repudiation of papal authority was much less important than the iron grip fastened on the

Church in England by the Crown. The wealth of the Church was a temptation which the impoverished monarch showed no desire to resist. The *Valor Ecclesiasticus* of 1535 gave the net annual income of the Church as £320,000. Allowing for omissions and under-estimates, the true figure was nearer £400,000, just over half being attributed to the monasteries. The current yield of the Crown lands was about £40,000 a year.[5]

The king appointed as Vicar-General of the Church his trusty minister Thomas Cromwell, who arranged for the Crown to receive, not only an annual tax of ten per cent of the valuation of Church income, but also the entire first year's net income on the appointment of a new monastic head, bishop, parson or chantry priest. These payments were known as 'the first fruits and tenths'. It was to further this scheme that the new valuation, the *Valor Ecclesiasticus*, was made in 1535.

Meanwhile commissioners had been touring the Yorkshire monasteries requiring their members to take oaths accepting the royal supremacy and the legitimacy of the children of the king's marriage to Anne Boleyn. Only one monk spoke out openly against the royal supremacy, George Lazenby of Jervaulx. He was executed in August 1535. Archbishop Lee wrote to Cromwell and the king in January 1536 about the trouble that he had encountered in persuading the Carthusians to conform. The prior of the London Charterhouse and several of his monks resisted, and were executed. Lee told Henry VIII that 'The priors of Hull and Mount Grace were sore bent to die' rather than take the required oaths, 'but I have persuaded both to change their opinions'.[6]

Cromwell appointed Doctors Layton and Legh to make a series of monastic visitations throughout the country. In a lightning tour they reported cases of slackness, corruption and immorality in house after house. When their letters to Cromwell were printed in 1843, the editor commented on 'the facility with which the inmates of the monasteries ... confessed to vices from the very name of which our imagination now recoils.... The great cause of the Reformation has been but ill served by concealing the depravities of the system which it overthrew.'[7]

Any visitation on the scale of that carried out by Layton and Legh, who went to at least twenty-four Yorkshire monasteries, could have been expected to find plenty of evidence that many of the inmates were, to quote the prophet Amos, 'too much at ease in Zion', following an easy-going routine. But these men, eager servants of ruthless and greedy masters, knew what they wanted to find. Any kind of gossip or rumour was grist to their mill. They reported, for example, that Alice Brampton, a nun of Handale, had had a child, but did not point out that she was seventy-three years old. Their reports of immorality can be relied upon only in the cases for which there is corroborative evidence. The accounts of superstitions, eg the girdles of the Blessed Virgin, the 'Virgin's milk' at Basedale, and the fragments of the Holy Cross at Nunkeeling and Bridlington, may be more reliable, as information about these would be freely available, leaving less need to invent.[8]

William Thirsk, who succeeded Marmaduke Huby as abbot of Fountains in 1526, was before long accused of scandalous behaviour. In or before 1530 Henry Percy, earl of Northumberland, wrote to a member of Cardinal Wolsey's staff, saying that Thirsk had misappropriated monastic property and was 'moch tedews [tedious] and uncharitable' in his conversation. If Wolsey would arrange a new election, the monks would give him 500 marks. The greasing of palms at this period was done without much subtlety. When Layton and Legh visited Fountains in January 1536 they persuaded Thirsk to resign, with an annual pension of 100 marks (£66 13s 4d). As his successor they recommended Marmaduke Bradley, 'the wisest [Cistercian] monk within England ... and well learned, twenty years officer and ruler of that house, a wealthy fellow, which will give you 600 marks to make him abbot there ...' Bradley had been in trouble in the days of Abbot Huby, but had been pardoned. He was currently living off a prebend (canonry) of Ripon Minster, just the kind of abuse which a genuine reform would have rooted out. He promised to pay the first fruits, about £1,000, within three years. Bradley was appointed, but refused to give up his canon's income of £40 a year until the first fruits had been paid.[9]

Henry VIII and Thomas Cromwell decided to confiscate the property of the smaller monasteries. The preamble to the 1536 Act shows that the suppression of the larger houses was not then envisaged:

> Forasmuch as manifest sin, vicious, carnal and abominable living is daily used and committed among the ... small abbeys, priories ... where the congregation of religious persons is under the number of twelve ... considering also that divers and great solemn monasteries ... wherein, thanks be to God, religion is right well kept and observed, be destitute of ... full numbers ... the Lords and Commons ... most humbly desire the King's Highness that he shall take into his possession all houses which have not ... above the clear yearly value of £200.

There was a strong case for putting the small, struggling houses such as Grosmont and Nunburnholme out of their misery, but all of the nunneries, half of the Augustinian priories and the three abbeys of white canons were valued at under £200. There were, however, various exemptions, general or particular. The mendicant friars were left alone at this stage, because they had virtually no property, and the Trinitarian friars at Knaresborough escaped because they shared the same label even though they owned land and churches. The Gilbertines were excluded, and fourteen of the twenty-three nunneries secured licences to continue, some by paying money. Thomas Cromwell's granddaughter was attending school at Wilberfoss Priory, which may have helped that nunnery to survive. The only Cistercian abbey to be closed under the 1536 Act was Sawley, but six houses of black canons, together with Easby and Coverham, went the same way. Egglestone Abbey, a poor house, was spared. It was easier to secure a licence if the property was not worth much.[10]

The suppression of the smaller monasteries, and fears of further seizures of Church property, brought to a head popular discontent which had been growing in Yorkshire from a variety of causes: disputes about rents and tenures and the enclosure of common land; heavy taxation; resentment about 'upstarts' such as Thomas Cromwell in positions of power; and hostility to both the royal supremacy and the 'new learning'. It was, in short, a conservative resistance to unwelcome change. A rising in Lincolnshire began on the 3rd October 1536, and touched off a similar movement in Yorkshire. It started in the East Riding on the 9th October and had spread within a week throughout the Pennine dales.

The main leaders of the Pilgrimage of Grace, so called because it was declared to be not a rebellion, but a movement to defend the Church and remove the 'evil' advisers who were leading the king astray, were Robert Aske, a lawyer whose home was at Aughton by the River Derwent, Lord Darcy and Sir Thomas Percy. On the 12th October the 'pilgrims' restored Sawley Abbey, which seems to have been the source of the marching song which began:

> Christ crucified, For thy wounds wide,
> Us commons guide, Which pilgrims be.
> Through God's grace, For to purchase,
> Old wealth and peace, Of the spirituality.

Other monasteries became actively involved, including Jervaulx, where William Thirsk was living in retirement. He asked the rebels to restore him to Fountains. Some of the canons of Warter returned to their suppressed priory. A Trinitarian from Knaresborough, Robert Ashton or Esch, who was stationed at Beverley to collect alms for the friary, encouraged people in the East Riding to join the movement. Dr John Pickering, prior of the York Dominicans, who was staying at Bridlington Priory at the time of the Pilgrimage, wrote a more cerebral poem for the rebels, 'O faithful people of the Boreal region'.[11]

Lord Darcy, elderly and in poor health, was a reluctant rebel. He sent several appeals from Pontefract Castle for supplies of ammunition and artillery. 'There is not one gun in Pomfret Castle ready to shoot.' On the 17th October, as the rebel forces approached, Darcy wrote to the king: 'We in the castle must in a few days either yield or lose our lives.'[12]

The 'Pilgrims' controlled most of Yorkshire. They were too numerous and disciplined for the forces loyal to the king to risk a battle. In December 1536 the duke of Norfolk, on behalf of the king, was forced to agree to a partial acceptance of the demands of the rebels, including the holding of a parliament at York to discuss their grievances, and a full pardon for all. The preamble to the pardon declared that the king was being merciful because the rebels had been misled by 'sundry false tales spitefully set abroad amongst you by certain malicious and perverse persons'.[13]

Henry VIII made no move to fulfil his promises to the rebels. He busied himself instead with military preparations, shipping munitions to Hull. Suspicions about his intentions led to a new rising on 16th January 1537. It was led by Sir Francis Bigod of Settrington, an enigmatic figure whose personality and behaviour are analysed at length by Professor Dickens. Bigod was sympathetic to the new learning. He wrote a book criticising the monasteries for idleness and luxurious living, and particularly for the appropriation of churches in which there was no properly-funded vicarage. When he was writing, between 1533 and 1536, Yorkshire had about 622 parish churches of which nearly two-thirds were appropriated, mainly by the monasteries. Over 100 of these churches were apparently served by salaried chaplains. Bigod had enthusiastically supported the royal supremacy, and was the man who arrested George Lazenby.[14]

Sir Francis Bigod resented the behaviour of Layton and Legh in pressurising the prior of Guisborough, James Cockerell, to resign. He began to see the Pilgrimage of Grace as a possible vehicle for a genuine reform of the monasteries, which he preferred to their suppression. However, his resumption of the rebellion was opposed by Robert Aske and other leaders, and soon collapsed. It provided an excuse for Henry VIII to dispose of those active in the Pilgrimage. Sir Francis Bigod, Robert Aske, Lord Darcy, Sir Thomas Percy and Sir Robert Constable were amongst the 200 men executed. The king ordered the duke of Norfolk to seek out all the monks and canons involved and hang them 'to the terrible example of others'.[15]

William Wood, prior of Bridlington, pleaded that he had become involved only because of threats from the bailiffs of two local manors which belonged to rebel leaders, Kilham (Darcy) and Nafferton (Percy). He argued in vain. Adam Sedber, abbot of Jervaulx, William Thirsk, James Cockerell and John Pickering were also executed. Abbot Bolton of Sawley was sentenced to death, but may have died from natural causes. The former sub-prior and kitchener of Warter Priory were sentenced to be hanged in chains in York, and the sub-prior of Watton suffered the same fate at his own monastery. The canons of Watton had been persuaded by the rebels to depose the prior, Robert Holgate. He was a friend of Cromwell and had some sympathy with the 'new learning'. He became Master of Sempringham and therefore head of the Gilbertine order by 1534, and with Cromwell's support became also prior of Watton shortly before the Pilgrimage. At the time of the latter he was in the south of England.[16]

Jervaulx Abbey and Bridlington Priory, and all their estates, were confiscated by the Crown because of the treason of their heads. The duke of Norfolk wrote to the king on the 10th May 1537, saying that he would personally supervise their suppression, 'as well because the countries about them be populous and the houses greatly beloved with the people, as also I think well stored of cattle and other things profitable that will not come all to light so well if I be absent as if I be present'. Sir Arthur Darcy told Cromwell in a letter that he had attended 'the suppression of Jervaulx, which house within the gate is covered wholly with lead, and there is one of the fairest churches that I have seen, fair meadows ... the best pasture in England, hard and sound of kind ... the breed of Jervaulx for horses was the tried breed in the north ...' By November all of the lead had been stripped off the roofs of Jervaulx and smelted into pigs.[17]

The rood screen and loft from Bridlington Priory were almost certainly moved at the suppression three miles away to Flamborough Parish Church, which belonged to the priory. (Prickett, Priory Church of Bridlington)

It was not long before Henry VIII and his ministers realised how easy it would be to seize the rest of the monasteries and their estates. Commissioners were appointed to negotiate the quiet surrender of the houses, in return for which pensions would be granted to all but the mendicant friars. They began their work in Yorkshire in 1538 and by the beginning of 1540 had received the surrender of all the remaining religious houses. The pensions for the heads of the houses were fixed in relation to the resources of the monastery. Abbot Bradley of Fountains received £100 a year, Thomas Kent, minister of the Knaresborough Trinitarians, £13 6s 8d. The prior (second-in-command) of Fountains was awarded an annual pension of £8, the other thirty monks, all priests, between £6 13s 4d and £6. At Watton the two prioresses received £5 and £4 respectively, the nuns pensions ranging between 53s 4d and 33s 4d, and the eight lay sisters 13s 4d. By far the largest prize for anyone inside the monastic system in Yorkshire was carried off by Robert Holgate. He had already been appointed bishop of Llandaff (in 1545 he succeeded Lee as archbishop of York), and in lieu of a pension was given a lease for life of Watton Priory and some of its manors. At the other end of the scale the mendicant friars received only small single payments. Those to the Franciscan friars at Richmond ranged from the 13s 4d paid to the warden, Dr Robert Sanderson, to 4s.[18]

Three kinds of decline have been identified in the substantial body of historical writing on the last years of the monasteries: in standards of discipline and morality; in the popularity of the houses with testators; and in the numbers attracted to the religious life. It has been argued above that in Yorkshire the first of these is doubtful, not so much because of sanctity in the sixteenth century as because of failings at earlier periods, and the second simply wrong. The third is also open to question.

In their study *Monks, Friars and Nuns in Sixteenth Century Yorkshire*, Claire Cross and Noreen Vickers have identified about 610 monks and canons, 200 friars and 230 nuns and sisters in the religious houses at the suppression. They point out that an unknown number left their houses shortly before they were closed. As the mendicant friars received no pensions, and records relating to them are incomplete, ' ... in consequence the estimate of 200 friars in the county may be especially low'. When due allowance is made for this, however, there is little doubt that their numbers had declined since the fourteenth century. The four friaries of the city of York had about 140 members in 1300. The dissolution list totalled only 59.

The situation of the other houses of men was quite different. Mount Grace, its accommodation limited to the number of cells, had a queue of applicants in the 1520s. Fountains Abbey had 34 monks in 1380-1, 32 in 1539. Selby had 27 monks in 1362, 24 in 1539. The Trinitarian friary at Knaresborough (more like a house of black canons than a mendicant friary) had 11 members in 1375, the same number in 1538. The variations in the numbers of nuns and lay sisters, ranging from 41 at Watton and 20 at Swine to only 4 at Nunburnholme, can be explained by the resource factor. Where there were fewer nuns and sisters than at an earlier period, a decline in the yield of the estates may be to blame. With a few exceptions the houses of monks, canons and nuns could still, in the 1530s, recruit about as many members as they could house, clothe and feed.[19]

Warter Priory from the south-east. The nineteenth century church stands on the site of the priory church. Only earthworks trace the outline of the other buildings of the Augustinian canons.
(Cambridge University)

When the monasteries passed to the Crown, the lead was stripped off the roofs, mainly for its market value but also to discourage any idea of a restoration, leaving the 'Bare ruin'd choirs, where late the sweet birds sang' of Shakespeare's seventy-third sonnet. Chalices, plate, vestments, glass, anything saleable was taken. Even graves were robbed to recover the chalice and paten buried with some priest-monks, although this may have been done by common thieves. Fountains Abbey enjoyed a stay of execution. A plan was drawn up to create a bishopric of Fountains, to include the archdeaconry of Richmond which extended into north Lancashire, Westmorland and Cumberland. It was to be staffed by a bishop, a dean and twelve canons, a master of the grammar and song schools, and other officers. The scheme was soon abandoned, in

favour of the incorporation of the archdeaconry into a new diocese of Chester, and Fountains was handed over to the despoilers.[20]

For the sale of monastic property the
normal arrangement was to make a new assessment of the annual value and multiply it
by twenty to determine the price. Quite
apart from the effects of the inflation which
was gathering pace, the valuations were on
the conservative side, so that investment in
monastic property could be very profitable.
It was possible to buy an estate and sell half
of it to the sitting tenants for the purchase
price of the whole. Some of the gentry and
aristocracy bought or leased the site and
lands of monasteries of which they were
'founders'. Easby and most of its estates
were leased by Lord Scrope, who had previously bought the abbey's herd of cattle.[21]

The suppression of the monasteries and
the subordination of the Church in England
to the power of the state effectively mark the
end of the Middle Ages. The confiscation and
subsequent sale of monastic property
amounted to the biggest shift in the pattern
of land ownership in Yorkshire since the
Norman Conquest. The tithe and other
rectorial income which had been given to the
monasteries, particularly the houses of canons, was not redeployed for religious purposes, but sold as an investment to laymen.

In 1530 Yorkshire had about eighty monasteries, not counting small dependencies,
the hospitals and the Knights Hospitallers.
Some of the buildings were pulled down to
provide the stone for new mansions; some,
especially in the towns, were quarried by
local people; the rest were left to decay.
Some of the monastic buildings were in a
poor state of repair, and others, such as
Basedale Priory with its thatched domestic
buildings, were probably undistinguished

architecturally. We need not weep for them
all. But taken as a whole, the destruction of
so many magnificent buildings and their art-
istic treasures — rood screens, stalls, stained
glass, pictures, statues, shrines and tombs —
represented the greatest act of cultural van-
dalism ever committed in this country in
peacetime.

It is appropriate to give the last word to
Robert Aske, in the statements he made during the long interrogation as a prisoner of
the Crown. He could be called naive, in
imagining that he would ever be allowed to
get away with a successful demonstration-
in-force, which is what the Pilgrimage of
Grace really was, and believing that the
word of Henry VIII could be trusted. He
may have seen the dangers clearly, but felt
that he had no choice. The religious and
social systems which he, as a conservative
rebel, was defending, were already doomed,
but his views probably reflect those of most
Yorkshire people at the time. His integrity
is not in doubt.

Aske argued that the system of 'first fruits
and tenths' would ruin the surviving monasteries, especially if vacancies occurred frequently through death or resignation. He
criticised two key policies of Henry VIII: the
royal supremacy over the Church, against
which 'all men murmured', as no king had
ever claimed such authority 'sith the Faith
comyn within the realm'; and the royal
divorce. Far from bowing the knee to the
king, Aske asserted that Princess Mary, made
illegitimate by the statute annulling the marriage between the king and her mother Queen
Catherine, was 'marvellously beloved by the
whole people'. (A few of the statements quot-
ed in the printed State papers have been left
in the original spelling, but for most the
spelling has been modernised.)

About the monasteries, Robert Aske had this to say. He dealt specifically with those which had been closed under the 1536 Act, although he may have feared for the survival of the remainder:

> ... the abbeys in the North gave great alms to poor men and laudably served God ... by the said suppression the service of God is much minished [diminished], great number of masses unsaid and the consecration of the sacrament now not used in those parts, to the decrease of the Faith and spiritual comfort to man's soul, the temple of God ruffed and pulled down, the ornaments and relics of the church irreverently used, tombs of honourable and noble men pulled down and sold ... Also several of these abbeys were in the mountains and desert places, where the people be rude of conditions and not well taught the law of God, and when the abbeys stood the people not only had worldly refreshing in their bodies but spiritual refuge, both by ghostly living of them and by spiritual information and preaching ...
>
> Also the abbeys was one of the beauties of this realm to all men and strangers passing through the same; also all gentlemen much succoured in their needs with money, their younger sons there succoured and in nunneries their daughters brought up in virtue, and also their evidences [title deeds] and money left to the uses of infants in abbeys' hands, always sure there, and such abbeys as were near the danger of seabanks great maintainers of seawalls and dykes, maintainers and builders of bridges and highways [and] such other things for the common wealth.[22]

GLOSSARY OF TERMS RELATING TO MONASTIC BUILDINGS

chapter house	meeting place for conducting the collective business of the monastery
choir, quire	the choir stalls of the monks/canons/friars/nuns
crossing	the junction of the transepts and the main east–west line of a cruciform church; in the larger churches often surmounted by a tower
dorter	dormitory
frater	refectory
lavatory, laver	washing troughs, located at the entrance to the frater and elsewhere in the monastic buildings
misericord	room where meat eating allowed
nave	the western arm of the church, used by the lay brothers and, in the case of monasteries with a parochial function, by the laity
parlour	room where necessary conversations allowed
pentice	covered way along the side of a building
pulpitum	screen at the west end of the choir stalls
presbytery	location of the high altar, to the east of the choir stalls
reredorter	latrines, positioned over a drain
rood screen and loft	screen separating the nave from the choir stalls; normally with a loft above it, carrying images including a crucifix
transepts	the north and south arms of a cruciform church

GAZETTEER

This list of all the post-1066 monastic sites in Yorkshire is arranged by Ridings, with the city of York given separately. All of the houses were closed in the period 1536-40 unless otherwise stated. Cross-reference to the text can be made by using the first section of the index. Map references are given for rural sites, and in some other cases where they may be useful. Map references in brackets indicate the centre of the village when the exact monastic site is not known.

The names of monasteries with significant remains which are accessible to the public are printed in capitals. Times of opening are not given, as they are subject to change. At the time of writing the following English Heritage sites are unstaffed, and open during daylight hours free of charge: Easby, Egglestone, Monk Bretton and Sawley. Private sites with features visible from public roads are noted. In all other cases either there are no significant remains, or what survives is private and not visible from a public road. Readers are asked to respect the privacy of the owners and occupiers of such sites.

EAST RIDING

Beverley (1) Dominican friary, established by 1240. TA038393. Domestic buildings now part of youth hostel, best seen from footbridge over railway near Beverley Station. The sixteenth century gateway has been moved to the west side of Eastgate.

(2) Franciscan friary, by 1267. First site High and Low Friars, TA029393, near Newbiggin Bar. Second site 1297, outside Keldgate Bar.

BRIDLINGTON PRIORY Augustinian canons, 1113-14. Nave of priory church in use as parish church. Gatehouse. Guidebook on sale in church.

Burstall Priory Alien priory, Benedictine monks, dependency of Aumale Abbey, 1115. Closed by 1395. Site south of Welwick and Skeffling, washed away by the sea.

Cottingham First site of Haltemprice Priory, 1322. Possibly near church, TA050332.

Ellerton Priory Ellerton on the Derwent, otherwise on Spalding Moor. Gilbertine canons, c1208. SE701399. Part of priory church survived until mid-nineteenth century, when present church built.

Haltemprice Priory Augustinian canons, second site after Cottingham, 1326. TA043310. Farmhouse incorporates some material from the priory. Private.

Hull   (1) Carmelite friary, 1289. First site within Wyke-upon-Hull (renamed Kingston-upon-Hull in 1299). Second site 1304, at west end of Whitefriargate.

(2) Austin friary, c1303, in Blackfriargate, south of Market Place.

(3) Carthusian priory, otherwise Charterhouse, Carthusian monks, 1377-78. Outside the north gate of town. (The building known after the suppression as the Charterhouse was actually the Maison Dieu, a hospital.)

KIRKHAM PRIORY   Augustinian canons, c1122. SE736657. English Heritage, guidebook on sale.

Meaux Abbey   Cistercian monks, 1150-51. TA092394. Extensive earthworks. The derelict cottage on the site was built of stones from the abbey.

North Ferriby Priory   Augustinian canons, c1140. Established as a cell of the Augustinian abbey of the Temple of the Lord in Jerusalem (no connection with the Knights Templars), but operated for most of its life as a small independent priory. Site probably near All Saints Church, SE988257.

Nunburnholme Priory   Benedictine nuns, 1154-89. SE853494. Earthworks. The parish church, with Norman nave, is at the opposite end of the village.

Nunkeeling Priory   Benedictine nuns, c1152. TA145501. The parish church, which adjoined the priory church, continued in use after the suppression, was rebuilt 1810, now a ruin.

SWINE PRIORY   Cistercian nuns, by 1153, double house with canons and lay brothers for a period. TA134358. Part of chancel of priory church in use as parish church. Contains eight of the original sixteen choir stalls,

and four monuments of the Hilton family. 'The finest collection of medieval monuments in the East Riding' (Pevsner & Neave).

Thicket Priory   Benedictine nuns, by 1180. SE697436. House built on the site 1844-7 has been used as a Carmelite nunnery since 1955. Private.

Warter Priory   Augustinian canons, c1132. SE870505. Affiliated to Arrouaise Abbey, France, for some years in the mid-twelfth century. Earthworks around the parish church, which was rebuilt in the nineteenth century on or near the site of the priory church.

Watton Priory   Gilbertine, double house of nuns and canons, 1150. TA024498. Prior's lodging, fourteenth and fifteenth centuries, survives as private house, Watton Abbey. Private, visible from road.

WILBERFOSS PRIORY   Benedictine nuns, by 1153. SE733510. Nave of priory church in use as parish church. Traces of other buildings to north.

NORTH RIDING

Arden Priory   Benedictine nuns, c1147. SE520906. Slight remains in and around Arden Hall, Harmby. Private.

Basedale Priory   Cistercian nuns, third site after Hutton Lowcross and Nunthorpe, c1189. NZ621067. Private.

Byland on the Moor   Now Old Byland, second site of Byland Abbey after Hood, 1142. SE550859. The church, which was given to the abbey, was built c1100.

BYLAND ABBEY   Cistercian monks (Savigniac until 1147), fourth site after Hood, Byland on the Moor and Stocking. 1177.

SE550790. English Heritage, guidebook on sale.

Coverham Abbey Premonstratensian canons, second site after Swainby, 1196-1202. SE109864. Three arcades of the nave, part of the north transept and a gateway survive, together with remains built into houses on the site. Private.

EASBY ABBEY Premonstratensian canons, 1151. NZ185003. English Heritage, unstaffed, plan on site. St Agatha's Church in use as parish church.

EGGLESTONE ABBEY Premonstratensian canons, by 1198. NZ062151. English Heritage, unstaffed, plan on site.

Ellerton-in-Swaledale Priory Cistercian nuns, ?1154-89. SE080974. Fifteenth century tower and part of walls of church, on private land, visible from road.

Eskdale *see* Grosmont.

Fors Savigniac, later Cistercian, monks, first site of Jervaulx Abbey. Advance party c1145, abbey 1150. SD933910. Became a grange (Dale Grange) after 1156. Private.

Foukeholme *see* Thimbleby.

Goathland Hermitage c1109-14, soon afterwards became cell of Whitby Abbey, reduced to vaccary by 1335. (NZ835013).

Grendale *see* Handale.

Grosmont Otherwise known as Eskdale. Grandmontine monks, c1204. Cell of Grandmont Priory until 1317; then priory, dependency of Grandmont Abbey until 1394; then independent Grandmontine priory. NZ828058. Young in his *History of Whitby*, 1824 edition, writes that most of buildings converted into farm buildings; 1840 edition, writes that the remaining structures of the priory had been destroyed to make way for a new farmhouse. Private.

GUISBOROUGH PRIORY Augustinian canons, c1119. NZ618161. Langbargh District Council for English Heritage. Guidebook on sale.

HACKNESS (St Peter's Church) Cell of Whitby Abbey c1080, uncertain role from late twelfth century. SE969905. In the later Middle Ages operated as a church and a manor. Oldest part of church first half of twelfth century.

Handale (otherwise **Grendale**) **Priory** Benedictine or Cistercian nuns, 1133. NZ725157. Farmhouse on site may incorporate one wall of priory church. Private.

Hood Hermitage; then first site of Byland Abbey, c1139, then first site of Newburgh Priory, 1142-43. SE505823. Farm on site. Private.

Hutton Lowcross First site of Basedale Priory, c1162. Probable site is NZ590140.

JERVAULX ABBEY Cistercian monks (Savigniac until 1147), second site after Fors, 1156. SE173858. Jervaulx estate. Open to public, guidebook on sale.

Keldholme Priory Cistercian nuns, c1135. SE710863. Private.

Kildale Chapel of St Hilda-in-the-Park, short-lived home, c1310-15, of Crutched Friars. Site uncertain.

LASTINGHAM CHURCH Crypt built and abbey church begun by Abbot Stephen and his monks from Whitby, from c1080 until the move to St Olave's, York, in 1086. SE728905.

MALTON PRIORY Gilbertine canons, 1150. SE797726. Part of nave of priory church in use as Old Malton parish church.

Marrick Priory Benedictine nuns, 1154-58. SE067978. Part of priory church extensively reconstructed early nineteenth century, using piers and arches to form a new division between nave and chancel in the restored section. Perpendicular east window and some of the Perpendicular windows on the north and south sides are original. Ruins of original east end to east of restored church. Now converted to Church of England youth centre. Private, visible from road.

Marton Priory   Augustinian canons, c1150. SE585695. Originally double house with nuns, who moved to Moxby by 1167. Earthworks, small stone fragments in front of farmhouse. Private.

Middlesbrough St Hilda   Priory cell of Whitby Abbey, early twelfth century. Church of St Hilda apparently demolished by c1700. New church of St Hilda built on the site 1838-40.

Moulton   Possible site of 'Richmond' cell of French abbey of Begar. (SE236038.) Property given to Mount Grace Priory c1414.

MOUNT GRACE PRIORY   Carthusian monks, 1398. SE449985. English Heritage for National Trust. Guidebook on sale.

Moxby Priory   Benedictine or Augustinian nuns. SE597668. Began as part of double house at Marton c1150, moved to separate nunnery at Moxby by 1167. Earthworks only. Private.

Newburgh Priory   Augustinian canons, second site after Hood, 1145. SE543765. Private house on site (open to the public on certain days) incorporates parts of priory.

Northallerton   Carmelite friary, 1356. At east end of town near church. Site called the Friarage.

Nunthorpe   Second site of Basedale Priory, c1167. Earthworks near Nunthorpe Hall, NZ542132, may mark the site.

Richmond   (1) St Martin's Priory, Benedictine monks, 1100-37. NZ177007. Dependency of St Mary's Abbey, York. Ruins on private land, visible from road.

(2) FRANCISCAN FRIARY, 1258. NZ171010. Late fifteenth century friary tower and fragments of church walls.

(3) Possible site of twelfth century nunnery, the evidence being royal grants to 'the nuns of Richmond', 1171-82. The nuns may actually have been nearby at Ellerton-in-Swaledale.

RIEVAULX ABBEY   Cistercian monks, 1132. SE577894. English Heritage, guidebook on sale.

Rosedale Priory   Cistercian nuns, by 1158. SE724959. Present church built 1839 on site of chancel of priory church. Fragments in nearby field may be the angle of the north transept of the priory church.

Scarborough   (1) Franciscan friary. First site in Old Town, exact location unknown, c1239; second site in Throxenby area, 1245; third site in Sepulcre Street, 1267-72.

(2) Dominican friary, c1252, Queen Street.

(3) Carmelite friary, 1319. To the south of the Dominican friary, and to the north of part of Newborough.

(4) St Mary's Church. Belonged to Citeaux Abbey from 1189 to the late fourteenth century. In thirteenth and fourteenth centuries two or three Cistercian monks stationed in Scarborough to oversee the collection of tithes and other income, the senior monk styled warden.

Stocking   Third site, 1147, of Byland Abbey. SE504798. Farm on site. Private.

Swainby   Parish of Pickhill. First site of Coverham Abbey, 1184-7. SE336858. Private.

Thimbleby   Otherwise known as Foukeholme. St Stephen's Priory, nuns, order unknown, c1200. Last reference 1349. Nun House Farm, SE446940, is the probable site. Private.

Wath   Alien cell, Benedictine monks, cell of Mont St Michel Abbey, by 1156. Closed by 1239. SE326772 (parish church).

WHITBY ABBEY   Benedictine monks, priory from c1077, abbey by 1109. NZ903112. English Heritage, guidebook on sale.

Wykeham Priory   Cistercian nuns, c1153. SE962819. Part of north wall of church stands east of the house called Wykeham Abbey. Private.

Yarm   Dominican friary, by 1266. Site in vicinity of Friarage House, on south side of town.

Yedingham Priory   Benedictine nuns, by 1163. SE897798. Lower part of south wall of nave survives; the inner side of this wall is visible from the road. Private.

WEST RIDING

Allerton Mauleverer Priory   Alien priory, Benedictine monks, dependency of Marmoutier Abbey, c1110. Closed c1414. St Martin's Church, SE416850, rebuilt mid-eighteenth century, may contain materials from the priory church.

Arthington Priory   Cluniac nuns, c1154-55. SE288052. House on site dated 1585. Private.

Barnoldswick   First site of Kirkstall Abbey, 1147. SD877468 (parish church).

BOLTON PRIORY   Augustinian canons, second site after Embsay, 1155. SE075542. Nave of priory church in use as parish church. Ruins of other buildings. Generally known as Bolton Abbey. Duke of Devonshire's estate. Pedestrian access free, charge for car parking. Guidebook on sale.

Doncaster   (1) Franciscan friary, by 1284. In Marsh Gate.
(2) Carmelite friary, 1350. High Street/St Sepulchre Gate.

Drax Priory   Augustinian canons, 1130-39. SE667285. Private. The parish church (part Norman) was separate.

Ecclesfield Priory   Alien priory, Benedictine monks, dependency of St Wandrille Abbey, 1100-35. Closed by 1386. SK353942. Chapel wing and other fragments survive in a house called the Priory on north side of churchyard. Private.

Embsay   First site of Bolton Priory, 1120. SE010543. A quarter of a mile north-west of St Mary's Church. Private.

Esholt Priory   Cistercian nuns, late twelfth century. Fragments in the basement of Esholt Hall. Private. The present church is nineteenth century.

FOUNTAINS ABBEY   Cistercian monks, 1132. SE275683. National Trust, guidebook on sale.

Hampole Priory   Cistercian nuns, by 1156. SE506104. A few stone fragments in vicinity. Private.

Headley Priory   Benedictine monks, dependency of Holy Trinity Priory, York and Marmoutier Abbey; Holy Trinity only from 1414. SE445414. A farm, Headley Hall, on the site. Private.

Healaugh Park Priory   Augustinian canons. Hermitage by 1184; apparently evolved into a community of canons; fully-fledged priory by 1218. SE484464. Part of priory buildings incorporated into farm buildings. Private.

Kirkby Malham   Cell of house of Premonstratensian canons, West Dereham, Norfolk,
before 1189. (SD894610.)

Kirklees Priory   Benedictine or Cistercian
nuns. Possibly before 1138, probably 1154-89.
SE175222. Private house on site. Gatehouse
is mainly post-suppression.

KIRKSTALL ABBEY   Cistercian monks, second site after Barnoldswick, 1152. SE260361. In
public park. Plan on display and guidebooks
for sale in nearby Abbey House Museum.

Knaresborough   St Robert's Friary or Priory. Trinitarian friars, 1152. SE361561. Stone
fragments only. St Robert's Cave is nearby,
by the riverside. (The cave-chapel near Low
Bridge was made in the early fifteenth
century, and has no connection with either
St Robert or the friary.)

MONK BRETTON PRIORY   Cluniac
monks c1155, became independent priory of
Benedictine monks c1279. SE374065. English
Heritage, unstaffed, plan on site.

Nostell Priory   Augustinian canons c1114,
local move to new site 1120. SE407173. Stood
to south-east of present house, which is
open to the public at certain times. No surviving buildings.

Nun Appleton Priory   Cistercian nuns,
1148-54. SE556400. House on site. Private.

NUN MONKTON PRIORY   Benedictine
nuns, 1147-53. SE512580. Nave in use as parish
church. No other survivals.

Pontefract   (1) Priory of Cluniac monks,
1090, became independent of Cluny Abbey
c1393. SE433226. North of All Saints Church,
no buildings or earthworks.

(2) Dominican friary, 1256. Excavations in
1963 revealed original structure of timber on
stone footings, rebuilt in stone in early

fourteenth century. Site now occupied by
Pontefract General Infirmary.

ROCHE ABBEY   Cistercian monks, 1147.
SK544898. English Heritage, guidebook on
sale.

SAWLEY ABBEY   Cistercian monks, 1148.
SD776464. English Heritage, unstaffed, plan
on site.

SELBY ABBEY   Benedictine monks, 1069-
70. Whole abbey church in use as parish
church. Guidebook on sale.

Sinningthwaite Priory   Cistercian nuns,
by 1155. SE462487. South range of cloister
now a house. Private.

Skewkirk   Cell of Nostell Priory (Augustinian canons), 1114-35. SE472542. Some stones
from the cell built into Skewkirk Hall, a
farm. Private.

SNAITH   Priory cell of Selby Abbey, 1101-
08. SE641222. Church, with Norman, Early
English and Decorated features, in use as
parish church.

Tickhill Friary   Austin friars, c1260. SK586928.
Part of domestic buildings incorporated into
two houses. Private.

WOODKIRK   Priory cell of Nostell Priory,
by 1135. SE272250. Church in use as parish
church. West tower is thirteenth century, the
rest c1831.

YORK

Benedictine monks

(1) **ST OLAVE'S CHURCH**   Marygate.
Used c1086-88 by monks in transit from Lastingham to St Mary's Abbey.

(2) **ST MARY'S ABBEY**   1088. Ruins in
Museum Gardens, gatehouse on Marygate

side. Nearby King's Manor consists of the abbot's lodging, extensively rebuilt in the sixteenth and seventeenth centuries, and belonging to the University of York. The ruins of St Leonard's Hospital are adjacent to the entrance to Museum Gardens.

(3) **All Saints' Church**   Fishergate. Priory cell of Whitby Abbey.

(4) **HOLY TRINITY PRIORY**   Micklegate. Alien priory, dependency of Marmoutier, 1089. Became independent Benedictine priory 1426. The present church consists of the monastic nave, less the north aisle, with a small modern chancel.

Benedictine nuns

Clementhorpe Priory   Otherwise **St Clement's Priory**, c1130. On south side of street called Clementhorpe.

Gilbertine canons

St Andrew's Priory   c1200. Between St George's Field and Fishergate.

Friaries

(1) **Dominican**   1227. Site of old railway station, north-west of end of Barker Lane.
(2) **Franciscan**   c1230. First site uncertain. Second site, 1243, between Tower Street and Friargate, west of the castle.
(3) **Carmelite**   By 1253. First site on north-east side of Bootham. Second site, 1295, bounded by Stonebow Lane, Fossgate and River Foss.
(4) **Austin**   By 1272. Between Lendal and the Guildhall.
(5) **Friars of the Sack**   c1260, closed by 1312. Site unknown.
(6) **Friars of the Holy Cross**, or **Crutched Friars**   c1307, closed c1310. Site unknown.

KNIGHTS TEMPLARS

All suppressed 1308-12. Houses marked * passed to Knights Hospitallers.

East Riding
Faxfleet, on River Humber between Goole and Brough, founded ?by 1220.

North Riding
East Cowton*, north-west of Northallerton, c1142.
Foulbridge*, on River Derwent, east of Yedingham Priory, by 1226.
Pen Hill*, in upper Wensleydale, c1142, in decay 1338.
Westerdale*, south-east of Guisborough, by 1203.

West Riding
Copmanthorpe, south-west of York, 1258. United with Ribstone c1292.
Ribstone*, north of Wetherby, c1217.
Temple Hirst, south of Selby, 1152.
Temple Newsham, east of Leeds, by 1181.
Wetherby, 1240 or later. United with Ribstone, date unknown.
Whitley, east of Pontefract, by 1248.

KNIGHTS OF THE HOSPITAL OF ST JOHN OF JERUSALEM, or KNIGHTS HOSPITALLERS

Other houses of the order, suppressed 1540.

East Riding
Beverley, c1201.

North Riding
Mount St John, north-east of Thirsk, c1148.

West Riding
Newland, west of Goole, c1199.

BIBLIOGRAPHY AND REFERENCES

The place of publication is London, unless otherwise stated.

Suggestions for Further Reading

For the benefit of readers who would like some more specific guidance on further study than is provided by the references, the following suggestions are made.

Two concise general accounts containing a good deal of Yorkshire material, which are useful for the design and architecture of the monasteries: Colin Platt, *The Abbeys and Priories of Medieval England* (Fordham University Press, New York, 1984); and Glyn Coppack, *Abbeys and Priories* (English Heritage, 1990).

Papers on two Yorkshire topics: Janet E Burton, *The Yorkshire Nunneries in the Twelfth and Thirteenth Centuries* (Borthwick Paper 56, BIHR, York, 1979); and Claire Cross, *The End of Medieval Monasticism in the East Riding of Yorkshire* (East Yorkshire Local History Society, 1993).

Studies of particular houses and their role in the community: R B Dobson, *Selby Abbey and Town* (Selby, 1993); and Janet E Burton, *Kirkham Priory from Foundation to Dissolution* (Borthwick Paper 86, 1995).

On the monastic economy: Ian Kershaw, *Bolton Priory, the Economy of a Northern Monastery* (1973); J H Tillotson, *Marrick Priory, a Nunnery in Late Medieval Yorkshire* (Borthwick Paper 75, 1989); and for general background with much Yorkshire detail, Colin Platt *The Monastic Grange in Medieval England* (1969).

For the study of the architecture of monasteries with substantial remains, the best initial source is normally the guidebook available on site from English Heritage or other custodians. A more substantial work in this field, incorporating the results of recent archaeological research, is Glyn Coppack, *Fountains Abbey* (English Heritage, 1993).

Note: Borthwick Paper 93, *The Franciscans in the Medieval Custody of York* by Michael Robson, dated 1997, was issued in May 1998, after the preparation of the text of this book had been completed. It deals with four of the five friaries of Yorkshire, but not Richmond, which was in the Custody of Newcastle.

Abbreviations

Arch J	*Archaeological Journal*
BIHR	Borthwick Institute of Historical Research, University of York
Brid Chart	W T Lancaster (ed), *Chartulary of Bridlington Priory* (Leeds, 1912)
Burton, Thesis	Janet E Burton, 'Origins and Development of Religious Orders in Yorkshire, c1069–c1200', York D Phil, 1977

CCR	*Calendar of Close Rolls*
CLR	*Calendar of Liberate Rolls*
C Papal R	*Calendar of Papal Registers*
CPR	*Calendar of Patent Rolls*
Chron Melsa	*Chronicle of the Abbey of Meaux*, 3 vols, RS 43
Cross and Vickers	YASRS 150, Claire Cross and Noreen Vickers, *Monks, Friars and Nuns in Sixteenth Century Yorkshire* (1995)
EYC	*Early Yorkshire Charters*, vols I–III ed W Farrer, vols IV–XII YASRS
Fount Chart	W T Lancaster (ed), *Chartulary of Fountains Abbey* (Leeds, 1915)
Graham, *Gilbertines*	Rose Graham, *St Gilbert of Sempringham and the Gilbertines* (1901)
Graham, *Malton*	Rose Graham, 'The Finances of Malton Priory, 1244-1257', in Graham, *English Ecclesiastical Studies* (1929), pp247-70
Greenway	Diane E Greenway (ed), *Charters of the Honour of Mowbray 1107-1191* (British Academy, Oxford, 1972)
Kershaw	Ian Kershaw, *Bolton Priory, the Economy of a Northern Monastery* (1973)
Knowles and Hadcock	D Knowles and R N Hadcock, *Medieval Religious Houses, England and Wales* (2nd edn, 1971)
Lanercost	H Maxwell (ed), *Chronicle of Lanercost Priory 1272-1346* (1913)
L & P Henry VIII	*Letters and Papers, Henry VIII*
Mems Fount	*Memorials of Fountains Abbey*, vols I and III, Surtees 42, 130
Monastic Notes	*Notes on the Religious and Secular Houses of Yorkshire* vols I and II, YASRS 17, 81
MO	D Knowles, *The Monastic Order in England* (Cambridge, 1950)
Monasticon	W Dugdale, *Monasticon Anglicanum* (1823)
Nidderdale	B Jennings (ed), *A History of Nidderdale* (3rd edn, York, 1992)
Reg Giffard	*Register of Archbishop Giffard*, Surtees 109
Reg Gray	*Register of Archbishop Gray*, Surtees 56
Reg le Romeyn	*Register of Archbishop le Romeyn*, vols I and II, Surtees 123, 128
Reg Wickwane	*Register of Archbishop Wickwane*, Surtees 114
Riev Chart	*Chartulary of Rievaulx Abbey*, Surtees 83
RO I–III	D Knowles, *The Religious Orders in England* (Cambridge, vols I–III, 1948-59)
RS	Rolls Series
Selby Coucher	*Coucher Book of Selby Abbey*, vols I and II, YASRS 10, 13
Surtees	Surtees Society Publications
Test Ebor	*Testamenta Eboracensia*, vols I–VI, Surtees 20, 30, 45, 53, 79,106
Val Eccl	Record Commission, *Valor Ecclesiasticus*, vol V
VCH Yorks III	*Victoria County History, County of York*, vol III
VCH YNR	*Victoria County History, Yorkshire North Riding*, vols I and II
Whitby Chart	*Chartulary of Whitby Abbey*, vols I and II, Surtees 69, 72
YAJ	*Yorkshire Archaeological Journal*
YAS	Yorkshire Archaeological Society
YASRS	Yorkshire Archaeological Society Record Series

References

Chapter 1

1. B Jennings, *The Grey Friars of Richmond* (Richmond, 1958), pp3-4.
2. For this and the next four paragraphs, see *MO, ROI* and Janet E Burton, *Monastic and Religious Orders in Britain 1100-1300* (Cambridge, 1994).
3. Knowles and Hadcock, pp467-87; D H Farmer (ed), Bede, *Ecclesiastical History of the English People* (Penguin, 1990), pp182, 184-5, 187, 196, 243-7, 267, 269, 303, 373.
4. *Whitby Chart I*, p2; Rosemary Cramp, 'Monastic sites', in D M Wilson (ed), *The Archaeology of Anglo-Saxon England* (1976), pp223-9.
5. Knowles and Hadcock, pp467, 471; Bede, pp345-8.
6. G W O Addleshaw, *The Development of the Parochial System from Charlemagne to Urban II* (St Anthony's Hall Publications no 6, York, 1954), pp13, 15.

Chapter 2

1. Knowles and Hadcock, pp5-8.
2. *Selby Coucher I*, pp4-18.
3. *EYC I*, pp358-9.
4. *Selby Coucher I*, p12; R B Dobson, 'The First Norman Abbey in Northern England' *Ampleforth Journal* vol 74, 1969, pp161-76.
5. *MO*, pp166-8; *Whitby Chart I*, pp1-2; *EYC XI* pp92-3; A Hamilton Thompson, 'The Monastic Settlement at Hackness and its relation to the Abbey of Whitby', *YAJ* vol 27, pp388-405.
6. *Ibid*; *Whitby Chart I*, p2; *VCH Yorks III*, p102.
7. Thompson; *Whitby Chart I*, pp li-lvii.
8. *VCH Yorks III*, pp101-2, 107-8.
9. Margaret Faull and Marie Stinson (eds), *Domesday Book, Yorkshire* (2 vols, Chichester, 1986), 4N1 (there are no page numbers); Thompson; *EYC II*, pp197-8.
10. *Whitby Chart I*, p5; *VCH Yorks III*, p102.
11. Thomas Merton, *The Waters of Silence* (1950), p5; Justin McCann (ed), *The Rule of St Benedict* (1972), p71.
12. *Ibid*, pp96-7, 186.
13. *Ibid*, p111.
14. Burton, pp3, 160-1; *The Rule of St Benedict*, p37.
15. Merton, p3.
16. A H Thompson, 'The Pestilences of the Fourteenth Century in the Diocese of York', *Arch J*, vol 71, 1914, pp102-3.
17. *VCH Yorks III*, pp194, 389.
18. Burton, p33.
19. Thompson 'The Monastic Settlement at Hackness', pp401-4; *EYC I*, pp363-4.
20. *VCH Yorks III*, p112.
21. Donald Matthew, *The Norman Monasteries and their English Possessions* (Oxford, 1962), pp29-31, 51-2; *VCH Yorks III*, pp388-91; *EYC III*, pp6-7, 12-13, 30-3; Barbara English, *The Lords of Holderness* (Oxford, 1979), p3.
22. *VCH Yorks III*, pp91-2.
23. *Ibid*, p110; *ROI*, ch 4; *ROII*, pp309-20.
24. J C Dickinson *The Origins of the Austin Canons and Their Introductions into England* (1950); G W O Addleshaw, *The Development of the Parochial System*, pp13, 15, and *The Beginnings of the Parochial System* (St Anthony's Hall Publications no 3, 2nd edn, York, 1959), pp11-15; R T Fieldhouse and B Jennings, *A History of Richmond and Swaledale* (Chichester, 1978), p72; *Nidderdale*, pp52, 372.
25. W Stubbs, *Select Charters* (9th edn, Oxford, 1921), p88; Addleshaw, *Development of Parochial System*, pp9-10, 14-15.
26. J R H Moorman, *A History of the Church in England* (1953), p62; *Brid Chart*, pp185-6; YASRS 62, *Yorkshire Fines 1218-31*, p146; *Nidderdale*, p377.
27. *VCH Yorks III*, pp208-10; Cross and Vickers, p270.
28. *Ibid*, pp244, 262-349; Knowles and

Hadcock, pp148 *et seq*; Dickinson, pp172, 181; *Val Eccl*, p624; *VCH Yorks III*, p119.

29. Cross and Vickers, *passim*; *Val Eccl*, pp120-1.

30. *MO*, pp191, 197-8, 203, 376 and ch XI; Merton, pp7-8; Knowles and Hadcock, p109; F M Thompson, *The Carthusian Order in England* (1930), ch 1.

31. L J Lekai, *The Cistercians, Ideals and Reality* (Kent State University, 1977), pp11-32; *MO*, pp199-216.

32. W Williams, *St Bernard of Clairvaux* (Manchester, 1935), ch 1; *MO*, p230.

33. *Ibid*, pp228-30; Williams, pp46-8.

34. D Nicholl, *Thurstan, Archbishop of York 1114-40* (York, 1964), pp156-70; L G D Baker, 'The Foundation of Fountains Abbey', *Northern History*, vol IV, 1969, pp29-43.

35. *Ibid*; *MO*, pp231-7; *Mems Fount I*, pp5-31, 51-3; Williams, pp54-5; Lekai, p38.

36. *MO*, pp250-1; *VCH Yorks III*, pp31-2; *EYC IX*, p204; Greenway, pp27-8, 190.

37. *Ibid*, pp31-5, 53-4; *EYC III*, pp444-5; Burton, Thesis, pp124, 180, 510-1.

38. *MO*, pp220-1.

39. *VCH Yorks III*, pp135, 149.

40. F M Powicke (ed), Walter Daniel, *The Life of Ailred of Rievaulx* (1950), pp14-16; Janet E Burton, *Kirkham Priory from Foundation to Dissolution* (Borthwick Paper 86, BIHR, York, 1995), pp4-11; *MO*, pp241-5; *VCH Yorks III*, pp219-20.

41. *Ibid*, pp138-9; Greenway, p125; *EYC IV*, pp23-7, V, pp35-6.

42. *VCH Yorks III*, pp139-40; *EYC IV*, p32, V, p215.

43. G D Barnes, *Kirkstall Abbey 1147-1539* (Thoresby vol 58, 1984), pp4-9; Thoresby vol IV, *Miscellanea*, p171; *VCH Yorks III*, pp142-3; *EYC III*, pp164-6; Baker, p42.

44. *VCH Yorks III*, pp153, 156.

45. *Chron Melsa I*, pp xiii-xvi, 76-81; English, *Lords of Holderness*, pp26-7; *EYC III*, pp89-92.

46. *MO*, pp247-8; Janet Burton, *Monastic and Religious Orders in Britain*, p66.

47. *Life of Ailred*, pp37-40; Lekai, pp39-40; *MO*, pp257-66.

48. Merton, pp26-7.

49. *MO*, p205; H M Colvin, *The White Canons in England* (Oxford, 1951), pp1-20.

50. *Ibid*, pp56-8; *EYC V*, pp72-3, 131-3; M Longhurst, 'The Easby Cross', *Archaeologia*, vol 81, 1931, pp43-7.

51. Colvin, pp33, 126-9; *EYC V*, pp27-8, 307.

52. Colvin, pp162-3, 304-5; *VCH Yorks III*, pp249-50.

53. Colvin, p36.

54. Graham, *Gilbertines*, pp1-14, 71.

55. *Ibid*, p36; A L Poole, *From Domesday Book to Magna Carta* (2nd edn, Oxford, 1955), pp143, 270-2; *RS 82, Chronicles of Stephen, Henry II and Richard II*, vol III, pp152 *et seq*.

56. Knowles and Hadcock, *passim*.

57. *Ibid*, p186; *EYC II*, pp404-8.

58. Graham, p37; Knowles and Hadcock p198.

59. *Ibid*, p173; Graham, pp35, 168; *VCH Yorks III*, pp251-2, 255-6.

Chapter 3

1. R B Dobson and Sara Donaghy, *The History of Clementhorpe Nunnery* (York Arch Trust, 1984), pp1-10; *EYC I*, pp278-9, II, p240.

2. Janet E Burton, *The Yorkshire Nunneries in the Twelfth and Thirteenth Centuries* (Borthwick Paper 56, BIHR, York, 1979), pp2-4, 17-20; Sharon K Elkins, *Holy Women of Twelfth Century England* (University of North Carolina, 1988), ch 5.

3. Greenway, pp xii, 20-1, 179; *EYC I*, pp413-5, 419-21; Noreen Vickers, 'The Social Class of Yorkshire Medieval Nuns', *YAJ* vol 67, pp127-8.

4. Burton, pp38-43.

5. W Brown, 'The Nunnery of St Stephen's of Thimbleby', *YAJ* vol 9, pp334-7; *VCH Yorks III*, p160; Pipe Roll Society, *Pipe Rolls 18-29 Henry II*.

6. *VCH Yorks III*, pp180, 239; *EYC I*, pp419-23; Elkins, p118.

7. *Ibid*, pp84-9; *EYC III*, p76; Sally Thompson, 'The Problem of the Cistercian Nuns in

the Twelfth and Early Thirteenth Centuries', in Derek Baker (ed), *Medieval Women* (Oxford, 1978), pp227-52.

8. Elkins, pp91-3, 170-1.

9. Cross and Vickers, pp366, 373, 408-9, 560.

10. YASRS 92, *The Chartulary of the Augustine Priory of St John the Evangelist of the Park of Healaugh*, pp x-xi; *VCH Yorks III*, p216.

11. *ROI*, pp114; J R H Moorman, *A History of the Franciscan Order from its origins to the year 1517* (Oxford, 1968), pp3-15, 54-5, 123.

12. B Jennings, *The Grey Friars of Richmond*, p5.

13. *ROI*, pp114-29; Moorman, pp18-19, 57-8; A Jessopp, *The Coming of the Friars* (1899), pp9-23.

14. *ROI*, pp146-52, 176-80; W A Hinnebusch, *The History of the Dominican Order*, vol I, (New York, 1965), chs 1 and 2; Moorman, p123.

15. *VCH Yorks III*, p283; Knowles and Hadcock, p220.

16. *Ibid*, p227; Moorman, p118; *VCH Yorks III*, pp287-8.

17. *Ibid*, p263; Knowles and Hadcock, p215; C F R Palmer, 'The Friars Preachers or Black Friars of Beverley', *YAJ* vol 7, pp32-43.

18. *ROI*, pp187-8; Moorman, p177; *EYC I*, p286; *VCH Yorks III*, pp274-5.

19. *Ibid*, pp274-5, 277.

20. *Ibid*, pp275, 277.

21. *ROI*, pp196-201; F Roth, *The English Austin Friars 1249-1538, vol I, History* (New York 1966), pp14-16.

22. *ROI*, p196; *VCH Yorks III*, pp291-2.

23. *Ibid*, pp280, 294; Roth, pp345-7, 360-1.

24. *VCH Yorks III*, pp190, 263-95.

25. *Ibid*, p269; E Gillett and K A MacMahon, *A History of Hull* (Oxford, 1980), pp4-5.

26. *VCH Yorks III*, p270; Knowles and Hadcock, p242; Roth, p174; East Riding Archaeological Society, *Newsletter*, No 43, Jan 1996, pp4-6.

27. Knowles and Hadcock pp236-7, 246; *VCH Yorks III*, pp267, 270-1, 279; Roth, p307.

28. *ROI*, pp221-3.

29. *VCH Yorks III*, pp270, 296; *VCH YNR II*, p253; Surtees 89, *Guisborough Chartulary II*, pp388-90.

30. B Jennings (ed), *A History of Harrogate and Knaresborough* (Huddersfield, 1970), pp98-103.

31. *VCH Yorks III*, pp213-4.

32. Thompson, *Carthusian Order in England*, pp199-207; *VCH Yorks III*, pp190-1.

33. Thompson, pp229-34; W Brown, 'History of Mount Grace', *YAJ* vol 7, pp473-9; W Brown, 'History of Mount Grace Priory', *YAJ* vol 18, pp252-8.

34. *ROII*, pp157-65; *VCH Yorks III*, pp194, 387-91.

35. R M Clay, *The Hermits and Anchorites of England* (1914), pp vi-xvii, 26-7, 60.

36. R M Clay, *The Medieval Hospitals of England* (1909), *passim*.

37. P H Cullum, *Cremetts and Corrodies: Care of the Poor and Sick at St Leonard's Hospital, York, in the Middle Ages* (Borthwick Paper 79, BIHR, York, 1991).

38. Knowles and Hadcock, pp25-8; *VCH Yorks III*, pp336-45.

Chapter 4

1. Dobson, 'The First Norman Abbey in Northern England', p174; *Selby Coucher I*, pp19-21.

2. *Ibid*, p22; *EYC I*, pp52, 363-4.

3. *Ibid*, pp362-3.

4. *Selby Coucher I*, pp22-3, II, p xxii*.

5. *Ibid*, pp vi-xii*.

6. *Selby Coucher I*, pp26-9.

7. *Ibid*, pp31-4; English, *Lords of Holderness*, pp18-21.

8. *Selby Coucher I*, pp44-6; *VCH Yorks III*, p99.

9. *Selby Coucher I*, p xii-xvii*.

10. R B Dobson, *Selby Abbey and Town* (Selby, 1993), p22; *EYC III*, pp225-7, 369-70, XII, pp66-72.

11. G S Heslop, 'The Abbot of Selby's Financial Statement for the year ending Michaelmas 1338', *YAJ* vol 44, pp159-72.

12. *Ibid*, pp159-67; *Selby Coucher I*, pp65-7; J H Tillotson, *Monastery and Society in the Later*

Middle Ages: Selected account rolls from Selby Abbey, Yorkshire 1398-1537 (Woodbridge, Suffolk, 1988), pp 11-23.

13. Thoresby vol 39, 1939, K L McCutcheon, *Yorkshire Fairs and Markets*, p161; Jennings, *Harrogate and Knaresborough*, pp37, 58, 74-6.

14. *Whitby Chart I*, p xxx; *VCH Yorks III*, pp102-4; *EYC II*, p222.

15. G Coppack, *Abbeys and Priories* (1990), pp41-5.

16. *Whitby Chart I*, p xxx; *VCH Yorks III*, pp102-4; *EYC II*, p233.

17. *Ibid*, pp210-11; *VCH YNR I*, p503.

18. *EYC II*, pp203-4, 229-30, XI, pp21-2, 295-6.

19. *EYC I*, pp307-11.

20. *EYC II*, pp55, 203, 211, 214, 228-9, 356-7, 370, III, p454, XI, p24.

21. *EYC I*, pp286, 293-5, II, pp102, 171-3, 177, 185, 229, 236-8, 246, 370, 378, 492, IV, p210, XI, pp24, 44, 117, 236-7.

22. *EYC I*, p201, XI, pp235-6; *Whitby Chart I*, p328.

23. *EYC II*, pp219-20, 222-3, 466.

24. *EYC IX*, p210; *Whitby Chart I*, p329.

25. *EYC II*, pp231-3; *VCH YNR I*, p515; M W Beresford and H P R Finberg, *English Medieval Boroughs: A Handlist* (Totowa, New Jersey, 1973), p189.

26. *VCH YNR I*, pp508-10; 'The Chronicle of the Canon of Bridlington', in RS 76, W Stubbs (ed), *Chronicles of the Reign of Edward I and Edward II*, vol II, p120.

27. *VCH Yorks III*, pp102-4; *VCH YNR I*, pp508-10.

28. *ROIII*, p10.

29. *ROI*, chs 2 and 7.

30. *Reg Gray*, pp327-8; C *Papal R, Papal Letters* vol I, 1198-1304, pp331-3; *VCH Yorks III*, pp96, 104, 109-10.

31. *Ibid*, p96; *Reg Giffard*, pp322-4.

32. *Reg Wickwane*, pp22-5.

33. *Selby Coucher II*, pp xxii-xxvii*; Heslop, 'The Abbot of Selby's Financial Statement', p165.

34. *Reg Giffard*, p325; Tillotson, *Monastery and Society*, p213.

35. *VCH Yorks III*, pp97-8; Dobson, *Selby Abbey*

and Town, p22; Royal Historical Society, Camden 3rd Series 47, *Chapters of the Black Monks II*, p144.

36. *Reg Wickwane*, p54; *Reg Romeyn I*, pp178-9; *VCH Yorks III*, pp102-3.

37. *Ibid*, p103.

38. R B Dobson, 'The Election of John Ousthorp as Abbot of Selby in 1436', *YAJ* vol 42, pp31-3; *Whitby Chart II*, pp665-6.

39. North Riding Record Series NS vol V, *Honour and Forest of Pickering IV*, pp12-20.

40. *ROII*, pp205-6; Camden 3rd Series 54, *Chapters of the Black Monks III*, pp63-8, 277-309.

41. *Ibid*, pp63-8; *Whitby Chart I*, p318, II, pp558-77.

42. Heslop, pp159-68.

43. Tillotson, pp74-8; Dobson, 'John Ousthorp', p38; *Selby Coucher II*, p xxxi*.

44. Tillotson, pp41, 47-73; *Chapters of the Black Monks III*, p281.

45. Tillotson, pp10, 53-4, 80.

46. *Ibid*, pp53, 81.

47. *ROII*, pp182-4.

48. *Ibid*, p296; Tillotson, pp23-4, 93; Dobson, 'John Ousthorp', pp39-54, and *Selby Abbey and Town*, p20.

Chapter 5

1. Powicke (ed), Walter Daniel, *The Life of Ailred of Rievaulx*, pp14-16; G Coppack, *Abbeys and Priories*, p46.

2. *Ibid*, p47; Coppack, *Fountains Abbey* (1993), pp26-33; *Mems Fount I*, pp lii, 97-102.

3. Coppack, *Fountains Abbey*, pp36-47.

4. *Riev Chart*, p lxxiii; J Weatherill, 'Rievaulx Abbey', *YAJ* vol 38, pp333-43; English Heritage, *Rievaulx Abbey* (1991), pp8-9.

5. *Riev Chart*, pp16-21; *EYC III*, pp441-3; *VCH YNR I*, p495.

6. *EYC II*, pp62, 144-5, 288-95, IX, pp99-100, 165-8, 203.

7. *EYC IX*, pp92, 209-19, 224-6, 228, 230-9, 242-5; *VCH YNR I*, pp521-3.

8. *EYC I*, pp264-5, 268, 277, 301-5, 314-6, 482.

9. *Ibid*, pp479-80.

10. *EYC II*, pp60, 63, 470-3, 485, 499-502, 514-6.

11. *EYC III*, pp329, 334-5.

12. H R Schubert, *History of the British Iron and Steel Industry c450 BC—AD 1775* (1957), pp100-4.

13. *EYC I*, pp440-2, *II*, pp22, 84-9, *IV*, pp120-30; *Riev Chart*, pp66-7, 216-7, 266; B Waites, 'The Monastic Settlement of North-East Yorkshire', *YAJ* vol 40, p489.

14. *Chron Melsa*, *passim*.

15. *EYC I*, p386, *XI*, pp31-2, 183-4; Jennings (ed), *A History of Harrogate and Knaresborough*, p37; *Fount Chart*, pp151-5.

16. *Ibid*, pp306-15, 746-63; YASRS 52, *Yorkshire Fines 1347-77*, p58.

17. *Fount Chart*, pp415, 564, 704-8; *EYC IV*, pp19-20, *V*, pp313-4.

18. Coppack, *Fountains Abbey*, pp32-3; *Mems Fount I*, pp102-8; Burton, Thesis, p165.

19. *EYC IV*, pp46-7, 56, 144-6, *V*, pp205-8, *XI*, p324; *Fount Chart*, pp90-101.

20. A Raistrick, *The Pennine Dales* (Arrow edn, 1972), pp71, 82-4; *Nidderdale*, pp26-36; B Jennings, 'The Study of Local History in the Pennines: the comparative dimension', *Trans Halifax Antiquarian Society* NS vol 3, 1995, pp15-19.

21. *Nidderdale*, pp37-8.

22. *EYC VII*, pp61-2, 71, 73-4, 191, *XI*, pp34-6, 458.

23. *Nidderdale*, pp37-41, 58.

24. *Ibid*, pp43, 58-61; *Fount Chart*, pp415, 646-63, 785.

25. *Nidderdale*, pp43-4.

26. YASRS 12, *Yorkshire Inquisitions I*, pp225-6; YASRS 21, *1301 Lay Subsidy*, pp96-7; YASRS 62, *Yorkshire Fines 1218-31*, pp2-4; Fieldhouse and Jennings, *History of Richmond and Swaledale*, p39.

27. *EYC VII*, pp187-8, *XI*, pp154-8, 162-8, 315-6.

28. YASRS 16, *1297 Lay Subsidy*, *passim*.

29. Coppack, *Fountains Abbey*, pp43-54.

30. *Mems Fount I*, pp117-24.

31. *EYC VII*, pp261-2; W H St John Hope, 'Fountains Abbey', *YAJ* vol 15, p393; R Gilyard-Beer, *Fountains Abbey* (guidebook, 1970), p69.

32. *Mems Fount I*, pp126-8; *VCH Yorks III*, p137; *Chron Melsa I*, p346; Gilyard-Beer, pp12, 20, 35-6; Coppack, *Fountains Abbey*, pp57-62.

33. *VCH YNR I*, pp496-8; English Heritage, *Rievaulx Abbey* (1991), p23; Marylyn J Parris, 'Rievaulx: the Architecture of its First Hundred Years', *Studia Monastica*, vol 22, no 1, 1980, pp89-99.

34. J Bilson, 'The Architecture of the Cistercians with special reference to some of their earlier churches in England', *Arch J* vol 66, 1909, pp187, 198-9, 205-6.

35. *Monastic Notes I*, pp95, 109.

36. C Platt, *The Monastic Grange in Medieval England* (1969), p76 and *passim*; B Waites, 'The monastic grange as a factor in the settlement of North-East Yorkshire', *YAJ* vol 40, pp627-56; R A Donkin, 'The marshland holdings of the English Cistercians before c1350', *Citeaux in de Nederlanden*, vol IX, 1958, Westmalle, Belgium, pp3-11; Schubert, *Iron and Steel Industry*, ch 6; A Raistrick and B Jennings, *A History of Lead Mining in the Pennines* (1965), pp31-6.

37. *Nidderdale*, pp61-6.

38. *Ibid*, pp63-4; Raistrick and Jennings, p27.

39. H E Wroot, 'Yorkshire Abbeys and the Wool Trade', *Thoresby Soc* vol 33, 1935, pp8-10; A Raistrick, *The Role of the Yorkshire Cistercian Monasteries in the History of the Wool Trade in England* (Wool Education Society, 1953); F A Mullin, *A History of the Work of the Cistercians in Yorkshire* (Washington, DC, 1932), pp37-8; J Z Titow, *English Rural Society 1200-1350* (1969), p45; *Chron Melsa II*, p xiv.

40. G D Barnes, *Kirkstall Abbey 1147-1539* (Thoresby vol 58, 1984), p43.

41. *VCH Yorks III*, pp135-6.

42. Barnes, pp43-4.

43. H S Lucas, 'The Great European Famine of 1315, 1316 and 1317', in E M Carus Wilson (ed), *Essays in Economic History* vol I (1954), pp49-72; Kershaw, pp39-46; *Lanercost*, pp217, 239-41; Record Commission, *Taxatio Ecclesiastica*, pp325, 329; 'The Chronicle of the Canon of Bridlington' (RS 76), pp55-8.

44. Ibid, pp79-81; *Lanercost*, pp239-41.

45. *Chron Melsa III*, p77; A Hamilton Thompson, 'The Pestilences of the Fourteenth Century in the Diocese of York', *Arch J* vol 71, 1914, pp97-154; *Nidderdale*, pp86-9, 483-5; B Jennings (ed), *Pennine Valley: A History of Upper Calderdale* (Otley, 1992), pp35-7.

46. British Library Add MS 40010, ff189, 215; Platt, *The Monastic Grange*, pp96-7.

47. *Ibid*, p100; *Mems Fount I*, pp203-4; *Calendar of Inquisitions Miscellaneous II*, pp445-6.

48. Mullin, pp30-3; *VCH Yorks III*, p144; *Chron Melsa III*, plx; *C Papal R, Papal Letters I*, p181, V, pp160-1.

49. *Riev Chart*, p355.

50. *VCH Yorks III*, pp141, 157; Graham, *Malton*, pp252-3.

51. *Reg Romeyn II*, pp66, 77; *Mems Fount I*, pp179-81, 185.

52. *Chron Melsa I*, pp lvii-lxx, III, pp87, 94, 110-1, 166-7, 229-32, 239-76; *VCH Yorks III*, p148.

53. E F Jacob, 'The Disputed Election at Fountains Abbey, 1410-16', in V Ruffer and A J Taylor (eds), *Medieval Studies Presented to Rose Graham* (Oxford, 1950), pp78-97.

54. Gilyard-Beer, *Fountains Abbey*, p16; Coppack, *Fountains Abbey*, p75; *VCH Yorks III*, p138; *Mems Fount III*, passim

55. Coppack, pp67-9.

56. *Ibid*, pp71-7; C T Clay, 'Bradley, a grange of Fountains', *YAJ* vol 29, p103.

57. Coppack, pp70-1; *Nidderdale*, pp103, 137.

58. *Ibid*, pp97-105; YASRS 140, D J H Michelmore (ed), *The Fountains Abbey Lease Book*, passim.

59. *Nidderdale*, p95; Raistrick, *The Pennine Dales*, p94.

60. *Nidderdale*, pp67-71.

Chapter 6

1. *EYC I*, pp131-2, II, pp427, 449, 461-2, 485, 495-6.

2. Margaret Faull and Marie Stinson (eds), *Domesday Book, Yorkshire*, passim.

3. *EYC II*, pp428, 439.

4. *EYC II*, pp439-48, III, pp40, 52, 82, V, p278, XI, p115.

5. *EYC II*, pp442-4, 447-8.

6. *EYC III*, pp80-2.

7. *EYC II*, pp150-1, 439-42.

8. *Ibid*, pp429-30; RS 75, 'History of John of Hexham', in Symeon of Durham, *History of the Kingdom*, vol II, p315; RS 82, William of Newburgh, *History of England*, pp47-8; English, *Lords of Holderness*, pp21-2; *EYC III*, pp34-5.

9. *EYC II*, pp450-1, 455-9, 488; *VCH East Riding II*, p312; *Brid Chart*, pp184-93.

10. *Ibid*, pp92-3; *EYC I*, pp290-1, II, pp471, 496-502; H L Gray, *The English Field Systems* (1915), p505.

11. *EYC I*, pp282-3, 504, III, pp40, 117; YASRS 67, *Yorkshire Fines 1232-46*, pp75, 84.

12. *Ibid*, pp71-2; *EYC V*, pp342-7; *Brid Chart*, pp248, 254-5.

13. *EYC V*, p347.

14. *EYC III*, pp125, 467, VII, pp55-7, XI, pp137, 176-8; A Hamilton Thompson, *Bolton Priory* (Thoresby vol 30, 1924), p56; YASRS 62, *Yorkshire Fines 1218-31*, p15; *Reg Gray*, pp60, 118, 120.

15. *EYC VII*, pp64-9; Kershaw, pp6-7.

16. *EYC VII*, pp128-30, 180-2; *Reg Gray*, pp94, 103.

17. Kershaw, pp34, 113-4; Thompson, pp85-6; Raistrick and Jennings, *Lead Mining in the Pennines*, p34.

18. Kershaw, pp35-42, 80-8.

19. Thompson, p129.

20. Kershaw, pp63-7; YASRS 132, I Kershaw (ed), *Bolton Priory Rentals and Ministers' Accounts 1473-1539*; *Taxatio Ecclesiastica*, pp303-7, 321-33.

21. Anon (ed), Robert of Bridlington, *The Bridlington Dialogue* (1960), pp22-4, 107, 154-5 and passim.

22. 'The Chronicle of the Canon of Bridlington', pp xvii-xxxi (RS 76, vol II); RS 47, *The Chronicle of Peter of Langtoft*; RS 82, William of Newburgh, *History of the Kingdom*.

23. *Reg Wickwane*, pp26, 87-8, 96.

24. *Reg Romeyn I*, pp199-202

25. *VCH Yorks III*, pp201-2.

26. 'The Chronicle of the Canon of Bridlington', pp79-81.

27. *Brid Chart*, pp19, 58, 301; *VCH Yorks III*, p305; *C Papal R, Petitions 1342-1419*, p7.

28. *Reg Giffard*, pp145-6, 153, 302-12; *Reg Wickwane*, pp131-3.

29. *Reg Romeyn I*, pp56-7; *VCH Yorks III*, p199; Kershaw, pp9-14; Thompson, *Bolton Priory*, pp76-7.

30. Kershaw, pp16-18, 40-2, 83-4, 98.

31. Thompson, pp130-80.

32. 'Survey of the Priory of Bridlington, 32nd Henry VIII', *Archaeologia*, vol 19, pp270-5; Jill A Franklin, 'Bridlington Priory: an Augustinian Church and Cloister in the Twelfth Century', in C Wilson (ed), *Medieval Art and Architecture in the East Riding of Yorkshire* (British Archaeological Assn, 1989), pp44-61; J R Earnshaw, *A Reconstruction of Bridlington Priory* (Bridlington, 1975).

33. M Prickett, *An Historical and Architectural Description of the Priory Church of Bridlington* (Cambridge, 1831), pp39-50 and engravings.

34. 'Survey of the Priory', p271.

35. J S Purvis, 'St John of Bridlington', *Journal of the Augustinian Society, Bridlington*, no 2, August 1924, pp12-15, 42.

36. *Ibid*, pp19-42; *C Papal R, Papal Letters V*, p460.

37. Purvis, pp48-9; *VCH Yorks III*, pp202-3.

Chapter 7

1. *EYC V*, pp113-21, 131-8.

2. *Ibid*, pp67-70, 118, 149-53, 161, 360.

3. *EYC II*, pp141-2, *V*, pp75-6, 103-4, 117, 125, 138, 158-61, 331.

4. *EYC V*, pp103-4, 117, 122, 160, 234, 262.

5. *VCH Yorks III*, p247; YASRS 21, *1301 Lay Subsidy*, pp89, 92; *Monastic Notes I*, p47.

6. W H St John Hope, 'On the Premonstratensian Abbey of St Agatha juxta Richmond', *YAJ* vol 10, pp117-58; A W Clapham, 'The Architecture of the English Premonstratensians', *Archaeologia* vol 73, pp124-6.

7. *EYC V*, p115.

8. St John Hope, pp119-25, 157.

9. *Lanercost*, pp210-1, 216, 226-7; *Taxatio Ecclesiastica*, pp306-9; *VCH Yorks III*, p250.

10. *Ibid*, p246; H M Colvin, *The White Canons in England*, pp297-8.

11. *CPR 1391-6*, pp224, 271, 1396-8, p489.

12. *C Papal R, Papal Letters V*, pp360, 375; *VCH Yorks III*, p247.

13. Colvin, pp306-7; Clapham, p128.

14. Colvin, pp271, 358-61.

15. *Ibid*, pp224-7.

16. *VCH Yorks III*, p247.

17. *Ibid*, p248.

Chapter 8

1. *EYC II*, pp403-6, 409-10.

2. *Ibid*, pp396-7, 402-3.

3. *EYC IX*, p193, *XI*, pp40, 296-7.

4. *EYC II*, pp37, 410-1, *III*, p500.

5. *EYC I*, pp463-5, *II*, pp254, 408-9, 526, *XII*, pp78-9, 82, 85; Cross and Vickers, p394; W H St John Hope, 'Watton Priory, Yorkshire', *Trans East Riding Antiquarian Society*, vol 8, 1901, p71.

6. *EYC VI*, p195, *IX*, p179; *VCH Yorks III*, p253; Graham, *Malton*, appx I.

7. *EYC VI*, pp191-5; Graham, *Malton*, p258.

8. *EYC I*, pp387-8; YASRS 16, *1297 Lay Subsidy*, pp145-9.

9. *EYC I*, p305, *II*, p80, *III*, pp498-9, *VI*, pp106, 148, 172-3; Graham, *Malton*, pp254-61.

10. Graham, *Gilbertines*, pp71-3.

11. *Ibid*, pp50-61; *Malton*, pp249-51.

12. *Gilbertines*, pp54-5.

13. *Ibid*, p69; Hope, 'Watton Priory', p90.

14. G Constable, 'Ailred of Rievaulx and the Nun of Watton', in D Baker (ed), *Medieval*

Women, pp205-26; Sharon Elkins, *Holy Women of Twelfth Century England*, pp106-11.

15. Constable, p223; Elkins, pp114-6.

16. Hope, 'Watton Priory', p85.

17. *Ibid*, pp70-107; *Chron Melsa I*, p107.

18. *VCH YNR I*, pp534-7; *1301 Lay Subsidy*, pp47, 52-3.

19. *VCH YNR I*, pp538-41.

20. Graham, *Malton*, p263.

21. *1301 Lay Subsidy, passim*.

22. *Monastic Notes I*, pp120-1.

23. Graham, *Gilbertines*, pp83-5; *Monastic Notes II*, p24; *VCH YNR I*, p532.

24. *Monastic Notes I*, p122; *Gilbertines*, pp137-9.

25. *Ibid*, p94.

26. *Ibid*, pp91-4; *VCH YNR I*, pp529-30; 'The Chronicle of the Canon of Bridlington', p180.

27. *Gilbertines*, pp146-7.

28. *VCH Yorks III*, p254; *Monastic Notes II*, p50.

29. *Ibid*, p50.

30. *VCH Yorks III*, pp252, 256; Cross and Vickers, pp373, 381, 384, 408-9.

Chapter 9

1. Rose Graham, 'The Order of Grandmont and its houses in England', *English Ecclesiastical Studies* (1929), p225.

2. *Ibid*, pp235-7; *Reg Gray*, pp22, 29.

3. Graham, p239; W Brown, 'Description of the Buildings of Twelve Small Yorkshire Priories at the Reformation', *YAJ* vol 9, pp213-5.

4. A W Clapham, 'The Order of Grandmont and Its Architecture', *Archaeologia* vol 75, pp204-6.

5. Graham, pp235-42; *VCH Yorks III*, pp193-4.

6. A fuller account of St Robert and the Trinitarian friary, with detailed references, is given in Jennings (ed), A *History of Harrogate and Knaresborough,* pp95-108.

7. W H St John Hope, 'Architectural History of Mount Grace Charterhouse', *YAJ* vol 18, pp291-6.

8. *Ibid*, pp295-6; H V Le Bas, 'The Founding of the Carthusian Order', *YAJ* vol 18, pp241-52; E M Thompson, *The Carthusian Order in England* (1930), pp116-7, 129.

9. *Ibid*, pp113-5, 488-91.

10. This and the next three paragraphs are based upon W Brown, 'History of the Priory', *YAJ* vol 18, pp252-69, and Hope, 'Architectural History', pp270-309.

11. Brown, pp254-63.

12. Thompson, pp335, 339-40, 518-9; R W Swanson, *Church and Society in Late Medieval England* (Oxford, 1989), p339; Carol B Rowntree, 'Studies in Carthusian History in Later Medieval England', York D Phil, 1981, pp195-202.

13. B Donaghey and K Shimonomito, 'Some Literary News: A Recent Development in the Heritage of Medieval Yorkshire', *Medieval Yorkshire* (YAS), No 25, 1996, pp18-33.

Chapter 10

1. Brown, 'Description of the Buildings of Twelve Small Yorkshire Priories', pp197-215, 321-33; G Poulson, *History of Holderness* (Hull, 1840), vol I, p386, vol II, pp210-1.

2. *Val Eccl, passim*.

3. *EYC III*, pp75-7.

4. Sir G Duckett, 'Charters of the Priory of Swine in Holderness', *YAJ* vol 6, pp113-24; *Chron Melsa I*, p110.

5. *EYC III*, p 116, *XII*, pp89-90, 112-3.

6. *EYC III*, pp76-7; *Taxatio Ecclesiastica*, p304.

7. *Chron Melsa I*, pp356-7.

8. YASRS 62, *Yorkshire Fines 1218-31*, p97; YASRS 67, *Yorkshire Fines 1232-46*, p43.

9. *Chron Melsa II*, pp12-22; *Val Eccl*, p114.

10. *EYC I*, pp412-5, *VII*, p155; *Reg Gray*, p2.

11. *Taxatio Ecclesiastica*, pp306, 309.

12. J H Tillotson, *Marrick Priory, A Nunnery in Late Medieval Yorkshire* (Borthwick Paper 75, BIHR, York, 1989), p10.

13. *EYC II*, p72, *V*, pp28-9, 219-20, 283;

J G Nichols (ed), *Collectanea Topographica et Genealogica*, vol V (1838), pp100-25, 221-39.

14. *EYC I*, p344, *II*, pp177, 192, 251-2; *Monasticon IV*, pp354-7; *Val Eccl*, p142.

15. H E Wroot, 'Yorkshire Abbeys and the Wool Trade' (*Thoresby* vol 33), pp9-10; W Cunningham, *The Growth of English Industry and Commerce during the Early and Middle Ages* (3rd edn, Cambridge, 1896), pp624-33.

16. *EYC II*, p72; Elkins, *Holy Women of Twelfth Century England*, pp170-1.

17. *EYC III*, pp75-8.

18. *Yorkshire Fines 1232-46*, p43; YASRS 82, *Yorkshire Fines 1246-72*, p48; *Chron Melsa II*, pp12-22.

19. *Reg Giffard*, pp146-8.

20. *Reg Romeyn I*, pp199, 203-4; *VCH Yorks III*, p180.

21. *Ibid*; *Reg Romeyn I*, pp203-4, 209, 211, 217.

22. *VCH Yorks III*, p142; *Reg Wickwane*, pp112-3.

23. *VCH Yorks III*, p126.

24. *Ibid*, pp117, 119, 166.

25. *Test Ebor I*, pp186-90.

26. *VCH Yorks III*, pp122-3; Eileen Power, *Medieval English Nunneries c1275 to 1535* (Cambridge, 1922), p77.

27. *Monasticon IV*, p354; *VCH Yorks III*, p126; *C Papal R, Papal Letters IV*, p393.

28. *Yorkshire Fines 1246-72*, pp157-9.

29. *VCH Yorks III*, p181.

30. *CPR 1317-21*, pp223, 237; *VCH Yorks III*, pp114, 175, 177, 239-40.

31. *Ibid*, pp120, 124-5, 127, 129, 161, 163, 172, 175.

32. *Ibid*, p123; *Test Ebor III*, pp161-8.

33. *Test Ebor I*, pp306-17.

34. *Test Ebor I and III*; Surtees 2, *Wills and Inventories, Northern Counties, Part I*.

35. *Test Ebor I*, pp133-4.

36. *VCH Yorks III*, p161; Tillotson, *Marrick Priory*, pp5-6.

37. *Ibid, passim*.

38. *VCH Yorks III*, pp114-5; Power, *Medieval English Nunneries*, pp86-7.

39. *VCH Yorks III*, pp120, 127, 168, 174-5, 183; *Test Ebor I*, p179, *II*, p13; 'Visitations in the

Diocese of York by Archbishop Edward Lee 1534-35', *YAJ* vol 16, pp424-58.

40. Power, pp293-4.

Chapter 11

1. L M Goldthorp, 'Franciscans and Dominicans in Yorkshire', *YAJ* vol 32, pp388-9; *CCR 1261-4*, p241; *CLR 1226-40*, p484; C F R Palmer, 'The Friars Preachers or Black Friars of Beverley', *YAJ* vol 7, pp32-3.

2. RS 61, *Letters from Northern Registers*, pp93-5; *Reg Romeyn I*, p113; Goldthorp, pp292, 370, 388.

3. *Reg Giffard*, pp226-7; J Hughes, 'The Administration of Confession in the Diocese of York in the Fourteenth Century', in D M Smith (ed), *Studies in Clergy and Ministry in Medieval England* (BIHR, York 1991), pp88-90.

4. Goldthorp, pp389-90; Surtees 98, *Beverley Chapter Act Books I*, p243.

5. Royal Commission on Historical Monuments, Supplementary Series 4, *Beverley, An Archaeological and Architectural Survey* (1982), pp11, 15; Surtees 108, *Beverley Chapter Act Books II*, p340.

6. Palmer, p35; *VCH Yorks III*, p263.

7. Palmer, p35; RCHM, *Beverley*, p48.

8. Palmer, pp36-7; Goldthorp, pp392-3; *Test Ebor I*, pp414-5.

9. Palmer, pp35-6; Goldthorp, pp392-4; *Test Ebor III*, pp227-9.

10. J R H Moorman, *A History of the Franciscan Order from its origins to the year 1517*, pp202, 513.

11. Palmer, pp37-42.

12. *Ibid*, p42.

13. B Jennings, *The Grey Friars of Richmond*, pp4-10.

14. Moorman, pp180, 239.

15. Jennings, p11.

16. *Ibid*, pp11-12.

17. *Test Ebor II*, p115.

18. Jennings, p13.

19. C Clarkson, *The History of Richmond* (Richmond, 1821), p216.

20. Jennings, p16; J R H Moorman, *The Franciscans in England* (1982), pp75, 96.

21. F Roth, *The English Austin Friars 1249-1538 – vol I, History*, pp346-7.

22. *Ibid*, p346; J Hunter, *South Yorkshire* (1828), vol I, p245; *Reg Giffard*, pp186, 198.

23. Roth, p348; *VCH Yorks III*, p280; *CPR 1272-81*, p164; *CCR 1272-79*, p339; YASRS 23, *Yorkshire Inquisitions II*, p11.

24. *CPR 1272-81*, pp73, 96.

25. Roth, p364; *VCH Yorks III*, p280; Hunter, vol I, pp245-6.

26. Roth, pp187-8, 235-6; *VCH Yorks III*, pp270, 281, 295; Hunter, vol I, pp245-6.

27. Roth, pp347, 364, 375; *VCH Yorks III*, pp280, 294.

28. *Test Ebor I*, pp57-61, 210-4, 272-8, 357-60, *III*, p247.

29. *Ibid*, pp246-8; T W Beastall, *Portrait of an English Parish Church: St Mary the Virgin, Tickhill* (Tickhill, nd), p19.

30. Roth, pp346-50; Peter F Ryder, *Medieval Buildings of Yorkshire* (Ash Grove Books, 1993), p60; H Thorold, *Collins Guide to the Ruined Abbeys of England, Wales and Scotland* (1993), p212.

31. *VCH Yorks III*, pp291-2.

32. *Ibid*, pp268, 292-3; *Test Ebor III*, pp304-10.

33. Helen M Jewell, *The North-South Divide* (Manchester, 1994), p186; *Monastic Notes II*, p91; *VCH Yorks III*, p292.

34. *Ibid*, pp269-70, 293.

35. *Test Ebor I and III*; Surtees 2, *Wills and Inventories, Northern Counties, Part I*.

Chapter 12

1. Eamon Duffy, *The Stripping of the Altars: Traditional Religion in England c1400-1580* (Yale UP, 1992), pp303-10, 328, 338-41.

2. M Prickett, *An Historical and Architectural Description of the Parish Church of Bridlington*, p30; A G Dickens, *Lollards and Protestants in the Diocese of York* (2nd edn, 1982), ch 2; J R H Moorman, *History of the Church in England*, p172; Camden Soc IV, *Plompton Correspondence*, pp231-2.

3. E W Crossley (ed), *Halifax Wills vol II* (Leeds, nd), p39; *Test Ebor V*, pp306-9.

4. 'Visitations in the Diocese of York by Archbishop Edward Lee 1534-35', *YAJ* vol 16, pp424-58.

5. W G Hoskins, *The Age of Plunder: The England of Henry VIII* (1976), pp121-9.

6. *L & P Henry VIII*, vol X, nos 93, 99.

7. Camden Soc 26, T Wright (ed), *Letters relating to the Suppression of Monasteries* (1843), preface.

8. *Ibid, passim; L & P Henry VIII*, vol X, nos 92, 364.

9. *Ibid*, no 137; Wright, pp100-2; *Mems Fount I*, pp252-3, 260-7, 280-1; Coppack, *Fountains Abbey*, pp98-9.

10. Cross and Vickers, p543.

11. *L & P Henry VIII*, vol XI, nos 622, 645, 705, 760, 784-5, 1047, XII(1), nos 6, 201, 369-70, 416, 910, 1012, 1022-3; Cross and Vickers, pp202, 574; Claire Cross, *The End of Medieval Monasticism in the East Riding of Yorkshire* (East Yorkshire Local History Society, 1993), pp23-6.

12. *L & P Henry VIII*, vol XI, nos 692, 760.

13. *Ibid*, no 884; M H and R Dodds, *The Pilgrimage of Grace* (1915), vol I, pp163 *et seq*, vol II, pp28-30.

14. A Hamilton Thompson, *The English Clergy and Their Organisation in the Later Middle Ages* (Oxford, 1947), pp115-6; Dickens, *Lollards and Protestants*, pp53-113.

15. *Ibid*, p91; L & P Henry VIII, vol XII(1), no 479; Fieldhouse and Jennings, *A History of Richmond and Swaledale*, pp80-6; A G Dickens, 'New Records of the Pilgrimage of Grace', *YAJ* vol 33, p298; Dodds, vol II, pp213-23.

16. Cross and Vickers, p395; Cross, *The End of Medieval Monasticism*, p26; *L & P Henry VIII*, vol XII(1), no 416; YASRS 48, *Yorkshire Monasteries, Suppression Papers*, p76.

17. *Ibid*, pp46-50; Wright, pp158-9, 164-5.

18. Cross and Vickers, *passim*.

19. *Ibid*, pp4-5, 502, 529 and *passim*; *VCH Yorks III*, pp99, 284, 288, 292, 294; Cross, *The End of Medieval Monasticism*, p32; Surtees 172, A G Dickens (ed), *Clifford Letters of the Sixteenth Century*, pp67-70; Coppack, *Fountains Abbey*, p63; *C Papal R, Papal Letters IV*, pp205-6; *Yorkshire Monasteries, Suppression Papers*, pp129-30.

20. Coppack, pp99-100; *VCH Yorks III*, p137.

21. *Yorkshire Monasteries, Suppression Papers*, pp100-1; *Nidderdale*, pp118-20.

22. *L & P Henry VIII*, vol XII(1), no 901.

INDEX

The index is in two parts. Part A lists the references to monasteries on pages 1-215, excluding the distribution maps on pages 5 and 30. Part B is a selective index of topics, people and places. For references to towns or villages which had a monastery, both parts should be consulted.

Part A: Yorkshire Monasteries

Part B: Topics, People and Places
Personal names, 'de' and 'of' are omitted